Memory and American History

EDITED BY

David Thelen

Memory
and
American
History

Indiana University Press

Bloomington and Indianapolis

First Midland Book edition 1990

© 1989 by the Organization of American Historians

The paper used in this publication meets the minimum requirements of American
National Standard for Information Sciences—Permanence of Paper for Printed
Library Materials, ANSI Z39.48-1984.

Manufactured in the United States of America

Library of Congress Cataloging-in-Publication Data

Memory and American history / edited by David Thelen.
    p.   cm.
    First appeared as a special issue of the Journal of American
history, v. 75, no. 4, Mar. 1989.
    ISBN 0-253-35940-6 (alk. paper).—ISBN 0-253-20570-0 (pbk. : alk. paper)
    1. United States—History—Methodology.   2. Oral history.
3. Memory.   4. Watergate Affair, 1972–1974—Sources.   I. Thelen,
David P. (David Paul)
E175.M46   1989
973'.01—dc20   89-24667
                                           CIP

Contents

INTRODUCTION: MEMORY AND AMERICAN HISTORY

David Thelen

The challenge of history is to recover the past and introduce it to the present. It is the same challenge that confronts memory. The starting place for this book is the conviction that topics and methods surrounding the workings of memory open fresh approaches to problems that have troubled many of the humanities and social sciences in the 1980s. This conviction led the *Journal of American History* to create a special issue on memory (March 1989) that became, in turn, the basis for this book.

Perhaps the best evidence that memory is emerging as a focal point for many developments in American history is that the special issue took shape around articles that came to the *Journal* in the ordinary rhythms of scholarship. We conceived a special issue on the theme of memory only after we could see that authors had already designed topics that converged on that theme and that dozens of referees, board members, and editors had independently applauded the articles. In contrast to the theme "The Constitution and American Life," which the *Journal* editors imposed on a special issue in December 1987, the theme of memory emerged naturally from the evolution of scholarship in American history.

The historical study of memory opens exciting opportunities to ask fresh questions of our conventional sources and topics and to create points for fresh synthesis, since the study of memory can link topics we have come to regard as specialized and distinct. Those questions grow so naturally out of everyday experiences that they point us toward bridges between our craft and wider audiences who have found professional history remote and inaccessible.

Since the memory of past experiences is so profoundly intertwined with the basic identities of individuals, groups, and cultures, the study of memory exists in different forms along a spectrum of experience, from the personal, individual, and private to the collective, cultural, and public. At one end of the spectrum are psychological issues of individual motivation and perception in the creation of memories. At the other end are linguistic or anthropological issues of how cultures establish traditions and myths from the past to guide the conduct of their members in the present. While history touches both ends of the spectrum, its concerns fall most comfortably on points between those ends. The territory between individual motivation and impersonal myth is natural for historians because its obvious units of study are the particular people and groups that have long been familiar objects of historical research. With a field defined by the exploration of change over time, historians naturally extend into more social contexts the conclusion of psychologists that individuals construct memories in response to changing circumstances.

Even more intriguing than the fresh perspectives that the study of memory can

David Thelen is professor of history at Indiana University and editor of the *Journal of American History*.

throw on particular topics are the new ways that study can connect separate points on the spectrum. By directing the same questions to different topics, the study of memory opens fascinating possibilities for synthesis. The same questions about the construction of memory can illuminate how individuals, ethnic groups, political parties, and cultures shape and reshape their identities—as known to themselves and to others. Those questions can explore how they establish their core identities, how much and what kind of variation they permit around that core, and what they rule out as unacceptable. The similarities and differences in the ways individuals and groups construct memories open new possibilities for exploring how individuals connect with larger-scale historical processes.

By reconnecting history with its origins in the narrative form of everyday communication, attention to memory transcends specialization by speaking the language of face-to-face association and firsthand experience. The construction and narration of a memory comes from the oral and epic traditions of storytelling, the same traditions that gave birth to the chronicle and then to history. "The storyteller," wrote Walter Benjamin, "takes what he tells from experience—his own or that reported by others. And he in turn makes it the experience of those who are listening to his tale." Storyteller and audience are partners in creating the memory to be told. In the course of everyday talk narrators fix their listeners very clearly in mind as they decide which elements to recollect, how to organize and interpret those elements, and how to make the memory public. "The events come out of the marrow of day-to-day living; traces of them are stored in the mind, and they return to life as they are elaborated when speaking to others or when thinking to oneself," observed Samuel Schrager. Schrager shrewdly speculated that "our own immersion in this talk as an ordinary activity is surely part of the reason it has proved so resistant to specification, so hard to pin down as a subject for study." [1] Scholars may indeed not recognize fresh scholarly approaches in the study of everyday talk precisely because it is so familiar and common, but promoters in 1988 founded a popular magazine, expecting that it would appeal to millions of American subscribers, and titled it *Memories.*

The study of how people construct and narrate memories may encourage a greater sensitivity in historians to wider audiences who might listen to (and help shape) the narratives we want to construct and tell. Appreciation for the crucial participation of listener, interviewer, or audience in the creation of a recollection represents a major contribution by oral historians to the historical study of memory. "Interviews are conversations," Ronald J. Grele reminds us. "The rhetorical necessity of the moment, the fancy of the memorist, in imaginations of both interviewer and interviewee will often determine what is and what is not discussed at any given moment, or the connections made between one event and another." Small wonder, then, that three articles in this book draw heavily from oral history. At a time when many historians believe that the narrative offers the most promising structure for solving intercon-

---

[1] Walter Benjamin, "The Storyteller: Reflections on the Works of Nikolai Leskov," in Walter Benjamin, *Illuminations*, trans. Harry Kohn (1955; reprint, New York, 1968), 87; Samuel Schrager, "What Is Social in Oral History?" *International Journal of Oral History*, 4 (June 1983), 77.

nected problems of specialization and interpretation, the study of memory may provide the most promising entrance to the possibilities in narrative.[2]

The fresh possibilities in the historical study of memory have two starting points, deeply embedded in historians' narrative traditions, that are now being hailed as major discoveries in other disciplines. The first is that memory, private and individual as much as collective and cultural, is constructed, not reproduced. The second is that this construction is not made in isolation but in conversations with others that occur in the contexts of community, broader politics, and social dynamics. Before we can explore further implications for historians in these starting points, we need to look at their origin in recent scholarship in other fields. That scholarship has forced a reconsideration of traditional assumptions about the workings of memory.

Historians have traditionally been concerned above all with the accuracy of a memory, with how correctly it describes what actually occurred at some point in the past. We compare different accounts of the same event and evaluate which is most accurate. Remembering, we tend to think, is a process by which people search some kind of storage system in their minds—a filing cabinet or computer "memory," perhaps—to see whether they can retrieve some objective record of a fact or experience they had learned or observed at some earlier point. We expect the accuracy of a memory to be shaped by the observer's physical proximity in time and space to the event. Memories fade over time. In the century since the modern science of memory began by studying how accurately, quickly, and durably subjects could remember nonsense syllables, experimental psychologists have searched for the mechanisms by which people sort and retrieve what they have learned and the locations in the brain where the memories are stored. When memory was believed to be an objective representation of a piece of information (like the text of the Fourteenth Amendment) or of an experience (like a conversation), the central issues for historians and psychologists alike did indeed pivot around how people stored and retrieved that objective representation. Any divergence between a person's recollection and the objective reality the recollection sought to describe reflected some physical, mental, or psychological disability in a person's storage and retrieval capacities.

During the 1980s a dramatic reconception of memory seemed to arise from the confluence of two lines of inquiry. The origins of this new approach reach back to Frederick C. Bartlett's classic, *Remembering* (1932). After asking subjects to remember and retell a complex tale several times over several months, Bartlett observed that it was "common to find the preliminary check, the struggle to get somewhere, the varying play of doubt, hesitation, satisfaction and the like, and the eventual building up of the complete story accompanied by the more and more confident advance in a certain direction." From this finding he concluded that "remembering appears to be far more decisively an affair of construction rather than one of mere reproduction." In

[2] Ronald J. Grele, "On Using Oral History Collections: An Introduction," *Journal of American History*, 74 (Sept. 1987), 570–78, esp. 570, 571. See also Alessandro Portelli, "The Peculiarities of Oral History," *History Workshop*, 12 (Autumn 1982), esp. 103–4. For an example of the call for narrative, see Thomas Bender, "Wholes and Parts: The Need for Synthesis in American History," *Journal of American History*, 73 (June 1986), 120–36.

each construction of a memory, people reshape, omit, distort, combine, and reorganize details from the past in an active and subjective way. They mix pieces from the present with elements from different periods in the past. "If we change the way we think about the world," explained Jean Piaget and B. Inhelder in 1973, "we automatically update memories to reflect our new understanding."[3]

While psychologists concluded that memory was a process of creative construction, biologists discovered that the brain had no central storage facility to hold bits of information. The fundamental unit for memory, they speculated, was a system of neurons, circuits, or loops that enable people to associate things endlessly with other things. Each localized loop or neuron changes through its association with others in what appears to be a new pattern each time. Instead of envisioning the physiology of memory as a hierarchical system driven by a central command unit, some investigators believe that the coordination among localized and specialized loops that creates memory is more akin to the way skilled players on a team cooperate to create a single play. Each player has a position, but each also has flexibility and judgment to meet new circumstances as a play unfolds.

Memory begins when something in the present stimulates an association. The association might be recognition of the circumstances or context of the thing in the present. Or it might be recall of an image or smell or emotion. In trying to remember a high school friend's name, for example, we often begin with associations: What did she look like? Who were her friends? How did I feel when I met her? What was the first letter in her last name? What did her name sound like? Each association then triggers another in a chain until we conclude that we have "remembered" enough for the situation. People can quit remembering at any point or can turn to expert help—psychoanalysis, hypnosis, or truth drugs, for example—if they want to push the associations further or deeper than they can on their own. The uncontrolled nature of many associations explains why people interrupt their associations with exclamations like "I forgot my point" or "I can't remember why I came into this room." It also explains why those powerful memory narratives, our dreams, often recruit for a single story actors who came from different periods in our lives and never met each other in the real past. While it will be many years before the precise nature of these loops or circuits is mapped for human memory (as they have been mapped for memory in sea snails), biologists now support the recent subjectivist thrust in psychology that envisions each memory as an active and new construction made from many tiny associations, not a passive process of storing and retrieving full-blown objective representations of past experiences.[4]

The starting place for the construction of an individual recollection is a present need or circumstance. When historians begin an evaluation of a narrative by wondering

[3] Frederick C. Bartlett, *Remembering: A Study in Experimental and Social Psychology* (1932; reprint, Cambridge, Eng., 1961), 205–9; for Jean Piaget and B. Inhelder's statement, see Edmund Blair Bolles, *Remembering and Forgetting: An Inquiry into the Nature of Memory* (New.York, 1988), 17.

[4] The most helpful layman's introduction to the major landmarks in the psychology and physiology of memory is Bolles, *Remembering and Forgetting*. Several psychological perspectives that emerge from the same new approach to memory are introduced in Ulric Neisser and Eugene Winograd, eds., *Remembering Reconsidered: Ecological and Traditional Approaches to the Study of Memory* (Cambridge, Eng., 1988).

about a person's motives or biases or mood or audience at the particular time and place when the person constructed the memory—rather than, say, proximity to the event being recalled—we focus on what psychologists now consider the crucial point. Likewise, people often begin their recollections with reminders, such as slides from a family vacation or notes taken at the moment one wants to recall. John Dean constructed his remarkable Watergate narrative from newspaper accounts that reminded him of public events that reminded him, in turn, of his actions and conversations on a particular day. Since an individual's starting points change as the person grows and changes, people reshape their recollections of the past to fit their present needs (as in recalling inaccurately that they had not spanked their children after it became unfashionable to spank children) and select from the present material that supports deeply held interpretations from the past (as in finding evidence in the newspaper to support long-standing political biases). People are often surprised when they first learn that friends plan to get a divorce, but then they reconstruct their associations with the couple and create a new pattern in which the divorce seems a more logical outcome of what they remembered. Since the reality is that an individual's needs and perceptions do change even as he or she remains the same person, people sometimes construct their personal life histories as a record of stability, continuity, and consistency (as when they feel warmly toward some past association) and sometimes as a record of change (as when they feel proud about losing weight or getting better grades or jobs). Instead of emphasizing how an individual conforms to an abstract or normative view of development, many personality theorists and therapists now emphasize how individuals construct their own scripts or life narratives as a way of ordering their pasts to shape their identities in the present. To simplify their associations, people conflate details from similar experiences into a generalized recollection or schema that can stand for a class of experiences. David C. Rubin has shown how generalized schemata are sufficient for ballad singers to remember and sing a particular ballad and for college students to remember and identify American coins. People can recall the structure of a foreign language for fifty years, but they quickly forget vocabulary words, the gender for nouns, and other details. In a probing evaluation of John Dean's vivid memory of his conversations with Richard M. Nixon, Ulric Neisser has shown that Dean incorrectly recalled most of the details and even the gist of the conversations but that he was correct about the basic fact that Nixon and his top aides were engaged in an elaborate cover-up to conceal their involvement in the Watergate break-in.[5]

A dramatic example of how people create memories is provided in this book by

[5] Michael Ross and Michael Conway, "Remembering One's Own Past: The Construction of Personal Histories," in *Handbook of Motivation and Cognition: Foundations of Social Behavior*, ed. Richard M. Sorrentino and E. Tory Higgins (New York, 1986), 122–44; Michael Ross et al., "Reciprocal Relation between Attitudes and Behavior Recall: Committing People to Newly Formed Attitudes," *Journal of Personality and Social Psychology*, 45 (Aug. 1983), 257–67; Dan P. McAdams and Richard L. Ochberg, eds., *Psychobiography and Life Narratives* (Durham, N.C., 1988), esp. 1–18, 105–38, 173–204; Wanda T. Wallace and David C. Rubin, "'The Wreck of the Old 97': A Real Event Remembered in Song," in Neisser and Winograd, eds., *Remembering Reconsidered*, 283–310; Rubin and Theda C. Kontis, "A Schema for Common Cents," *Memory & Cognition*, 11 (July 1983), 335–41; Harry P. Bahrick, "Semantic Memory Content in Permastore: Fifty Years of Memory for Spanish Learned in School," *Journal of Experimental Psychology: General*, 113 (March 1984), 1–26; Ulric Neisser, "John Dean's Memory: A Case Study," *Cognition*, 9 (Feb. 1981), 1–21.

Robert E. McGlone. John Brown's children, McGlone shows, continually distorted what they had done (and not done) at Harpers Ferry in 1859 as they reshaped their memories to create a family identity for themselves in the decades that followed their father's "treasonous" raid to free the slaves. Instead of viewing their efforts as dishonest or immoral or the products of defective recall, McGlone suggests that the Browns' reconstructions reflect typical processes by which people construct and reconstruct memories.

The ways that individuals shape, omit, distort, recall, and reorganize their memories—as the case of the Brown family illustrates—grow at least as much from interactions with others as from solitary construction. In his pathbreaking exploration *The Collective Memory,* first published in 1925, Maurice Halbwachs maintained that individuals required the testimony and evidence of other people to validate their interpretations of their own experiences, to provide independent confirmation (or refutation) of the content of their memories and thus confidence in their accuracy. Confirmation of a person's recollection by a second—and independent—eyewitness or source is the standard technique used to establish accuracy by journalists, lawyers, and historians. When people look to others to assist them in deciding whether their associations have yielded an accurate narrative of an event or experience, they acknowledge the need for a check on the subjective process by which they create a recollection. Michael Schudson has recently underscored how realities of the past constrict the range within which people are able to create new interpretations of that past.[6]

For our purposes the social dimensions of memory are more important than the need to verify accuracy. People depend on others to help them decide which experiences to forget and which to remember and what interpretation to place on an experience. People develop a shared identity by identifying, exploring, and agreeing on memories. The cautious and mutual discovery by two people of shared memories "is in and of itself the very elixir of friendmaking," observed Fred Davis. New spouses form an identity for their own new family, wrote Halbwachs, through "a great mutual effort full of surprises, difficulty, conflict, and sacrifice" by which they identify which memories from their earlier separate families they want to make defining features of their own new identity. People seek to freeze or preserve memories by taking pictures that remind them of shared moments or people from the past. In discussing which pictures to frame or place in albums, people literally decide what image of their pasts they want to show others (including historians, if we would use such sources). In the course of taking a picture or creating an album they decide what they want to remember and how they want to remember it.[7]

[6] Michael Schudson, "The Present in the Past versus the Past in the Present," *Communication*, 11 (No. 2 1989), 105–13.

[7] Maurice Halbwachs, *The Collective Memory*, trans. Francis J. Ditter, Jr., and Vida Yazdi Ditter (1950; reprint, New York, 1980), 22–49, esp. 121; Nathan Wachtel, "Memory and History: Introduction," *History and Anthropology*, 2 (Oct. 1986), 207–21; Fred Davis, *Yearning for Yesterday: A Sociology of Nostalgia* (New York, 1979), 43; David Lowenthal, *The Past Is a Foreign Country* (Cambridge, Eng., 1985), esp. 196–97. On eyewitnesses, the pioneering exploration is Elizabeth F. Loftus, *Eyewitness Testimony* (Cambridge, Mass., 1979). On the importance of pictures as people grow older, see Mihaly Csikszentmihalyi and Eugene Rochberg-Halton, *The Meaning of Things: Domestic Symbols and the Self* (Cambridge, Eng., 1981), 67–68, 112.

The ways that people depend on others to shape their recollections thus create an apparent paradox. People refashion the past to please the people with whom they discuss and interpret it, but they also depend on the accuracy of accounts by others to gain confidence in the accuracy of their own memories.[8] That paradox may explain why people reshape their memories even as they often insist that their memories are vivid, unchanging, and accurate. In the recollections of the discovery of the Watergate tapes published in this book, Alexander Butterfield and Scott Armstrong graphically illustrate how people cherish the sense of a vivid and unchanging recollection even as they reshape the content of their recollections. The ways that Butterfield, for example, reconstructed his account of the past in response to new audiences are similar to the ways historians reconstruct their accounts of the past to address new audiences while insisting that the new account is a more accurate depiction of the past. Like people in ordinary conversation, historians move backward and forward between present and past as they create their accounts of the past. My conversations with Butterfield illustrate how the give-and-take between two particular people influences what parts of a memory get repeated by rote, what parts get reopened for fresh consideration, and what parts get reshaped. What is important is that the memory be authentic for the person at the moment of construction, not that it be an accurate description of a past moment.

The historical study of memory would be the study of how families, larger gatherings of people, and formal organizations selected and interpreted identifying memories to serve changing needs. It would explore how people together searched for common memories to meet present needs, how they first recognized such a memory and then agreed, disagreed, or negotiated over its meaning, and finally how they preserved and absorbed that meaning into their ongoing concerns.

Since collective memories are constructed and modified by individuals who must be able to recognize their own pasts in the group's shared memory, the historical study of memory can provide fresh perspectives on how individuals and smaller groups shaped and were shaped by larger groups and processes. What in their circumstances led them to seek out others with whom to share memories? What did individuals emphasize, reinterpret, and abandon from their own memories in order to create a shared identity with others? People whose ancestors brought very local and specific memories of lives in County Cork, Tuscany, a Yoruban village, or a Kentucky hollow to their new circumstances in, say, Chicago soon discovered, as they found others with whom to share their lives, that their families' defining memories had actually been "Irish," "Italian," "African," or "Appalachian." Tamara K. Hareven has suggested that many immigrants and their descendants were driven by assimilationist pressures in the United States to make a more self-conscious search for "roots" and shared experiences after their particular groups ceased to be replenished with new migrants. To construct and participate in that larger memory, however, they had to abandon or reinterpret

---

[8] E. Tory Higgins and William S. Roles, "'Saying Is Believing': Effects of Message Modification on Memory and Liking for the Person Described," *Journal of Experimental Social Psychology*, 14 (July 1978), 363–78.

elements of their own pasts. The experience of enslavement in an English-speaking environment, Sterling Stuckey has explained, led African Americans to search among their varied religious, tribal, and linguistic memories for common sources from which to construct a shared English-speaking slave culture. In a similar vein men and women have drawn on diverse experiences with gender relationships, as Joan Scott has argued, to construct new definitions, identities, and interactions at different times and places. Far from determining single perspectives, race, ethnicity, and gender provide individuals and groups with richly varied memories from which they construct new meanings and identities.[9]

As intriguing as the ways people negotiated a larger collective identity out of many smaller pieces are the ways they reached back to some very remote past to recover a feeling or memory to meet present needs. What led people who no longer practiced languages or customs from their families' places of origin to decide that they wanted their children to learn Gaelic or Hebrew outside the home? How did they build group identities in the United States around struggles for an Irish free state, a Zionist homeland, abolition of apartheid in South Africa, or Serbian or Armenian independence? Under what immediate circumstances did evangelicals suddenly reject parts of their secular lives and instead draw on or even invent memories of past, and presumably more fundamental, religious practice or enthusiasm as newfound guides to belief and conduct? What connections between present and past, between private memory and public identity, inspired individuals and groups to campaign to "preserve" environment or neighborhood or culture or architectural landmark? What remembered pasts were they trying to preserve, and why?

Since politicians must by trade find memories that still have private resonance for large numbers of voters, politics opens many ways for exploring how individuals connected (or failed to connect) their private memories with the defining memories of larger groups and associations. In the decades after the Civil War, politicians urged voters to "vote the way your father shot." The Democratic party gained a generation's hold over voters by linking its present appeal to people's private memories of the Great Depression and Franklin D. Roosevelt (and Herbert Hoover). When those memories ceased to be defining experiences in the private recollections of many voters, the Democrats seemed to lose public purpose and vision. Since appeals to memories have long saturated political discourse, voters have learned to tell when politicians are making routine, calculated, and rhetorical uses of memory and when they are describing memory in the same vivid, personal, defining ways that voters use it to meet their present needs. A spectacular example of that difference occurred during the vice-presidential debate of 1988 when Dan Quayle sought votes from people with positive memories of John F. Kennedy by suggesting that he and Kennedy had shared experiences (and generations). Lloyd Bentsen answered Quayle's familiar kind of rehearsed appeal by vivid and authentic memory rooted in firsthand experience: "I served with

[9] Tamara K. Hareven, "The Search for Generational Memory: Tribal Rites in Industrial Society," *Daedalus*, 137 (Fall 1978), 137, 147–49; Sterling Stuckey, *Slave Culture: Nationalist Theory and the Foundations of Black America* (New York, 1987), 3–97; Joan Wallach Scott, *Gender and the Politics of History* (New York, 1988), esp. Introduction and chs. 1 and 2.

Jack Kennedy. I knew Jack Kennedy. Jack Kennedy was a friend of mine. Senator, you're no Jack Kennedy." [10] Watchers (and pundits) gasped. They knew the difference between a memory that a person constructed on the spot out of a vivid experience and in response to an immediate present need and a rehearsed appeal that floated lazily out in hopes that listeners somewhere might somehow connect it with their own personal memories.

Since people seem to use common patterns in constructing memories in response to change, social history opens promising fields for the study of memory. Perhaps the most familiar theme of social history is that people have resisted rapid, alien, and imposed change by creating memories of a past that was unchanging, incorruptible, and harmonious. They mobilize those memories to resist change. In exploring how Malaysian peasants resisted economic changes in their communities, James C. Scott argued that villagers "collectively created a *remembered village* and a *remembered economy* that served as an effective ideological backdrop against which to explore the present." "Their memory," wrote Scott, "focuses precisely on those beneficial aspects of tenure and labor relations that have been eroded or swept away over the last ten years. That they do not dwell upon other, less favorable, features of the old order is hardly surprising, for those features do not contribute to the argument they wish to make today." [11] In this book John Bodnar shows how the same process took place in more familiar settings. On the basis of interviews with former Studebaker employees in South Bend, Indiana, many years after they lost their jobs in the plant's 1963 closing, Bodnar shows how individuals constructed a chronology in which a stable past defined by a friendly workplace gave way to a contentious time of change and conflict that ended in the plant's closing.

When the central issue about these recollections becomes their construction, not their accuracy, old issues become moot and new ones becomes urgent. When Herbert Gutman and many of his followers interpreted workers' struggles as attempts to preserve warmly remembered and stable traditions in the face of change, they were often criticized for inaccurate and romantic characterizations of the past. In a study of memory the important question is not how accurately a recollection fitted some piece of a past reality, but why historical actors constructed their memories in a particular way at a particular time. The hunt for the moment when life (or work) was "traditional" is pointless, as folklorist Dell Hymes has observed, because all peoples "traditionalize" some aspects of their experience to meet social needs in the present. Instead of dismissing the construction of imagined pasts as romantic, escapist, inaccurate, or neurotic, we should try to understand why it is so common. Why did people in the relatively prosperous 1970s recall the 1930s, not as a time of misery and struggle, but as a time when people had been closer to each other, warmer and more caring, more "like a family" to each other? Why did they "traditionalize" familylike warmth when they recalled their pasts for oral historians or when they watched television programs like "The Waltons"? Why did they "forget" the public combat and private misery?

---

[10] Quoted by David Broder, *Columbia* (Missouri) *Tribune*, Oct. 6, 1988, p. 1.
[11] James C. Scott, *Weapons of the Weak: Everyday Forms of Peasant Resistance* (New Haven, 1985), 178–79; Lowenthal, *The Past Is a Foreign Country*, 40–41.

Why did some southern whites energize their resistance to Reconstruction with memories of a "Lost Cause"? [12]

Since people's memories provide security, authority, legitimacy, and finally identity in the present, struggles over the possession and interpretation of memories are deep, frequent, and bitter. Like George Orwell's Big Brother, powerful creators and imposers of historical change fear that they will fail to win popular approval for their changes so long as people combine their private memories of a warm and unchanged past with the local customs and folkways of community, workplace, and religion. Big Brother could triumph only when he persuaded people that they could no longer trust the authenticity of their memories as a yardstick against which to evaluate his assertions. "The struggle of man against power is the struggle of memory against forgetting," wrote Milan Kundera of the attempts by many Czechoslovakians to preserve their culture in the face of a Soviet drive to obliterate memories and compel the silence, if not the loyalty, of those whose land they occupied. [13] David W. Blight illustrates the wisdom of Kundera's maxim in his essay for this book. Blight shows how Frederick Douglass fought for thirty years to keep alive among northern whites the memory of the Civil War as an emancipatory struggle. That memory, Douglass believed, was the freedmen's best weapon for resisting southern white schemes to establish more oppressive race relations.

Faced with people's tendency to widen and deepen their positive associations with remembered realities when confronted by imposed change, leaders have invented traditions and myths whose repetition will, they hope, at least weaken the confidence of tradition-minded peoples in their memories. "It is the contrast between the constant change and innovation of the modern world and the attempt to structure at least some parts of social life within it as unchanging and invariant, that makes the 'invention of tradition' so interesting for historians of the past two centuries," wrote Eric Hobsbawm in a pathbreaking introduction to the problem. In the late 1940s the promoters and advertisers for the new medium of television confronted the strong likelihood that they would be unable to sell their sponsors' products, argues George Lipsitz, because many potential buyers had emerged from the depression and war with deep collective memories of ethnic and working-class experiences that were alien to an individualistic ethic of consumption. The promoters' solution was to create situation comedies such as "The Honeymooners," "Amos N' Andy," "Life of Riley," "Mama," "Hey Jeannie," "Life with Luigi," and "The Goldbergs" in which characters with working-class and ethnic backgrounds resolved the problems of work and family life by buying happiness in the form of consumer goods and not by waging collective battles against powerful interests in their lives. [14]

[12] Herbert G. Gutman, *Work, Culture and Society in Industrializing America: Essays in American Working Class and Social History* (New York, 1977), esp. 3–117; Dell Hymes, "Folklore's Nature and the Sun's Myth," *Journal of American Folklore*, 88 (Oct.–Dec. 1975), 353–54; Studs Terkel, *Hard Times: An Oral History of the Great Depression* (New York, 1970), 41, 100; Jacquelyn D. Hall, "Politics and Poetics: Writing the History of Southern Workers," paper delivered at the conference "(Re-) Writing American Literary History," University of Frankfurt, West Germany, June, 1988 (in David Thelen's possession).

[13] Milan Kundera, *The Book of Laughter and Forgetting*, trans. Michael Henry Heim (New York, 1981), 3.

[14] Eric Hobsbawm, "Introduction: Inventing Traditions," in *The Invention of Tradition*, ed. Eric Hobsbawm and Terrence Ranger (Cambridge, Eng., 1984), 1; George Lipsitz, "The Meaning of Memory: Family, Class, and Ethnicity in Early Network Television Programs," *Cultural Anthropology*, 1 (Nov. 1986), 355–87.

The struggle for possession and interpretation of memory is rooted in the conflict and interplay among social, political, and cultural interests and values in the present. The actors appeal for popular support by claiming the sanction of the past. People test such public appeals against their personal and private memories, and to support their recollections, however distorted, they form and re-form conclusions, connecting and disconnecting public appeals in ever-changing ways to their private memories. If the line between the personal and the political is as indistinct as many scholars argue, these everyday conversations about "private" memory are at least tinged with political meaning and can lead to participation. From actors' conflicts and negotiations over memory are born traditions, legends, myths, rituals, and more formalized cultural expressions of collective memory. Hoping to win popular approval for their plans for massive economic development of the continent, Richard Slotkin argues, American developers invented the myth of the frontier as the source for American exceptionalism and hoped that myth would tap popular memories and experiences. A focus on memory would lead us to treat myths, not as disembodied values, but as creations of people with real needs. Earlier historians' discoveries of American myths of the virgin land, the agrarian past, the machine and the garden, the self-made man, and, above all, the myth of progress itself might be reinterpreted as products of the struggle over memory. And the myths might be revisited to discover how people reshaped—and ignored—them so they would better connect (or fail to connect) with their private memories. [15]

Popular negotiations over memory were more like an endless conversation than a simple vote on a proposition. Each construction of a new memory, like that of a myth, grew from earlier associations and conversations. Different elements got repressed, forgotten, and reshaped only to reemerge later in the conversation in a new form. The difficulty of accepting military and political defeat in Vietnam led many Americans, as Michael Frisch has argued, to deny that experience and any lessons that might be learned from it and applied to policy toward other Third World countries. [16] And yet, as Freud pointed out, it is very hard to keep even the most painful memory from coming back in some new form. So often did Oliver North refer to Vietnam in his summer 1987 testimony in support of his Iran-Contra deal that he sounded more interested in defending the Vietnam policy of 1967 than the Nicaraguan policy of 1987.

The creation of the Vietnam Veterans Memorial may exemplify the most common resolution of the tension between participants' private memories of an event and elites' preferences for turning the past into myths that promote uniformity and stability. Supporters and opponents of the war remembered it as a political or a military folly, depending on viewpoint, that had embarrassed the United States in the world and sapped its political will at home. To the men and women who fought the war, the ones whose sacrifice was to be remembered, however, there was no single "war in Vietnam." There were, rather, thousands of different experiences and memories that veterans felt

---

[15] Richard Slotkin, *The Fatal Environment: The Myth of the Frontier in the Age of Industrialization, 1800–1890* (New York, 1985), chs. 2 and 3, esp. pp. 33–45.

[16] Michael Frisch, "The Memory of History," in *Presenting the Past: Essays on History and the Public*, ed. Susan Porter Benson, Stephen Brier, and Roy Rosenzweig (Philadelphia, 1986), 5–17.

no one wanted to hear when they returned home. Maya Lin designed a memorial that brilliantly allowed those with large political agendas and those with intimate private memories to come together. She envisioned a simple wall on which would be carved the names of Americans who had died in Vietnam. To those with policy agendas the sheer number of names was an overwhelming reminder of folly. To veterans the names triggered a different scale and kind of memory. "If I can touch the name of my friends who died," wrote a former infantryman, "maybe I will finally have time to react. Maybe I will end up swearing, maybe crying, maybe smiling, remembering a funny incident. Whatever it is, I will have time and the focal point to do it now. There just wasn't the emotional time in Nam to know what happened." [17] The tension between invented traditions and private memories may finally resolve into one of scale. Big memorials may legitimate elites' conduct in their own eyes, but they also provide space for people to nurture the intimate memories of the most searing experiences in their individual lives.

The debate over whether and how to remember Vietnam overlaps and parallels the debate about "American Memory." What do—and should—Americans remember from the nation's past as the defining experiences that shape our present? We are indebted to conservatives, as Michael Frisch shows in this book, for raising the question of how and why Americans "remember" so few so-called landmarks of Western and American civilization. It is less clear that conservatives are correct in believing that the cause of this "forgetting" is the democratization of culture and curriculum in the 1960s and the alleged accompanying consequences of undisciplined thinking at the expense of rigorous memorization and of "fringe" subjects, such as black literature or women's studies, at the expense of presumed core topics. Frisch cites his own polls to demonstrate that the alleged changes of the 1960s have not much influenced the content of "American Memory" at all.

The debate over "American Memory" returns us to two central concerns in creating this book. While most discussion has centered on what content students should be required to learn, there is at least as important a question about how to teach about memory itself. What names and facts should students be required to memorize and then retrieve as signposts for the rest of their lives? That approach to memory nicely fitted the view that memories were objective representations, passively stored, but it simply does not fit the view of memory as a subjective process of active construction. If we wanted a history curriculum that taught people how to use memories, we would focus on how memories are constructed. We would help students learn how to get honest and accurate feedback for their own constructions even as they followed their natural wishes to find support for their conclusions. We would encourage them to learn how to challenge, adapt, and construct memories instead of accepting interpretations that others seek to impose on them, how to test appeals to the past instead of accepting them on faith and authority. We would explore the social and communal contexts in which memories are created, reshaped, and forgotten. We would illustrate

---

[17] Jan C. Scruggs and Joel L. Swerdlow, *To Heal a Nation: The Vietnam Veterans Memorial* (New York, 1985), 70–71, 99, esp. 126.

how their memories can lead as naturally to progressive constructions and ideologies as to conservative ones.

The debate over "American Memory" is finally about audiences for American history. Frisch found that the remembered signposts of the past in the 1980s were pretty much what they would have been in the 1950s. The Right's fears of radical transformation of popular historical consciousness are apparently unfounded. While we need to explore why, we also need to explore how his finding fits with an equally intriguing development. Frisch, like many others, is understandably troubled by the gap between the content that amateur audiences associate with "American History" and the content that is presently taught in most graduate departments of history. There is undoubtedly a chasm between popular and professional approaches to the past, as David Lowenthal suggests in this book, that will be very hard to bridge. Why, for example, has the new social history had so little impact on popular memories? How can we connect our craft with the wider audiences that clearly like history when the memories of those audiences are so different from the memories of professional historians?

We hope that this book will point to an approach that underscores similarities in the ways people construct and reconstruct memories of the past regardless of the ways they earn their incomes. And we hope those similarities will help bridge gaps among the many different people who make their historical understanding in many different settings.

This book is truly a collective effort by many people. It is first of all a collective effort by the superb staff of the *Journal of American History*. Only those who have worked with them can appreciate the tremendous contributions of Susan Armeny, Richard Blackett, Nicole Etcheson, Mary Jane Gormley, Paul Murphy, Ricky Newport, Dotti Riggins, Barbara Scales, Steven Stowe, Greg Sumner, and Mary Ann Wynkoop. I would also like to thank several people for encouragement, ideas, criticism, and suggestions along the course of thinking about, writing, and revising this chapter and book: Susan Armeny, Richard Blackett, Casey Blake, John Bodnar, Michael Frisch, Robert Griffith, Jacquelyn Hall, Jackson Lears, Richard Shiffrin, Esther Thelen, and Herbert Thelen.

American History and the Structures of Collective Memory: A Modest Exercise in Empirical Iconography

Michael Frisch

For over a decade now, I have been accumulating some fascinating data on the images of American history that my students have carried around in their heads before entering my classroom. The term *data* may be misleadingly scientific, and I am not even sure my hunting and gathering process deserves to be called research, since it began playfully, as little more than a tonic designed to fortify student recruits setting out on their uncertain trek across the arid reaches of the standard survey course. Increasingly, however, I have come to sense that there may be some broader meaning, or at least interest, in the picture gradually emerging from this experimentation.

That sense has been recently sharpened by loud alarums—the very lively debate about American education's role in the ominously accelerating historical amnesia reportedly afflicting high school and college students. As it happens, my modest experiments in what can be called "empirical iconography," conducted well before that debate emerged, address its concerns quite directly, providing a certain reassurance in the face of the jeremiads while raising some disturbing questions of a rather different sort.

Let me begin with some brief frame-setting observations about the problem at hand. I will then turn to a straightforward unfolding of my quasi-scientific data combined with some unlicensed flights of exegetical excess. I will conclude by returning to the contemporary debate about American education and historical memory, in order to see how different it may appear after our excursion into the realm of the collective historical subconscious, or at least that portion of it embodied in the responses of over one thousand students at the State University of New York at Buffalo (SUNY-Buffalo) over the past decade.

As a general matter, discussions of historical memory have not been very clear about the relation of individual-level processes—what and how we remember, whether about our own or more broadly historical experience—and the processes of collective memory, those broader patterns through which culture may shape the

Michael Frisch is professor of history and American studies at the State University of New York at Buffalo and editor of the *Oral History Review*. An earlier version of this paper was presented at the "Symposium on Memory and History" at Baylor University in February 1988.

1

parameters, structure, and even the content of our sense of history. My impression is that the two levels of discussion have remained relatively separate, the former engaging more those concerned with psychology, education, language, and to an extent oral history, the latter of interest to cultural historians.

The current debate about history, culture, and education in American life has brought these differing aspects of memory together, since it focuses on what individuals know about history, how they come to know (or not know) it, and what this says about our collective culture, in terms of both cause and broader effect. I will presume a certain familiarity with the recently discovered crisis of cultural illiteracy, which seems to have struck a genuine chord of some kind. Two basic texts by the prophets Allan Bloom and E. D. Hirsch, Jr., have been improbable best sellers for many months, and there has been widespread discussion of documents such as *A Nation at Risk*, the report of the National Commission on Excellence in Education, and *American Memory: A Report on the Humanities in the Nation's Public Schools*, by Lynne V. Cheney, the chairman of the National Endowment for the Humanities. All have worked their way into newsweekly cover stories and extensive television news reports. The most recent sensation, Diane Ravitch and Chester E. Finn, Jr.'s *What Do Our Seventeen-Year-Olds Know?* has seemed to offer the hard epidemiological evidence on which the declaration of a cultural health emergency has been based.[1]

This literature is far from uniform, but for present purposes it is possible to identify at least three linked propositions sounded consistently in all these works, and others in the same vein. The first, already noted, is that our students and young adults are woefully ignorant of the most basic orienting facts of history, particularly our own American history, much less its larger meanings, with the result that the strings of a shared cultural memory have been cut. The second proposition is that this severing of memory is a direct consequence of a failure of education, of the diminished place of history education in the curriculum at every level, and of a deterioration in the pedagogy by which we teach whatever history has managed to survive. The final proposition, a derivative of the first two, is that unless there is a drastic change in the quantity and quality of the teaching of history, the only issue will be whether we collapse from internal disintegration before we are overwhelmed by economic and political threats from without. Indeed, the most apocalyptic critics mirror the homophobic Right in its view of Acquired Immune Deficiency Syndrome

---

[1] The best sellers, of course, are E. D. Hirsch, Jr., *Cultural Literacy: What Every American Needs to Know* (New York, 1987); and Allan Bloom, *The Closing of the American Mind: How Higher Education Has Failed Democracy and Impoverished the Souls of Today's Students* (New York, 1987). The 1987 study by the chairman of the National Endowment for the Humanities is Lynne V. Cheney, *American Memory: A Report on the Humanities in the Nation's Public Schools* (Washington, 1987), which follows the 1983 report of the National Commission on Excellence in Education, *A Nation at Risk: The Imperative for Educational Reform* (Washington, 1983). Both are available from the U.S. Government Printing Office. The new study is Diane Ravitch and Chester E. Finn, Jr., *What Do Our Seventeen-Year-Olds Know? A Report on the First National Assessment of History and Literature* (New York, 1987). For a representative example of the mass-mediated digestion of this debate, see the cover story, "What Americans Should Know," *U.S. News and World Report*, Sept. 28, 1987, pp. 86–94.

(AIDS), seeing the amnesia epidemic as at once a threat to our survival and a kind of divine judgment on a culture gone wrong.

All three propositions involve history and memory, and all turn out, on close examination, to be something short of self-evident, at least in the sense in which they are usually advanced. The last mentioned, of course, is so dependent on a particular ideological world view as to be beyond the critical discussion appropriate in this forum. The first two, however, can be stated in objective, even quantitative, form, and are amenable to both internal and external test.

The evidence I present today is offered in this empirical spirit. As for the first, root proposition, my data challenge the amnesiac conclusion itself, quite directly. While my tables can lay little claim to scientific validity, in at least one respect they address the central question more squarely than most of the well-funded research on which the current debate rests. Ravitch and Finn's title notwithstanding, the major survey work has pursued a kind of inversion of Howard Baker's famous Watergate query: What don't the students know and since when haven't they known it? But to answer such questions, even assuming the validity of the dubious survey instrument, is not necessarily to discover the other side of the coin, to see and understand what they *do* know.[2] However inadvertently, my somewhat whimsical investigation may have stumbled on some very different results because it began as an attempt to map that very terrain, to explore an interior historical landscape exactly as presented by students.

In fact, the expedition has revealed an environment so strikingly uniform as to cast a significant shadow over the remaining proposition — that pedagogy and curriculum are critical variables in the structuring of American memory. My evidence suggests that our students' historical memory may not, in fact, be shaped so much by their education or lack of it as by collective cultural mechanisms and structures we need to understand better. In that sense, the research bears quite directly on a central focus of recent cultural studies, the concept of "civil religion." Those studies argue the existence in American culture of a set of shared beliefs, myths, "meaning systems," and historical images forming a functionally religious structure, and inquire into the content, origins, and functions of the complex, both as a general cultural concept and in terms of its particular American meaning.[3]

Because so much prior discussion has relied on literary, rather than empirical, evidence of the very existence, much less shared acceptance, of such core cultural beliefs, my data may help advance the inquiry. Cultural analysis, in turn, has much to contribute to our understanding of the broader relation of history to memory. Unless we can bring those two far-from-identical concepts together in a clearly demarcated arena, we will have difficulty penetrating an increasingly strident public

---

[2] See two useful reviews of Ravitch and Finn, *What Do Our Seventeen-Year-Olds Know?* that develop this point: Deborah Meier and Florence Miller, "The Book of Lists," *Nation*, Jan. 9, 1988, pp. 25–27; and Etta Moser, "What They Do Know," *ibid.*, 27–28.

[3] The best single discussion, as well as the best case study application, is Catherine L. Albanese, *Sons of the Fathers: The Civil Religion of the American Revolution* (Philadelphia, 1976). See also Hirsch, *Cultural Literacy*, 98–103, for a discussion especially relevant to the context of this essay.

discourse in which they are being pressed into the service of some not-so-hidden agendas. But if the debate is approached with careful curiosity and the conceptual tools commonly found in our scholarly workshops, it may be possible to get closer to the core of legitimate concern in it. Even more, I believe this may be one of the rare instances where the benefits flow both ways—where the heat of a particular polemic can generate light sufficient to illuminate some of the issues.

Let me describe my classroom laboratory. Over a decade ago, I was first assigned to take my turn conducting the first semester of our standard year-long American history survey course, from the beginning through the Civil War. As one who had been teaching the relatively exotic specialty of urban and social history, I realized that this would be an initiation in which I would have to teach materials that most of my students had previously encountered, in what I presumed to be high school versions that were parochial at best and grossly distorted at the expected worst. With all the arrogance of a beginner, I expected my major task to be the clearing of a forest of facts, names, dates, and conventional concepts in order to build, out of the logs of American experience, a city of insight and understanding.

As a way to survey the wilderness before me, I began the very first class with a spot quiz: I asked the students to take out blank paper and to write down, without undue reflection, the first ten names that popped into their heads in response to the prompt "American history from its beginning through the end of the Civil War." Assuming that the lists would be predictably presidential, starting with George Washington, after the students had finished I suggested that the experiment be repeated, but this time excluding presidents, generals, statesmen, or other figures in official public life. I hoped that the two lists in combination would be a reasonable approximation of the image of American history brought into the class. The quiz was anonymous, I assured them, simply a way to obtain, via free association, a kind of collective portrait of our starting point. My intention was to fashion, out of the collated answers, an opening lecture contrasting this high school image to the university-level alternative we would develop during the semester.

The results were in some ways quite surprising, which encouraged me to repeat the quizzes each time I taught the course. I have now run eight such surveys, between 1975 and 1988, involving over 1,000 students in groups ranging from 40 to 270. That is a sufficiently substantial base, I think, to justify taking a close look at the results.

Tables 1.1 and 1.2 present two representative surveys' tally for the first question, one from 1984 and the other from my current class in the fall 1988 semester. The parenthetic figures are the number of students mentioning each name. (About 95 took the quiz in 1984 and 220 in 1988.) I should note that the free association mechanism worked dramatically. Many students listed only five or six names and then froze, their minds a blank, although they realized on seeing the lists later that they "knew" virtually every name anybody had mentioned. It is, of course, the difference between those names recognized and those immediately leaping to mind that stu-

Table 1.1
Responses to Question One: 1984

(Question One: Write down the first ten names that you think of in response to the prompt, "American History from its beginning through the end of the Civil War.")

Rank	Name	Frequency	Rank	Name	Frequency
1	G. Washington	83	21	T. Paine	5
2	A. Lincoln	76	22	J. Davis	4
3	T. Jefferson	70	23	N. Hale	4
4	B. Franklin	52	24	J. Monroe	4
5	R. E. Lee	37	25	B. Arnold	3
6	U. S. Grant	31	26	J. Cabot	3
7	J. Adams	30	27	C. Cornwallis	3
8	C. Columbus	22	28	G. A. Custer	3
9	P. Revere	22	29	George III	3
10	J. Hancock	16	30	Lafayette	3
11	J. Smith	10	31	F. Magellan	3
12	A. Jackson	9	32	S. Adams	2
13	J. Q. Adams	7	33	D. Boone	2
14	J. W. Booth	7	34	A. Burr	2
15	A. Hamilton	7	35	H. Clay	2
16	B. Ross	7	36	T. Edison	2
17	P. Henry	6	37	F. S. Key	2
18	J. Madison	6	38	D. Madison	2
19	A. Jackson	5	39	Pocahontas	2
20	Lewis & Clark	5	40	H. Tubman	2

dents of culture, with backing from the psychologists, may find most interesting. The phenomenon also helps compensate for a methodological deficiency: In a more serious analysis, it would be important to analyze the order of mention as well as the frequency, but as that was beyond my statistical resources, I sought an approximation by limiting the time available and by encouraging students to stop when their minds began to go blank, rather than to fill up all ten places through more deliberate concentration.

The first tables are unsurprising, an array of mostly political and military figures crystallizing around the major defining events of United States history, the Revolution and the Civil War. There is little here to suggest anything other than the dutiful, civics-focused high school history courses whose residue I had expected to find. But as we shall see, the other results cast the lists in a somewhat different light.

Table 1.3 presents an eight-time comparison of answers to this question. The lists are of unequal length because of frequent ties, and because each survey rank orders all those names receiving at least three to six mentions, depending on the size of the class—wherever it falls ordinally, the last name marks a dropping-off point; all those below it received only relatively isolated mentions.

Table 1.2
Responses to Question One: 1988

(Question One: Write down the first ten names that you think of in response to the prompt, "American History from its beginning through the end of the Civil War.")

Rank	Name	Frequency	Rank	Name	Frequency
1	G. Washington	197	22	H. Tubman	8
2	A. Lincoln	192	23	George III	7
3	T. Jefferson	140	24	F. S. Key	7
4	B. Franklin	102	25	T. Edison	6
5	J. Adams	78	26	P. Henry	6
6	U. S. Grant	70	27	J. P. Jones	6
7	R. E. Lee	64	28	J. Q. Adams	5
8	A. Jackson	58	29	Lafayette	5
9	C. Columbus	49	30	W. T. Sherman	5
10	J. Hancock	37	31	A. Burr	4
11	J. Madison	25	32	F. Douglass	4
12	P. Revere	25	33	T. J. Jackson	4
13	A. Hamilton	22	34	A. Johnson	4
14	T. Paine	19	35	W. Penn	4
15	B. Ross	17	36	H. B. Stowe	4
16	G. A. Custer	11	37	D. Boone	3
17	J. Smith	11	38	C. Cornwallis	3
18	B. Arnold	9	39	S. Douglas	3
19	J. W. Booth	9	40	N. Hale	3
20	J. Monroe	9	41	Lewis & Clark	3
21	S. Adams	8	42	D. Madison	3
			43	M. Standish	3

The results confirm the initial impression of any one year, but the uniformity is quite striking. Considering first the "top ten" of each list, we find six names appearing every year (Washington, Thomas Jefferson, Abraham Lincoln, Ulysses S. Grant, John Adams, and Benjamin Franklin). As charted in table 1.4, four other names rank in the top ten in five of the eight years: Robert E. Lee, Paul Revere, John Hancock, and Andrew Jackson.

All told, only 14 different names appear in the 80 slots (10 each year for eight years) at the top of the lists. To be in social-scientific fashion, I have calculated measures of the diversity and consensus on these lists. (See table 1.5.) The maximum number of possible top ten names (80) minus the minimum possible (10) yields a maximum "spread" of 70. Subtracting from the actual total number of names in the 80 slots (14) that same minimum (10) yields an *actual* spread of 4. To provide a standardized base for comparison, dividing actual spread by the potential maximum yields an index on a scale where 0.00 represents total lack of diversity (the same ten names each year) and 1.00 represents total diversity (no names appearing

Table 1.3
Question One: Eight Samples

(Question One: Write down the first ten names that you think of in response to the prompt, "American History from its beginning through the end of the Civil War.")

1975	1976	1978	1982	1983	1984	1985	1988
1. G. Washington	1. G. Washington	1. G. Washington	1. G. Washington	1. G. Washington	1. G. Washington	1. G. Washington	1. G. Washington
2. T. Jefferson	2. T. Jefferson	2. T. Jefferson	2. A. Lincoln	2. A. Lincoln	2. A. Lincoln	2. A. Lincoln	2. A. Lincoln
3. A. Lincoln	3. A. Lincoln	3. A. Lincoln	3. T. Jefferson	3. T. Jefferson	3. T. Jefferson	3. T. Jefferson	3. T. Jefferson
4. U. S. Grant	4. B. Franklin	4. B. Franklin	4. B. Franklin	4. B. Franklin	4. B. Franklin	4. J. Adams	4. B. Franklin
5. R. E. Lee	5. J. Adams	5. U. S. Grant	5. J. Adams	5. U. S. Grant	5. R. E. Lee	5. B. Franklin	5. J. Adams
6. J. Adams	6. U. S. Grant	6. R. E. Lee	6. U. S. Grant	6. R. E. Lee	6. U. S. Grant	6. U. S. Grant	6. U. S. Grant
7. B. Franklin	7. P. Revere	7. J. Adams	7. A. Jackson	7. J. Adams	7. J. Adams	7. P. Revere	7. R. E. Lee
8. J. Madison	8. J. Hancock	8. A. Jackson	8. J. Hancock	8. J. Hancock	8. C. Columbus	8. R. E. Lee	8. A. Jackson
9. A. Hamilton	9. A. Jackson	9. C. Columbus	9. R. E. Lee	9. P. Revere	9. P. Revere	9. A. Jackson	9. C. Columbus
10. J. Smith	10. A. Hamilton	10. P. Revere	10. P. Revere	10. A. Jackson	10. J. Hancock	10. J. Hancock	10. J. Hancock
11. C. Columbus	11. R. E. Lee	11. J. Hancock	11. J. Madison	11. C. Columbus	11. J. Smith	11. C. Columbus	11. J. Madison
12. B. Ross	12. B. Ross	12. J. Smith	12. C. Columbus	12. J. Madison	12. A. Jackson	12. A. Hamilton	12. P. Revere
13. P. Revere	13. P. Henry	13. George III	13. G. A. Custer	13. A. Hamilton	13. J. Q. Adams	13. J. Madison	13. A. Hamilton
	14. J. Madison	14. J. Madison	14. T. Paine	14. J. Monroe	14. J. W. Booth	14. J. Smith	14. B. Ross
	15. C. Columbus	15. B. Arnold	15. A. Hamilton	15. J. P. Jones	15. A. Hamilton	15. J. Q. Adams	15. G. A. Custer
				16. G. A. Custer	16. B. Ross	16. George III	16. J. Smith
				17. P. Henry	17. P. Henry	17. J. Monroe	17. B. Arnold
					18. J. Madison	18. B. Ross	18. J. W. Booth
						19. J. W. Booth	19. J. Monroe

Table 1.4

Question One: Eight Sample Summary

(Question One: Write down the first ten names that you think of in response to the prompt, "American History from its beginning through the end of the Civil War.")

	Name	1975	1976	1978	1982	1983	1984	1985	1988	Years on List
					Rank in Year:					
1	G. Washington	1	1	1	1	1	1	1	1	8
2	A. Lincoln	3	3	3	2	2	2	2	2	8
3	T. Jefferson	2	2	2	3	3	3	3	3	8
4	B. Franklin	7	4	4	4	4	4	5	4	8
5	U. S. Grant	4	6	5	6	5	6	6	6	8
6	J. Adams	6	5	7	5	7	7	4	5	8
7	R. E. Lee	5	11	6	9	6	5	8	7	8
8	P. Revere	13	7	10	10	9	9	7	12	8
9	C. Columbus	11	15	9	12	11	8	11	9	8
10	J. Madison	8	14	14	11	12	18	13	11	8
11	A. Jackson		9	8	7	10	12	9	8	7
12	J. Hancock		8	11	8	8	10	10	10	7
13	A. Hamilton	9	10		15	13	15	12	13	7
14	J. Smith	10		12			11	14	17	5
15	B. Ross	12	12				16	18	15	5
16	G. A. Custer				13	16			16	3
17	P. Henry		13			17	17			3
18	J. Monroe					14		17	20	3
19	J. W. Booth						14	19	19	3
20	T. Paine				14				14	2
21	J. Q. Adams						13	15		2
22	George III			13				16		2
23	B. Arnold			15					18	2
24	J. P. Jones						15			1

on more than one year's list). This I will declare, only slightly tongue-in-cheek, to be the Diversity Index: for question one's top ten, it is a minuscule 0.057.

The Consensus Index is less complex—those names appearing *every* year in the top ten as a percentage of all names appearing *any* year in the top ten: 42.9 percent. Perhaps more indicative is the Five-Plus Consensus Index: 71.4 percent of the names that ever appeared in the top ten did so in five or more of the eight years surveyed.

Moving from the top ten to consider the full lists, we find slots for 132 names, but only 24 different ones appearing, resulting in a Diversity Index of 0.036—*lower* than that for the top ten. This is an important indication that the degree of diversity does not increase as one proceeds down the list. Of the 24 names, 10 (41.7 percent) appear every year and 15 (62.5 percent) in five of the eight years. Both the Diversity Index and the Consensus Index, then, suggest that the overall similarity of the lists

Table 1.5
Eight Sample Analysis

Question One		*Top Ten*	*Total List*
A	Total Names	14	24
B	Maximum Possible Names	80	132
C	Minimum Possible Names	10	20
D	Maximum Possible Spread (B-C)	70	112
E	Actual Spread (A-C)	4	4
F	Diversity Index (E/D)	0.057	0.036
G	Names on List All Eight Years	6	10
H	Eight-Year Consensus Index (G/A)	42.9%	41.7%
I	Names on List Five Years or More	10	15
J	Five-Plus Consensus Index (I/A)	71.4%	62.5%
K	Consensus Decay Index [(J.1-J.2)/J.1		0.125

is hardly accounted for by the very famous names at the top but spreads relatively evenly through the full range of names my students list year after year.

Perhaps the most culturally revealing characteristic of the lists is their almost exclusively political and military cast, focused on epochal events. In class discussion, we have frequently noted the kinds of people missing from the survey: religious figures, for instance, or artists, philosophers, or scientists. It is hard to imagine a similar poll in England or Italy or China or Chile being quite so relentlessly political, public, and heroic. That narrow focus certainly seemed to say something about American culture, but it is not inconsistent with my original expectation that what I was measuring was the result of high school history curricula focused on our civic traditions and formal institutions. The dramatic uniformity from year to year, however, suggested something else — perhaps an unexpected level of indoctrination, or a deeper set of cultural structures at work on the collective imagination of students year after year.

The results of the second set of surveys offer some powerful evidence for the latter hypothesis, and some provocative suggestions as to the content and meaning of those cultural structures. The most recent surveys are presented in tables 2.1 and 2.2, a compendium of near-legendary characters whom most Americans encounter in grade school, if anywhere on the educational spectrum; more generally, the figures on the list are the stuff of popular culture rather than school curricula.

I must admit that the first time I encountered such results, I was quite surprised. Indeed, the students were surprised and a little embarrassed themselves: again, they all claimed to "know" something about the more sophisticated names mentioned even once. Yet it seemed clear that when confronting the blank page, many of them had reached back beyond their recent experience and listed figures imaginatively encountered a good bit earlier, or outside of school altogether.

This impression is confirmed, to put it mildly, by comparing the answers to this

Table 2.1

Responses to Question Two: 1984

(Question Two: Write down the first ten names that you think of, excluding presidents, generals, statesmen, etc., in response to the prompt, "American History from its beginning through the end of the Civil War.")

Rank	Name	Frequency	Rank	Name	Frequency
1	B. Ross	37	19	A. G. Bell	3
2	P. Revere	25	20	G. W. Carver	3
3	H. Tubman	15	21	F. Douglass	3
4	Lewis & Clark	14	22	J. Hancock	3
5	J. W. Booth	11	23	W. Penn	3
6	D. Madison	10	24	M. Standish	3
7	J. Smith	10	25	M. Washington	3
8	F. S. Key	8	26	S. B. Anthony	2
9	Pocahontas	8	27	C. Attucks	2
10	H. B. Stowe	7	28	A. Burr	2
11	D. Boone	6	29	D. Crockett	2
12	T. Edison	6	30	N. Hale	2
13	B. Franklin	6	31	C. McCormick	2
14	R. Fulton	6	32	F. Nightingale	2
15	B. Arnold	5	33	T. Paine	2
16	C. Barton	5	34	M. Pitcher	2
17	J. Brown	5	35	Sacajawea	2
18	J. P. Jones	4	36	W. Scott	2

second survey in the eight different years. (See table 2.3.) The lists are so consistent in character, and even in individual composition, as to suggest that they stem from something beyond the high school classroom. They suggest, as a closer examination can illustrate, that the free association method was opening to view evidence of a very particular cultural imprinting independent of whatever degree of sophistication the students had encountered in high school. To explore the nature and content of that particularity, we need to examine this ad hoc pantheon more closely.

At first glance, it is the uniformity that is the most striking. In fact, given the absence of the focusing presence of Lincoln, Washington, and Jefferson, the similarity of the lists is really astonishing. To repeat the previous analysis, we find here that only 20 different names appear in the top ten for the eight years, out of the 80 possible, for a Diversity Index of 0.14 — not as low as for question one, but still strikingly diminutive.

Two of the top ten are the same in all eight years: Betsy Ross, the apocryphal creator of the first American flag, and Paul Revere, the horseback-borne messenger of revolution. Another six rank in this grouping in at least five of the seven years: Christopher Columbus; John Smith, the leader of the first successful colonial settle-

Table 2.2

Responses to Question Two: 1988

(Question Two: Write down the first ten names that you think of, excluding presidents, generals, statesmen, etc., in response to the prompt, "American History from its beginning through the end of the Civil War.")

Rank	Name	Frequency	Rank	Name	Frequency
1	B. Franklin	124	21	M. Washington	9
2	B. Ross	74	22	Pocahontas	8
3	Columbus	63	23	E. Whitney	8
4	P. Revere	63	24	P. Henry	7
5	J. Hancock	33	25	G. W. Carver	6
6	H. Tubman	33	26	M. Standish	6
7	Lewis & Clark	25	27	D. Madison	5
8	T. Edison	17	28	F. Nightingale	5
9	J. W. Booth	16	29	N. Turner	5
10	F. S. Key	15	30	A. G. Bell	4
11	T. Paine	13	31	J. Brown	4
12	S. B. Anthony	12	32	A. Burr	4
13	N. Hale	12	33	D. Crockett	4
14	A. Hamilton	12	34	George III	4
15	J. Smith	12	35	J. P. Jones	4
16	F. Douglass	10	36	S. Clemens	3
17	H. B. Stowe	10	37	J. Jay	3
18	B. Arnold	9	38	Dred Scott	3
19	D. Boone	9	39	M. Twain	3
20	W. Penn	9	40	Uncle Tom	3

ment in Virginia; Eli Whitney, inventor of both interchangeable parts and the cotton gin and hence a symbol of the rise of both northern industry and southern slave society; Meriwether Lewis and William Clark, explorers of the American West who are counted as one—they have become almost a fused individual in the memories of students, always listed together as "Lewis & Clark" or, more than once, Lewis N. Clark; the frontiersman Daniel Boone; and Harriet Tubman, the heroic escaped slave who returned to lead others to freedom, whose presence is the one sign that a century-old pantheon has begun to respond to the recent recognition of blacks as agents of change, not merely objects of misfortune, in American history.

Considering the entire list, in a total of 168 possibilities, only 46 different names are listed, and of them 17 appear in at least five of the eight years and 5 appear every year. Our Diversity Index for question two's full list is thus 0.15, inconsequentially higher than the 0.14 for the list's top ten. The diversity and consensus indexes for question two are of course considerably lower than for the canonical list of question one, but that is unsurprising since the second question prompts responses unconstrained by the familiar political pantheon. In fact, it is remarkable that the indexes are as low as they are, given the infinite range of possible responses. It is especially significant that the diversity and consensus in the top ten list for question two do not alter very much when the full range of responses is considered. Indeed, by at least one measure (which in a last fit of social science I will call the Consensus Decay Index, or CDI), there is more consistency between the top ten and the full list on question two (a CDI of 0.076) than on question one (a CDI of 0.125, nearly 65 percent higher). That is to say, on question two there is a slower increase than on question one in the variation encountered as we move away from the most popular images at the top. This means there is actually more consistency in the images students have offered over the years in response to the second question.

It is hard to know how much we can generalize from the uniformity of these lists, or how much interpretive weight they can bear. Perhaps all this is merely an artifact of my western New York sample, or the curriculum of New York State's primary and secondary schools; I would be the first to concede that a similar survey in Waco, Texas, for example, would produce a somewhat different list. But I believe regional variation would be far less than might be expected, and that the consistency of the lists—arguably closer to the heart of their significance than the precise content—might well be as striking. I think the free association producing the lists is tapping a very particular kind of cultural memory, one whose hold is general rather than a product of particular associations. For instance, the most famous local citizen in national life—Millard Fillmore, a lamentable president but a great Buffalonian, whose name inescapably graces city streets, districts, and public institutions—has not made the list even once. Beyond that, Buffalo is a heavily ethnic city, and many of our students come from a highly self-conscious Polish-American community; Casimir Pulaski is paraded every year and his name is certainly well known to such students. Yet he has rarely been mentioned on any list *at all*, nor do the tallies suggest much imprint of any other ethnic identification.

There is some more positive and empirical support for my claim of generality in one carefully controlled replication of the survey in another locale. After learning of my experiment and discussing it in correspondence, the cultural geographer Wilbur Zelinsky tried it on a large group of his own students at the Pennsylvania State University—an institution not terribly far from Buffalo, but not in an identical culture area either, and one whose students are shaped by a different precollege curriculum. Even with the accumulating weight of my own evidence, we were both astounded by the results in Pennsylvania: on questions one and two alike, thirteen of the top fifteen names were identical to those on my Buffalo surveys, appearing in nearly identical rank order, headed once again by the unsinkable Betsy Ross. The tiny differences in the lists almost disappeared in the fuller list of twenty or so: William Penn turns out to be the only figure who holds a very different place in the Pennsylvania rankings. Zelinsky's lists even reproduce some of the peculiarities of mine, such as the curiously misplaced presence of George Washington Carver and Thomas Edison, who belong in a different time period, and the Americanization of Florence Nightingale, who belongs on another continent.

In addition, Zelinsky added one methodological flourish whose products bear

Table 2.3
Question Two: Eight Samples

(Question Two: Write down the first ten names that you think of, excluding presidents, generals, statesmen, etc., in response to the prompt, "American History from its beginning through the end of the Civil War.")

1975	1976	1978	1982	1983	1984	1985	1988
1. B. Ross	1. B. Ross	1. B. Ross	1. B. Ross	1. B. Ross	1. B. Ross	1. B. Ross	1. B. Franklin
2. P. Revere	2. P. Revere	2. E. Whitney	2. P. Revere	2. P. Revere	2. P. Revere	2. P. Revere	2. B. Ross
3. C. Columbus	3. C. Columbus	3. D. Boone	3. J. Smith	3. Lewis & Clark	3. H. Tubman	3. H. Tubman	3. C. Columbus
4. J. Smith	4. E. Whitney	4. P. Revere	4. T. Edison	4. J. Smith	4. Lewis & Clark	4. C. Columbus	4. P. Revere
5. Pocahontas	5. T. Paine	5. Pocahontas	5. E. Whitney	5. T. Edison	5. J. W. Booth	5. F. S. Key	5. J. Hancock
6. B. Arnold	6. H. Tubman	6. C. Columbus	6. D. Crockett	6. J. W. Booth	6. D. Madison	6. J. Smith	6. H. Tubman
7. Lewis & Clark	7. J. Smith	7. Lewis & Clark	7. C. Columbus	7. H. Tubman	7. J. Smith	7. Pocahontas	7. Lewis & Clark
8. D. Boone	8. Lewis & Clark	8. J. Smith	8. H. Tubman	8. E. Whitney	8. F. S. Key	8. Lewis & Clark	8. T. Edison
9. E. Whitney	9. B. Arnold	9. R. Fulton	9. D. Boone	9. D. Boone	9. Pocahontas	9. E. Whitney	9. J. W. Booth
10. D. Crockett	10. D. Boone	10. T. Edison	10. F. S. Key	10. T. Paine	10. H. B. Stowe	10. B. Franklin	10. F. S. Key
11. F. S. Key	11. Pocahontas	11. A. Hutchinson	11. N. Turner	11. Pocahontas	11. D. Boone	11. J. W. Booth	11. T. Paine
12. T. Paine	12. F. S. Key	12. D. Crockett	12. F. Nightingale	12. M. Washington	12. T. Edison	12. T. Paine	12. S. B. Anthony
13. J. P. Jones	13. J. Brown	13. F. Douglass	13. T. Paine	13. C. Columbus	13. B. Franklin	13. M. Washington	13. N. Hale
14. N. Hawthorne	14. J. P. Jones	14. C. McCormick	14. J. W. Booth	14. B. Arnold	14. R. Fulton	14. C. Attrucks	14. J. Smith
15. H. B. Stowe	15. Lafayette	15. N. Hawthorne	15. P. De Leon	15. A. Burr	15. B. Arnold	15. J. Brown	15. F. Douglass
16. R. Williams	16. J. W. Booth	16. H. Tubman	16. Sitting Bull	16. F. Douglass	16. C. Barton	16. G. W. Carver	16. H. B. Stowe
17. M. Standish	17. D. Crockett	17. H. B. Stowe	17. M. Washington	17. Sitting Bull	17. J. Brown	17. S. B. Anthony	17. B. Arnold
18. G. W. Carver	18. R. Fulton	18. V. Balboa	18. E. Allen	18. J. Hancock	18. J. P. Jones	18. D. Boone	18. D. Boone
	19. G. W. Carver	19. G. W. Carver	19. G. W. Carver	19. F. S. Key	19. A. G. Bell	19. N. Hale	19. W. Penn
				20. G. W. Carver	20. G. W. Carver	20. P. Henry	20. M. Washington
					21. F. Douglass	21. M. Pitcher	21. Pocahontas
					22. J. Hancock	22. M. Standish	22. E. Whitney
					23. W. Penn	23. H. B. Stowe	23. P. Henry
					24. M. Standish		24. G. W. Carver
					25. M. Washington		25. M. Standish

usefully on the broader issues I raised earlier: he asked his students to note whether they had ever taken a college American history course before (roughly 30 percent had, and 70 percent had not). Given the cultural importance that many attach to exposure to history courses in the curriculum, it is interesting to ask what changes when Zelinsky's responses are tallied under these headings.

The answer is absolutely nothing; the lists compiled by both groups of students are virtually identical in composition and even rank order. Some individual names obtain slightly higher support from students exposed to college history courses (Samuel Adams and Jefferson Davis on question one, Davy Crockett and John Wilkes Booth on question two), while others gain proportionally more of their votes from students without that background (George Washington Carver and William Penn). But the breakdown of support for most of the names shows only the most modest divergence from the breakdown of the class as a whole. There is a final poetic justice in the fact that the one figure on question two at absolute dead center, listed in absolutely identical proportions by history and non-history students alike, is none other than Betsy Ross. Whatever students may or may not have learned in college history courses (and, as I shall argue, high school history courses) seems to have little to do with the images drawn forth by this exercise.[4]

Having mollified the gods of empiricism, let us turn to the task of explaining in broader cultural terms the patterns we have uncovered. Each list profiles a strikingly consistent pantheon of generally received and recalled cultural heroes, legends, and near-mythic figures. Quite apparently, we are examining here evidence of cultural transmission, perhaps as mediated through the primary schools and popular culture. Accordingly, my introductory lecture has had less to do with the high school curricula I had expected to engage in battle than with what I came to pose, for the students, as a kind of anthropological question: "If all you knew about American culture was what you could deduce from this list, what would you know?"

Thus viewed as a cultural artifact, the profile offered in each list is anything but random. Rather, it stands as a dramatic elaboration of what Catherine L. Albanese has termed the "presumption of newness" at the core of the American myth.[5] Indeed, what we see here is a broadening of that theme into an ongoing fixation on creation myths of origin and innovation.

In this, myth must be understood as the driving force behind history: John Smith and Pocahontas were real, of course, but manifestly it is the mythic scene in which the "love" of the Indian "princess" saves the explorer from a "savage" death that accounts for the high-ranking presence of both figures in the imagination of my students. Such a mythic framework reaches out to the explorers, from Columbus

---

    [4] I much appreciate Professor Zelinsky's interest in the problem and his sending me the data from his March 1, 1984, survey of a Geography 1 class of 115 students. This material is discussed and presented with his kind permission. Wilbur Zelinsky to Michael Frisch, March 5, 1984 (in Michael Frisch's possession).
    [5] Albanese, *Sons of the Fathers*, 9, 28.

Table 2.4

Question Two: Eight Sample Summary

(Question Two: Write down the first ten names that you think of, excluding presidents, generals, statesmen, etc., in response to the prompt, "American History from its beginning through the end of the Civil War.")

	Name	1975	1976	1978	1982	1983	1984	1985	1988	Years on List
1	B. Ross	1	1	1	1	1	1	1	2	8
2	P. Revere	2	2	4	2	2	2	2	4	8
3	J. Smith	4	7	8	3	4	7	6	14	8
4	D. Boone	8	10	3	9	9	11	18	18	8
5	G. W. Carver	18	19	19	19	20	20	16	24	8
6	C. Columbus	3	3	6	7	13		4	3	7
7	Lewis & Clark	7	8	7		3	4	8	7	7
8	H. Tubman		6	16	8	7	3	3	6	7
9	E. Whitney	9	4	2	5	8		9	22	7
10	Pocahontas	5	11	5		11	9	7	21	7
11	F. S. Key	11	12		10	19	8	5	10	7
12	J. W. Booth		16		14	6	5	11	9	6
13	T. Paine	12	5		13	10		12	11	6
14	T. Edison			10	4	5	12		8	5
15	B. Arnold	6	9				14	15	17	5
16	H. B. Stowe	15		17			10	23	16	5
17	M. Washington				17	12	25	13	20	5
18	R. Fulton		18	9			14			4
19	D. Crockett	10	17	12	6					4
20	F. Douglass			13		16	21		15	4
21	M. Standish	17					24	22	25	4
22	B. Franklin						13	10	1	3
23	J. Hancock					18	22		5	3
24	J. P. Jones	13	14				18			3
25	J. Brown		13				17	15		3
26	S. B. Anthony							17	12	2
27	N. Hawthorne	14		15						2
28	N. Hale							19	13	2
29	Sitting Bull				16	17				2
30	W. Penn						23		19	2
31	P. Henry							20	23	2
32	J. Madison						6			1
33	A. Hutchinson		11							1
34	N. Turner				11					1
35	F. Nightingale				12					1
36	C. McCormick			14						1
37	C. Attucks							14		1
38	P. De Leon				15					1
39	A. Burr					15				1
40	Lafayette		15							1
41	R. Williams	16								1
42	C. Barton						16			1
43	E. Allen				18					1
44	V. Balboa			18						1
45	A. G. Bell						19			1
46	M. Pitcher							21		1

Table 2.5
Eight Sample Analysis

Question Two		Top Ten	Total List
A	Total Names	20	46
B	Maximum Possible Names	80	168
C	Minimum Possible Names	10	25
D	Maximum Possible Spread (B-C)	70	143
E	Actual Spread (A-C)	10	21
F	Diversity Index (E/D)	0.14	0.15
G	Names on List All Eight Years	2	5
H	Eight-Year Consensus Index (G/A)	10.0%	10.9%
I	Names on List Five Years or More	8	17
J	Five-Plus Consensus Index (I/A)	40.0%	37.0%
K	Consensus Decay Index [(J.1-J.2)/J.1]		0.076

to the Siamese-twin Lewis & Clark, who define the nation by "beginning" its history, their "discovery" of space really a beginning of America's historical time, again and again. It includes both the revolutionary progenitors and the practical inventors like Whitney who are remembered as initiators of America's distinctive epoch of technological time.

It is interesting, in this regard, to note the rank of the inventor Edison, in fourteenth place on the question two summary tally, near the top, and the place of the black botanist Carver, who brings up the rear almost every time and who is the only figure *never* to appear in the top ten who *always* ranks on the overall list. (On Zelinsky's poll, he is the single figure most disproportionately listed by students who had not taken history courses.) As figures from the late nineteenth and early twentieth centuries, both Edison and Carver represent an overriding of the instructions to focus on an earlier time period. It hardly seems coincidental, given contemporary anxiety about ungraspable technological change and uncontrollable corporate organization on a worldwide scale, that the *only* regularly repeated chronological "mistakes" are these comfortable symbols of practical genius and human-scale progress.

And for a white society shuttling between racial guilt and fear, the symbol of Carver has always offered an additional all-too-convenient balm. The myth of the patient experimenter, the "credit to his race" who discovered manifold new uses for the lowly peanut, has long obscured the reality of a man whose acquiescence in the racism of the early twentieth-century United States stands in dramatic contrast to the resistance offered by contemporaneous black leaders like W. E. B. Du Bois and even Booker T. Washington. One wonders if that posture may have contributed more than his modest scientific accomplishments to Carver's not-quite-natural selection for immortality in the evolution of American memory.

There is also something beyond coincidence in the recurrence of John Wilkes Booth and Benedict Arnold, who represent for an innocent nation the serpent-traitors whose evil also sets history in motion — necessary preludes to the transcendent triumph of good. As these observations suggest, the list is not only composed of quasi-mythic figures: as a collective portrait, it has a kind of mythic structure and completeness itself, a character confirmed by its re-creation year after year in nearly identical terms.

But the most compelling indication of this character is the nearly unshakable hold of Betsy Ross on the first place position — she tops the list in seven of the eight classes, and her decline to second place this past semester is actually the exception that proves the rule. My graduate assistant notes that I seem to have omitted the "statesmen" prompt from the list of those to be excluded on question two's list, thus accounting for Franklin's triumph and John Hancock's uncharacteristically high rank on question two. (Always fixtures on question one, both were usually omitted from the second list by students given the intended exclusionary prompt in other years.) In any event, Betsy Ross's position at the top is truly phenomenal, a record that cries out for explanation as it has occasioned a good deal of discussion in my classes each year. Even given everything said so far, it is still not immediately apparent why this *particular* mythic figure has been discovered so much more frequently than others by the searching beam of free association memory.

Part of the explanation may lie in a kind of psychological/feminist interpretation generated by one class discussion. Perhaps the command to produce names of those not in positions of public power led the genderized imaginations of students through the following sequence: Nonpublic means domestic and private; domestic and private means women; women means Betsy Ross. I think there may be something to this, though it still begs a number of questions. The framework of civil religion and comparative mythology provides some additional insights, however, and all combined may serve to make the Betsy Ross hegemony less mystical and more instructive.

The flag, of course, is the primary symbol of what is distinctive about the United States. It represents the core of our nationality — that political identity declared and constituted in the epochal revolutionary experience whose artifactual, yet genuine, religious content Albanese has documented so powerfully. As Marshall Smelser has written, the flag "has assumed a moral value transcending the mundane purposes of national identification. As a tribal totem, it satisfies the real and almost universal hunger for a public symbol of spiritual kinship above and invulnerable to the contentions and changes of politics — and for which no other totem is available to the United States."[6] If that is true, there is a nice logic to Betsy Ross's preeminent place in a structure of creation myth figures and heroic progenitors; she represents the most inclusive symbol of national identity, an identity perhaps more fragile and in need of shoring up than other national identities because of its uniquely political character.

The Ross hegemony also helps to bring the presidential list of question one within the interpretation developed here, for its figures are also more powerful as symbols

[6] *Ibid.*, 261–62n51.

of political cohesion and identity than as historical figures per se. Indeed, Washington himself "absorbed and unified the elements from the classical and Christian past, becoming for Americans, a divine man."[7] Beyond helping us to respect, and thereby understand, a sometimes ludicrous apotheosis that began even in Washington's lifetime, Albanese's discussion provides a context for some final reflections on the essentially religious meaning of Betsy Ross's place in this collective portrait.

Albanese documents how the revolutionary sons made themselves into Founding Fathers, with Washington the *primus inter pares*, literally the spiritual Father of the Nation. She also shows how his spiritual meaning came to obscure his real existence: his wife Martha faded from legendary image and relatively speaking from our memories, because "kindred as was the soul of the father of his country to his wife, it had proved to be far more closely interfused with the structures of meaning and value of his countrymen. Washington . . . had become a grand collective representative, a tribal totem." And in the process, fictive and symbolic kin came to replace his real family in popular imagination: thus the common celebration of the marquis de Lafayette as the "beloved and 'adopted son.'"[8]

Albanese could go no further with the myth, but evidence of the symbolic role of Betsy Ross allows us to complete the picture. To this end, it is important to note that the Betsy Ross story is a product of a late nineteenth-century style of religio-mythic craftsmanship. The actual Betsy Ross had, demonstrably, no role whatsoever in the actual creation of any actual first flag. But more important, her story itself played no part in revolutionary-era tradition or mythmaking even at its most instrumental. In fact, the flag story emerged only a century later in Philadelphia, when her descendants sought to create a tourist attraction around the time of the centennial exposition of 1876. The reasons for the emergence of the tale were thus prosaic, not to say mercenary; but as Albanese reminds us, however intentional and instrumental, such self-consciousness does not exclude deeper levels of cultural meaning and expression.[9]

It is hard to avoid the speculation that the latter-day invention of the mythic Betsy Ross—and her immediate public enshrinement—came as a kind of needed supplement to the revolutionary myth, a final step in the humano-centric articulation of essentially religious beliefs and experiences. If George is the Father of the Country—of the nation, of all the American sons and daughters—then surely Betsy Ross exists symbolically as the Mother, who gives birth to our collective symbol.

One can go further. If Washington is, indeed, a surrogate for God the Father, the meaning of Betsy Ross is unmistakable: she stands for the Blessed Virgin Mary in the iconography of our civil religion. A plain woman is visited by a distant god and commanded to be the vehicle, through their collaboration, of a divine creation.

---

[7] *Ibid.*, 158–59.
[8] *Ibid.*, 172, 170.
[9] See the full and interesting account in Joseph Jackson, *Encyclopedia of Philadelphia* (Harrisburg, 1931), 1054–55.

The certificate records a contribution to the "Endowment Fund for the preservation of the Historic House in which the First Flag of the United States of America was made." Wreath-encircled representations of Betsy Ross's house and grave flank a painting (enlarged below). Behind it the sun rises; on its beams rides an American eagle, clutching arrows and the E Pluribus Unum streamer.

This reproduction of *Birth of Our Nation's Flag* appears on the elaborate certificate of membership (above) that the American Flag House and Betsy Ross Memorial Association issued to Charlotte Kromm in 1919. The certificate has sobering relevance to the politics of past and present cultural literacy campaigns: Kromm, a German American, may have taken out membership less to advance historic preservation than to affirm the loyalty of German Americans, much impugned during World War I.
Certificate courtesy of Donald A. Ritchie.

This advertisement, appearing widely in American magazines in 1986,
presents a visual pun on the historical imagery captured in *Birth of Our Nation's Flag* (opposite).
It conveys advertisers' confidence that readers recognize and understand cultural icons,
jeremaids on cultural illiteracy from on high notwithstanding.

And indeed, in the classroom pageants enacted by generations of American school-children over the past century, that is exactly what we see: Washington calls on the humble seamstress Betsy Ross in her tiny home and asks her if she will make the nation's flag, to his design. And Betsy promptly brings forth—from her lap!—the flag, the nation itself, and the promise of freedom and natural rights for all man-kind.

There is a final note of confirmation for this hypothesis in the rather after-the-fact addition of Betsy Ross to our national mythology. For the cult of the Virgin Mother was itself a rather late development in Christian theology, a medieval elaboration of an undeveloped dimension of the Gospels, a statement, perhaps, that for a fully satisfying religious symbolism, Sons and Fathers were not quite enough. If I seem to overinterpret what are, after all, trite relics from grade school primers, then I ask you to remember Albanese's caution that the contrivance or superficiality of myth-making does not necessarily deny, and may even tend to confirm, its deeper cultural functions.

That observation provides a pivot on which to return to our initial questions—the relevance of this exploration in historical trivia for the august debates on history and education that loom so large in contemporary discussion.

On one level, my results can be read as a confirmation of the diagnosis that some-thing is seriously wrong. If college students cannot come up with lists showing more depth and grasp than these; if college courses—as Zelinsky's data suggest, or even high school courses, as the overall survey demonstrates—have so little impact, then surely we are in some kind of trouble. The almost childish character of the revealed pantheon seems quite consistent with the diagnosis that we are producing genera-tions for whom a meaningful national history in even some of its richness and com-plexity is not an accessible resource. And as such, the survey can only reinforce the resonance many history teachers must feel when they encounter the documented ignorance that so exercises former Secretary of Education William J. Bennett, Diane Ravitch, Lynne Cheney, et al. Everyone who teaches history must have his or her own horror story that seems to confirm the ominous collapse of rope bridges across the generation gap.[10]

As I have argued, however, the surveys are more interesting when taken as evi-dence of what students do know, rather than what they don't. If the results say little one way or the other about how much history the students surveyed may actually know, they are evidence that cultural imagery seems to be reproduced in our young people with startling consistency and regularity. And this conclusion casts some-

---

[10] My personal favorite is Professor Manning Marable's report of the black student in a black studies class who came up to ask, "Now, who is this Malcolm the Tenth, and what was he king of, anyway?" (Professor Marable confirmed this anecdote in a conversation in Buffalo in February 1987.) This is instructive in indicating that the problem of cultural loss, whatever else it may mean, is a shared one, not simply a matter, as usually presented, of the dominant culture's heritage being insufficiently respected by those held to be in need of its ministrations.

thing of a shadow over the current jeremiads, whose core concerns, I would argue, are at bottom more fundamentally cultural and political than educational. This point is worth at least brief examination by way of conclusion.

The sermons being preached in this crusade are difficult to deal with as texts, because they slide so fluidly along a spectrum of analysis ranging from the high-minded and humanistic to the crudely political and instrumental. At the former end, we find the calls for exposure to the complexity of historical studies, for the cultivation of the critical mind, and for provision of the basic orientation to the real world and its history that citizens need to understand the present and make intelligent choices in the future. It is hard to see how anyone could fail to be shocked by the documented effects on students of an almost willful indifference to the value of historical consciousness and training, and the effects on teachers, especially in the secondary schools, of decades of overemphasis on pseudoprofessional training programs and methods at the expense of subject and substance.

It is a different matter when those unexceptionable themes are given a more particular emphasis: that students need not just more of history, but rather more of "our" national history. To a degree, the argument still holds: citizenship in a democracy requires the critical skills that such training should provide, and a certain core familiarity with the history and geography of one's country is arguably essential to knowing what the society is all about. But in most formulations, the educational critique is sufficiently expansive to suggest a different animus behind it: the problem is that our students are spending too much time on "them"—the rest of the world, global and comparative studies, and so forth—rather than on the "us" at home. And to the extent they do study "us," it is the wrong us—too much emphasis on social history, people outside ruling elites, minorities, and women, rather than on the political and military core of national tradition.

That emphasis is held to be problematic, both symptom and cause of a fragmentation of national unity, cohesion, and will in the face of grave political, economic, and military threats from without, and even from within. Virtually every one of the core documents slips into this mood sooner rather than later, after the appropriate genuflections at the altar of humanism and the critical spirit. The issue is put starkly in terms of American competitiveness, the Cold War, and the danger of ethnic and linguistic pluralism run rampant.

Since I haven't the time to demonstrate this point by citing chapter and verse from the new scriptures, let me instead offer a single picture. This lead page from a 1985 *New York Times Magazine* article by Ravitch touches every base. The headline announces the problem in its most generalized form—the "Decline and Fall of Teaching History." The subhead slides into the Americanization of the cultural literacy problem, masking the shift of focus with syntax that raises concern about plain old literacy at the *Times*: "An ignorance or indifference about studying our past has become cause for concern." And finally, there is the picture, suspended between the two: a teacher leads a small group discussion in a global studies course that is, elsewhere in the article, an object of ridicule. Manifestly, the picture is in-

New York Times Magazine, November 17, 1985, p. 50.
Courtesy Jeanne Strongin © 1987 and
The New York Times Company © 1985.

tended to illustrate both "decline and fall" and "ignorance and indifference." Yet the class seems lively and intense; the lesson plan on the blackboard behind the teacher carries the outline for what could be a satisfying history lecture in any college course. What, then, is the picture doing here? Could it have anything to do with the fact that the teacher is black, the students black and perhaps Hispanic, and the planned lesson a discussion of Russia on the eve of the 1917 Revolution?[11]

I submit that the page captures perfectly the tension between the explicit text, couched in broadly acceptable abstract terms about history, and the deeply political subtext of the current educational crusade. Beneath the huffing and puffing about historical studies lies a fear not dissimilar to that propelling the "Americanization" efforts that so dominated education and politics in the United States in the early years of the twentieth century, fueled by a terror of immigrant cultures and concern for the future of the Anglo-Saxon race and heritage. It is fascinating how often, in the current litany, those educational efforts are taken to represent a kind of golden age to which we should return.

If all this has a quaint ring so soon after the Statue of Liberty centennial, the explicit cold war fixation strikes a much more ominous tone: Secretary Bennett has grounded his own critique of the schools, for example, on the proposition that they have embraced the doctrine of, in Jeane Kirkpatrick's term, "moral equivalence," willfully offering education "designed to prevent future generations of American intellectuals from telling the difference between the U.S. and the U.S.S.R."[12]

In such formulations, educational reform has been given a highly ideological definition: the point of education is not individual but national; the object of improvement in training in history is the production of obedient, patriotic citizens who share a set of presumptions about the United States, its people, economy, and relation to the other nations of the world. The argument has traveled a long way from its humanistic origins, arriving at a point where education and indoctrination — cultural and political — seem almost indistinguishable.

Indeed, in one of the more remarkable documents in the current literature, they *are* indistinguishable. Sidney Hook's 1984 lecture "Education in Defense of a Free Society" is a kind of *Ur-text* of the cultural literacy movement, outlining a set of themes that reappear again and again, less baldly, in the writings and speeches of Bennett, Ravitch, Cheney, and others. To Hook the issue is "whether we possess the basic social cohesion and solidarity today to survive the challenge to our society . . . posed by the global expansion of Communism"; the role of the schools — primary and secondary especially — is to generate sufficient loyalty through what he freely acknowledges is an embrace of propaganda and indoctrination (critical thought comes later, he says). In the final analysis, "no institutional changes of themselves will develop that bond of community we need to sustain our nation in times of crisis without a prolonged schooling in the history of our free society, its martyrology, and its national tradition."[13]

---

[11] Diane Ravitch, "Decline and Fall of Teaching History," *New York Times Magazine*, Nov. 17, 1985, pp. 50, 52, 54, 56, 101, 117.

[12] Walter Goodman, "Conservatives' Theme: The West is Different," *New York Times*, May 5, 1985, sec. 1, p. 21, a report on an anticommunism conference, the first event sponsored by the State Department's new and controversial Office for Public Diplomacy.

[13] Sidney Hook, "Education in Defense of a Free Society," *Commentary*, 78 (July 1984), 17–22, esp. 21, 22. Hook delivered the speech on receiving the Jefferson award for "intellectual achievement in the humanities," bestowed as its highest honor by the National Endowment for the Humanities.

Hook's explicit reference to martyrology, tradition, and the need for cultural in-doctrination in the primary and secondary schools brings us back to Betsy Ross and the tables of data I have been discussing here. According to Hook, Bennett, Cheney, Ravitch, and others in what William Greider has called the "Bloom and Doom" school, we are in trouble on every front: the crisis of historical amnesia, the decline of formal studies in history, and the deterioration of critical thinking are taken to be linked to a presumed corrosion of national spirit and will, evidenced in a declining respect for and awareness of the binding symbols of national tradition at the most basic levels. Such critics see no contradiction in calling for both patriotic indoctrination under the umbrella of a culturally binding nationalism and intellec-tually challenging studies in history. The assumption is that a shared cultural memory and historical consciousness ought to be close to the same thing, or at least linked in some developmental or cumulative sense.[14]

The evidence I have presented suggests that this philosophically dubious proposi-tion is also without foundation empirically. Whatever the deeper knowledge and grasp of history among my students, there is no indication in the data that the chords of cultural memory, in terms of the hold of national historical symbols, have weakened in the slightest. In fact, the consistency and extraordinary uniformity in the images offered up by these students indicates that the president, Secretary Ben-nett, and their followers have little cause for concern: the structure of myth and heroes, martyrs and mothers, is firmly in place.

This does not mean there is no crisis in the teaching of history, no deficiency in the historical consciousness with which our young people perceive the swiftly changing world around them. It does suggest, however, that frantic injections of cul-tural symbolism are not needed and almost certainly will not be the solution to the epidemic; if anything, the lesson is that indoctrination and education need to be more effectively decoupled, not conflated. For students who already hold lists of heroes deep in their imaginations need a sense that history is populated by three-dimensional human beings, the famous as well as the forgotten, who live in and act on a real world that is always changing.

In the tension between such a vision and the grade-school pantheon students du-tifully remember for my surveys each year, there is a suggestion of what most history teachers in the trenches already know: that alienated students cannot be bullied into attention or retention; that authoritarian cultural intimidation is likely to be met by a further and more rapid retreat; and that there may well be, in that alienation itself, statements about the claims of the present on the past worth our respect, at-tention, and response. I have concluded in my own teaching that the evidently mas-sive, uniform subsurface reefs of cultural memory are, in this sense, part of the problem, not resources for a solution.

---

[14] The reference is to a witty review of Bloom, *Closing of the American Mind*: William Greider, "Bloom and Doom," *Rolling Stone*, Oct. 8, 1987, pp. 39–40. For other relevant critiques, see Martha Nussbaum, "Undemocratic Vistas," *New York Review of Books*, Nov. 5, 1987, pp. 20–26; and Robert Pattison, "On the Finn Syndrome and the Shakespeare Paradox," *Nation*, May 30, 1987, pp. 710–20.

As such, however, those structures merit immense respect from pedagogic navigators. They tell us a great deal about our culture, its resources, and its often problematic hold on the imagination of students—and on citizens as well, to judge from the power in the 1988 presidential campaign of some of the very icons discussed in this essay. My ongoing experiment in the survey course has convinced me that we need to realize what we are up against, in the classroom and in political life more broadly. We must understand the depth of the cultural symbolism our students and fellow citizens carry inside them long before entering our classrooms, if ever they do. Appreciating the powerful grip of collective cultural memory becomes a necessary first step if we are to help our students to understand the real people and processes of history, to locate its reality in their lives, and to discover the power and uses of historical imagination in the present.

"For Something beyond the Battlefield": Frederick Douglass and the Struggle for the Memory of the Civil War

David W. Blight

> Fellow citizens: I am not indifferent to the claims of a generous forgetfulness, but whatever else I may forget, I shall never forget the difference between those who fought for liberty and those who fought for slavery; between those who fought to save the Republic and those who fought to destroy it.
> —Frederick Douglass, "Decoration Day," 1894

> We fell under the leadership of those who would compromise with truth in the past in order to make peace in the present and guide policy in the future.
> —W. E. B. Du Bois, *Black Reconstruction*, 1935

> What you have as heritage,
> Take now as task;
> For thus you will make it your own.
> —Goethe, *Faust*, 1808

In the first week of January 1883, on the twentieth anniversary of the Emancipation Proclamation, a distinguished group of black leaders held a banquet in Washington, D.C., to honor the nineteenth century's most prominent Afro-American intellectual, Frederick Douglass. The banquet was an act of veneration for Douglass, an acknowledgment of the aging abolitionist's indispensable role in the Civil War era, a ritual of collective celebration, and an opportunity to forge historical memory and transmit it across generations. The nearly fifty guests comprised a who's who of black leadership in the middle and late nineteenth century. For the moment, rivalries and ideological disputes were suppressed. Sen. Blanche K. Bruce chaired the event. Robert Smalls, Edward Blyden, the Reverend Benjamin T. Tanner,

David W. Blight is assistant professor of history and Afro-American studies at Harvard University. An earlier version of this article was delivered at the annual meeting of the Organization of American Historians, Reno, Nev., March 26, 1988. For their many helpful criticisms and suggestions, the author wishes to thank Daniel Aaron, Susan Armeny, Karin Beckett, Ira Berlin, Richard Blackett, Randall Burkett, Melvin Dixon, David Herbert Donald, Genevieve Fabre, Nathan I. Huggins, Michael Kammen, Alan Levy, Waldo E. Martin, David Thelen, Clarence Walker, the reviewers for the *Journal of American History*, and especially the members of the Working Group on History and Memory in Afro-American Culture, W. E. B. Du Bois Institute, Harvard University.

Frederick Douglass, *Courtesy Library of Congress.*

Professor Richard T. Greener, the young historian George Washington Williams, and the journalist T. Thomas Fortune were just a few of the notables who took part. The celebrants included men from many backgrounds: college professors, congressmen, state politicians, bishops, journalists, and businessmen. Virtually every southern state and six northern states were represented. After a sumptuous dinner, numerous toasts were offered to Douglass, and to nearly every major aspect of black life: to "the colored man as a legislator"; to "the Negro press"; to "the Negro author"; to "the Republican Party"; and so forth. Douglass himself finally ended the joyous round of toasts by offering one of his own: to "the spirit of the young men" by whom he was surrounded. Many of the most distinguished guests had come of age only since the Civil War. For them slavery, abolitionism, and even the war itself were the history beyond memory. Douglass had captured an essential meaning of the occasion; the young had gathered in tribute to the old. As they met to celebrate and to understand the pivotal event in their history—emancipation—the meaning of that event was being passed to a new generation of black leaders.[1]

In his formal remarks at the banquet, Douglass demonstrated that during the last third of his life (he lived from 1818 until 1895), a distinguishing feature of his leadership was his quest to preserve the memory of the Civil War as he believed blacks and the nation should remember it. Douglass viewed emancipation as the central reference point of black history. Likewise the nation, in his judgment, had no greater turning point, nor a better demonstration of national purpose. On the twentieth anniversary, Douglass sought to infuse emancipation and the war with the sacred and mythic qualities that he had always attributed to them. "This high festival . . . ," Douglass declared, "is coupled with a day which we do well to hold in sacred and everlasting honor, a day memorable alike in the history of the nation and in the life of an emancipated people." Emancipation day, he believed, ought to be a national celebration in which all blacks—the low and the mighty—could claim a new and secure social identity. But it was also an "epoch" full of lessons about the meaning of historical memory. "Reflection upon it (emancipation) opens to us a vast wilderness of thought and feeling," Douglass asserted. "Man is said to be an animal looking before and after. To him alone is given the prophetic vision, enabling him to discern the outline of his future through the mists of the past." Douglass challenged his fellow black leaders to remember the Civil War with awe. "The day we celebrate," he said, "affords us an eminence from which we may in a measure survey both the past and the future. It is one of those days which may well count for a thousand years." This was more than mere banquet rhetoric. It was Douglass's attempt to inspire his colleagues with the idea Robert Penn Warren would later express when he wrote that "the Civil War is our only *felt* history—history lived in the national imagination."[2]

Douglass's effort to forge memory into action that could somehow save the legacy of the Civil War for blacks—freedom, citizenship, suffrage, and dignity—came at a time when the nation appeared indifferent or hostile to that legacy. The richly

---

[1] *People's Advocate*, Jan. 6, 1883, Leon Gardiner Collection (Historical Society of Pennsylvania, Philadelphia). The banquet was organized by Professor J. M. Gregory of Howard University.

[2] *Ibid.*; Robert Penn Warren, *The Legacy of the Civil War: Meditations on the Centennial* (Cambridge, Mass., 1983), 4. Douglass's imagery here reflects his apocalyptic view of history. On his apocalyptic conception of the Civil War, see David W. Blight, "Frederick Douglass and the American Apocalypse," *Civil War History*, 31 (Dec. 1985), 309–28.

symbolic emancipation day banquet of 1883 occurred only months before the United States Supreme Court struck down the Civil Rights Act of 1875, sacrificing the Civil War amendments, as the dissenting Justice John Marshall Harlan put it, and opening the door for the eventual triumph of Jim Crow laws across the South. The ruling in *United States v. Stanley*, better known as the *Civil Rights Cases*, declared that the equal protection clause of the Fourteenth Amendment applied only to states; a person wronged by racial discrimination, therefore, could look for redress only from state laws and courts. In effect, the decision would also mean that the discriminatory acts of private persons were beyond the safeguards of the Fourteenth Amendment. At a mass meeting in Washington, D.C., immediately after the decision, Douglass tried to capture the sense of outrage felt by his people. "We have been, as a class, grievously wounded, wounded in the house of our friends," Douglass proclaimed. In the Supreme Court's decision, Douglass saw "a studied purpose to degrade and stamp out the liberties of a race. It is the old spirit of slavery, and nothing else."[3]

Douglass interpreted the *Civil Rights Cases* as a failure of historical memory and national commitment. Reflecting on the Supreme Court decision in his final autobiography, Douglass contended that "the future historian will turn to the year 1883 to find the most flagrant example of this national deterioration." White racism, among individuals and in national policy, he remarked, seemed to increase in proportion to the "increasing distance from the time of the war." Douglass blamed not only the "fading and defacing effects of time," but more important, the spirit of reconciliation between North and South. Justice and liberty for blacks, he maintained, had lost ground from "the hour that the loyal North . . . began to shake hands over the bloody chasm."[4] Thus, Douglass saw the Supreme Court decision as part of a disturbing pattern of historical change. Historical memory, he had come to realize, was not merely an entity altered by the passage of time; it was the prize in a struggle between rival versions of the past, a question of will, of power, of persuasion. The historical memory of any transforming or controversial event emerges from cultural and political competition, from the choice to confront the past and to debate and manipulate its meaning.

Ever since the war Douglass had exhibited an increasingly keen sense of history. "I am this summer endeavoring to make myself a little more familiar with history," Douglass wrote to Gerrit Smith in 1868. "My ignorance of the past has long been a trouble to me." From the early days of Reconstruction, but especially by the 1870s, Douglass seemed acutely aware that the postwar era might ultimately be controlled by those who could best shape interpretations of the war itself. Winning the peace would not only be a matter of power, but also a struggle of moral will and historical

---

[3] Rayford W. Logan, *The Betrayal of the Negro: From Rutherford B. Hayes to Woodrow Wilson* (New York, 1965), 114–18; Frederick Douglass, "The Civil Rights Case: Speech at the Civil Rights Mass-Meeting Held at Lincoln Hall, October 22, 1883," in *The Life and Writings of Frederick Douglass*, ed. Philip S. Foner (5 vols., New York, 1950), IV, 393, 402.

[4] Frederick Douglass, *The Life and Times of Frederick Douglass, Written by Himself: His Early Life as a Slave, His Escape from Bondage, and His Complete History* (1892; reprint, New York, 1962), 539.

consciousness. In the successful rise of the Democratic party, Douglass saw evidence that the South was beginning to win that struggle. In 1870 he complained that the American people were "destitute of political memory." But as he tried to reach out to both black and white readers with his newspaper, Douglass demanded that they not allow the country to "bury dead issues," as the Democrats wished. "The people cannot and will not forget the issues of the rebellion," Douglass admonished. "The Democratic party must continue to face the music of the past as well as of the present."[5]

Some of Douglass's critics accused him of living in the past. American politics, declared a Liberal Republican newspaper in 1872, would "leave Mr. Douglass behind . . . vociferating the old platitudes as though the world had stopped eight years ago." To such criticisms Douglass always had a ready answer: he would *not forgive* the South and he would *never forget* the meaning of the war. At the Tomb of the Unknown Soldier in Arlington National Cemetery in 1871, on one of the first observances of Memorial Day, Douglass declared where he stood.

> We are sometimes asked in the name of patriotism to forget the merits of this fearful struggle, and to remember with equal admiration those who struck at the nation's life, and those who struck to save it—those who fought for slavery and those who fought for liberty and justice. I am no minister of malice . . . , I would not repel the repentant, but . . . may my tongue cleave to the roof of my mouth if I forget the difference between the parties to that . . . bloody conflict . . . I may say if this war is to be forgotten, I ask in the name of all things sacred what shall men remember?[6]

Douglass often referred to the preservation of the Union in glowing, nationalistic tones. But in the last third of his life, he demonstrated that the Civil War had also left many bitter elements of memory. Around the pledge to "never forget," Douglass organized his entire postwar effort to shape and preserve the legacy of the Civil War.

By intellectual predilection and by experience, Douglass was deeply conscious that history mattered. As the author of three autobiographies by the 1880s, he had cultivated deep furrows into his own memory. In a real sense, the Frederick Douglass who endures as an unending subject of literary and historical inquiry—because of the autobiographies—is and was the creature of memory. Moreover, Douglass deeply understood that peoples and nations are shaped and defined by history. He knew that history was a primary source of identity, meaning, and motivation. He seemed acutely aware that history was both burden and inspiration, something to be cherished and overcome. Douglass also understood that winning battles over policy or justice in the present often required an effective use of the past. He came to a realization that in late nineteenth-century America, blacks had a special need for a usable past. "It is not well to forget the past," Douglass warned in an 1884

[5] Frederick Douglass to Gerrit Smith, Aug. 24, 1868, in *Life and Writings of Frederick Douglass*, ed. Foner, IV, 210; *New National Era*, Nov. 24, 1870.

[6] *Golden Age*, quoted in *New National Era*, Aug. 8, 1872; Frederick Douglass, "Address at the Grave of the Unknown Dead," May 30, 1871, reel 14, Frederick Douglass Papers (Manuscript Division, Library of Congress).

speech. "Memory was given to man for some wise purpose. The past is . . . the mirror in which we may discern the dim outlines of the future and by which we may make them more symmetrical."[7]

To all who look to history for meaning, those premises may seem obvious. But in the 1880s, according to Douglass, blacks occupied a special place in America's historical memory, as participants and as custodians. He understood his people's psychological need not to dwell on the horrors of slavery. But the slave experience was so immediate and unforgettable, Douglass believed, because it was a history that could "be traced like that of a wounded man through a crowd by the blood." Douglass urged his fellow blacks to keep *their* history before the consciousness of American society; if necessary, they should serve as a national conscience. "Well the nation may forget," Douglass said in 1888, "it may shut its eyes to the past, and frown upon any who may do otherwise, but the colored people of this country are bound to keep the past in lively memory till justice shall be done them." But as Douglass learned, such historical consciousness was as out of date in Gilded Age America as the racial justice he demanded.[8]

In his retrospective thought about the Civil War, Douglass's intention was to forge enduring historical myths that could help win battles in the present. The deepest cultural myths—ideas and stories drawn from history that, through symbolic power, transcend generations—are the mechanisms of historical memory. Such myths are born of divergent experiences and provide the cultural weapons with which rival memories contest for hegemony. Douglass hoped that Union victory, black emancipation, and the Civil War amendments would be so deeply rooted in recent American experience, so central to any conception of national regeneration, so necessary to the postwar society that they would become sacred values, ritualized in memory. Douglass dearly wanted black freedom and equality—the gift from the Union dead who were memorialized every Decoration Day—to become (as Richard Slotkin puts it) one of those "usable values from history . . . beyond the reach of critical demystification."[9] Douglass's hope that emancipation could attain such in-

[7] Frederick Douglass, "Speech at the Thirty-Third Anniversary of the Jerry Rescue," 1884, reel 16, Douglass Papers. On the nature and importance of historical memory, see Hayden White, *Tropics of Discourse: Essays in Cultural Criticism* (Baltimore, 1978), 26–50; Eric Hobsbawm and Terence Ranger, eds., *The Invention of Tradition* (New York, 1983); Jaroslav Pelikan, *The Vindication of Tradition* (New Haven, 1984); Michael Kammen, *A Season of Youth: The American Revolution and the Historical Imagination* (New York, 1978); Ulric Neisser, ed., *Memory Observed: Remembering in Natural Contexts* (San Francisco, 1982); and David Lowenthal, *The Past Is a Foreign Country* (London, 1985). On the Civil War in the northern memory, see Daniel Aaron, *The Unwritten War: American Writers and the Civil War* (New York, 1973); Oscar Handlin, "The Civil War as Symbol and as Actuality," *Massachusetts Review*, 3 (Autumn 1961), 133–43; Kammen, *Season of Youth*, 256–59; Paul H. Buck, *The Road to Reunion, 1865–1900* (New York, 1937), 228–309; and James M. McPherson, *The Abolitionist Legacy: From Reconstruction to the NAACP* (Princeton, 1975), 95–139, 333–38.

[8] Douglass, "Speech at the Thirty-Third Anniversary of the Jerry Rescue"; Frederick Douglass, "Address Delivered on the Twenty-Sixth Anniversary of Abolition in the District of Columbia," April 16, 1888, reel 16, Douglass Papers.

[9] Richard Slotkin, *The Fatal Environment: The Myth of the Frontier in the Age of Industrialization, 1800–1890* (New York, 1985), 19. My understanding of the structure of cultural myth, and its uses and misuses by historians, is derived from *ibid.*, 3–32; Bruce Kuklik, "Myth and Symbol in American Studies," *American Quarterly*, 24 (Oct. 1972), 435–50; Sacvan Bercovitch, *The American Jeremiad* (Madison, 1978), xi–xii, 132–220; Clifford Geertz, *The*

delible mythic quality was rooted in his enduring faith in the doctrine of progress and in his moral determinism, a belief that in a society of egalitarian laws good will outweigh evil in the collective action of human beings. Repeatedly, Douglass criticized the claim that emancipation came only by "military necessity" during the war. "The war for the Union came only to execute the moral and humane judgment of the nation," he asserted in 1883. "It was an instrument of a higher power than itself." What drew northerners to Memorial Day observances, Douglass maintained in 1878, was the "moral character of the war . . . , the far-reaching . . . , eternal principles in dispute, and for which our sons and brothers encountered . . . danger and death."[10] By continuing to stress that sacred and ideological legacy of the war, Douglass exposed both his deepest sense of the meaning of the conflict and his fear that such meaning would not successfully compete with rival memories (in both North and South) and could, therefore, be lost.

Douglass's pledge to "never forget" the meaning of the Civil War stemmed from at least five sources in his thought and experience: his belief that the war had been an ideological struggle and not merely the test of a generation's loyalty and valor; his sense of refurbished nationalism made possible by emancipation, Union victory, and Radical Reconstruction; his confrontation with the resurgent racism and Lost Cause mythology of the postwar period; his critique of America's peculiar dilemma of historical amnesia; and his personal psychological stake in preserving an Afro-American and an abolitionist memory of the war. Douglass never softened his claim that the Civil War had been an ideological conflict with deeply moral consequences. He abhorred the nonideological interpretation of the war that was gaining popularity by the 1880s. The spirit of sectional reunion had fostered a celebration of martial heroism, of strenuousness and courage, perhaps best expressed by Oliver Wendell Holmes, Jr., and later popularized by Theodore Roosevelt. Holmes experienced and therefore loathed the horror of combat. But to him, the legacy of the Civil War rested not in any moral cause on either side, but in the passion, devotion, and sacrifice of the generation whose "hearts were touched with fire." To Holmes, the true hero — the deepest memory — of the Civil War was the soldier on either side, thoughtless of ideology, who faced the "experience of battle . . . in those indecisive contests." War almost always forces people to ask the existential question *why*? Massive organized killing compels the question, but it seldom reveals satisfying answers. Indeed, the very face of battle, suffering, and death can blunt or deny ideology altogether. Teleological conceptions of war are rarely the luxury of individual soldiers; the veteran's memory rarely focuses on the grand design. Ideology, though always

---

Interpretation of Cultures: Selected Essays by Clifford Geertz (New York, 1973), 28–30, 33–141, 213–20; Kammen, *Season of Youth*, 3–32, 221–58; and Warren I. Susman, *Culture as History: The Transformation of American Society in the Twentieth Century* (New York, 1984), 3–26.

[10] Frederick Douglass, "Speech on Emancipation Day," September 1883, reel 15, Douglass Papers. For Douglass's attacks on the idea of "military necessity," see also [Frederick Douglass], "The Black Man's Progress on This Continent," *New National Era*, July 27, 1871. Frederick Douglass, "Speech in Madison Square," Decoration Day, 1878, reel 15, Douglass Papers.

at the root of war, is left to the interpreters, those who will compete to define the meaning and legacy of the wartime experience. "In the midst of doubt, in the collapse of creeds," said Holmes, "there is one thing I do not doubt, and that is that the faith is true and adorable which sends a soldier to throw away his life in obedience to a blindly accepted duty, in a cause which he little understands, in a plan of campaign of which he has no notion, under tactics of which he does not see the use." By the 1880s Holmes's memory of the war became deeply rooted in American culture. What mattered most was not the content of the cause on either side but the acts of commitment to either cause, not ideas but the experience born of conflict over those ideas. Whoever was honest in his devotion was *right*.[11]

Douglass resisted such an outlook and demanded a teleological memory of the war. His Memorial Day addresses were full of tributes to martial heroism, albeit only on the Union side; but more important, they were testaments to the abolitionist conception of the war. The conflict, Douglass insisted in 1878, "was a war of ideas, a battle of principles . . . a war between the old and new, slavery and freedom, barbarism and civilization." After Reconstruction Douglass was one of a small band of old abolitionists and reformers who struggled to sustain an ideological interpretation of the Civil War. His speeches were strikingly similar to the writings of the novelist and former carpetbagger, Albion Tourgée. Satirically, Tourgée attempted to answer the Holmesian version of an ideology-free veteran's memory. "We have nothing to do with the struggle that followed" the outbreak of war, wrote Tourgée in 1884. "History hath already recorded it with more or less exactitude. It was long and fierce because two brave peoples fought with the desperation of conviction. . . . It was a wonderful conflict." What people should remember of the war, Tourgée contended, was "*not* the courage, the suffering, the blood, *but only the causes that underlay the struggle and the results that followed from it.*" Like Douglass, Tourgée considered emancipation the great result of the war. He also rejected a core concept of the national reunion: that the South's war effort was honest and, therefore, just as heroic as the Union cause. "Because an opponent is honest," Tourgée asserted, "it does not follow that he is right, nor is it certain that because he was overthrown he was in the wrong." Thinkers like Douglass and Tourgée were not merely trying to "keep alive conflict over issues time was ruthlessly discarding," as Paul H. Buck wrote in 1937.[12] Belligerence was not the primary motive of those who argued for an ideological memory of the Civil War. Theirs was a persuasion under duress by the 1880s, a collective voice nearly drowned out by the chorus of reconciliation. They understood the need for healing in the recently divided nation; they could acknowl-

[11] Mark De Wolfe Howe, ed., *The Occasional Speeches of Justice Oliver Wendell Holmes, Jr.* (Cambridge, Mass., 1962), 4–5, 76. Excellent discussions of Holmes are found in George M. Fredrickson, *The Inner Civil War: Northern Intellectuals and the Crisis of the Union* (New York, 1965), 218–21; Cruce Stark, "Brothers At/In War: One Phase of Post-Civil War Reconciliation," *Canadian Review of American Studies*, 6 (Fall 1975), 174–81; and Aaron, *Unwritten War*, 161–62.

[12] Albion W. Tourgée, *An Appeal to Caesar* (New York, 1884), 37, 44; Buck, *Road to Reunion*, 242. On Tourgée, see Otto H. Olsen, *Carpetbagger's Crusade: The Life of Albion Winegar Tourgee* (Baltimore, 1965); Richard Nelson Current, *Those Terrible Carpetbaggers: A Reinterpretation* (New York, 1988), 367–82, 401–6; and Aaron, *Unwritten War*, 193–205.

edge the validity of veterans' mutual respect. But they distrusted the sentimentalism of both North and South, and they especially feared Holmes's notion of the "collapse of creeds." Most of all, those northerners who stressed ideas in the debate over the memory of the war saw America avoiding—whether benignly or aggressively—the deep significance of race in the verdict of Appomattox.

Douglass's voice was crucial to the late nineteenth-century debate over the legacy of the Civil War. As Edmund Wilson wrote in analyzing the significance of "detached" American writers of the Civil War era: "They also serve who only stand and watch. The men of action make history, but the spectators make most of the histories, and these histories may influence the action." Douglass had acted in history, but now his principal aim was to help shape the histories. Unlike Holmes and many others, Douglass had not served on the battlefield. But he had served in slavery, he had served on the abolitionist platform, and he had served with his pen and voice as few other black leaders had during the war. Douglass's war was an intellectual and spiritual experience; his action had been more of an inner struggle than a physical test. Perhaps his remoteness from the carnage enabled him to sustain an ideological conception of the war throughout his life. Answering the appeal of the veterans' memory, Douglass maintained that the war "was not a fight between rapacious birds and ferocious beasts, a mere display of brute courage and endurance, but it was a war between men of thought, as well as of action, and in dead earnest for something beyond the battlefield."[13]

The second source of Douglass's quest to preserve the memory of the Civil War was his refurbished nationalism. At stake for the former fugitive slave was the sense of American nationhood, the secure social identity that he hoped emancipation and equality would one day offer every black in America. Douglass expressed this connection between nationalism and memory in his famous speech at the unveiling of the Freedmen's Memorial Monument to Abraham Lincoln in Washington, D.C., in April 1876. The Freedmen's Memorial speech is too easily interpreted as merely eulogistic, as simply Douglass's contribution to the myth of Lincoln as Great Emancipator. Attended by President Ulysses S. Grant, his cabinet, Supreme Court Justices, and numerous senators, the ceremony was as impressive as the bright spring day, which had been declared a holiday by joint resolution of Congress. After a reading of the Emancipation Proclamation and the unveiling of the statue (which Douglass later admitted he disliked because "it showed the Negro on his knees"), Douglass took the podium as the orator of the day. His address included strong doses of the rail-splitter Lincoln image, the "plebeian" who rose through honesty, common sense, and the mysterious hand of God to become the "great liberator." But Douglass understood the significance of the occasion; he knew it was a moment to forge national memory and to practice civil religion. Through most of the speech he spoke to and for blacks; the monument had been commissioned and paid for

---

[13] Edmund Wilson, *Patriotic Gore: Studies in the Literature of the American Civil War* (Boston, 1984), 669; Douglass, "Speech in Madison Square." On the conflict between ideological and nonideological conceptions of the war, see Fredrickson, *Inner Civil War*, 196–98, 217–38.

almost entirely by blacks. But the monument was not only to Lincoln; rather, it was to the *fact* of emancipation. The occasion honored Lincoln, but Douglass equally stressed the *events* that transpired "under his rule, and in due time." Most important, Douglass staked out a claim to nationhood for blacks. "We stand today at the national center," he said, "to perform something like a national act." Douglass struck clear notes of civil religion as he described the "stately pillars and majestic dome of the Capital" as "our church" and rejoiced that "for the first time in the history of our people, and in the history of the whole American people, we join in this high worship." Douglass was, indeed, trying to make Lincoln mythic and, therefore, useful to the cause of black equality. But the primary significance of Douglass's Freedmen's Memorial address lies in its concerted attempt to forge a place for blacks in the national memory, to assert their citizenship and nationhood. "When now it shall be said that the colored man is soulless . . . ," Douglass concluded, "when the foul reproach of ingratitude is hurled at us, and it is attempted to scourge us beyond the range of human brotherhood, we may calmly point to the monument we have this day erected to the memory of Abraham Lincoln." What Lincoln himself had once called the "mystic chords of memory" as a source of devotion to the Union, Douglass now claimed as the rightful inheritance of blacks as well. He did so through language, the essence of cultural myth, and the only secure means he possessed.[14]

The third cause of Douglass's concern over the memory of the Civil War was the resurgent racism throughout the country and the rise of the Lost Cause mentality. Since its origins as a literary and political device immediately after the war, the Lost Cause has been an enigmatic phrase in American history. Historians have defined the Lost Cause in at least three different ways: as a public memory, shaped by a web of organizations, institutions, and rituals; as a dimension of southern and American civil religion, rooted in churches and sacred rhetoric as well as secular institutions and thought; and as a literary phenomenon, shaped by journalists and fiction writers from the die-hard Confederate apologists of the immediate postwar years through the gentle romanticism of the "local color" writers of the 1880s to the legion of more mature novelists of the 1890s and early twentieth century who appealed to a national audience eager for reconciliation.[15] Dividing the movement into the "inner" and "national" memories is also useful in making sense of the Lost Cause.

---

[14] On the Freedmen's Memorial speech, see Benjamin Quarles, *Frederick Douglass* (New York, 1968), 276–78. Quarles maintains that the speech was "distinctly not one of [Douglass's] best." See also Nathan I. Huggins, *Slave and Citizen: The Life of Frederick Douglass* (Boston, 1980), 102–3. Frederick Douglass, "Oration in Memory of Abraham Lincoln," April 14, 1876, in *Life and Writings of Frederick Douglass*, ed. Foner, IV, 317–19, 314, 310–11, 319. For the "mystic chords" quotation, see Abraham Lincoln, "First Inaugural Address," March 4, 1861, in *The Collected Works of Abraham Lincoln*, ed. Roy P. Basler (8 vols., New Brunswick, 1953), IV, 271. On black attitudes toward Lincoln during the war, see Benjamin Quarles, *Lincoln and the Negro* (New York, 1962).

[15] Gaines M. Foster, *Ghosts of the Confederacy: Defeat, the Lost Cause, and the Emergence of the New South, 1865–1913* (New York, 1986), 4–5, 36–46, 104–14; Charles Reagan Wilson, *Baptized in Blood: The Religion of the Lost Cause, 1865–1920* (Athens, Ga., 1980), 12–14, 37–78; Thomas L. Connelly and Barbara L. Bellows, *God and General Longstreet: The Lost Cause and the Southern Mind* (Baton Rouge, 1982), 39–72. See also C. Vann Woodward, *The Origins of the New South, 1877–1913* (Baton Rouge, 1951), 154–58.

Freedmen's Memorial Monument to Abraham Lincoln by Thomas Ball.
Courtesy Louis A. Warren Lincoln Library and Museum, Fort Wayne, Indiana.

The "inner" Lost Cause, argue Thomas L. Connelly and Barbara L. Bellows, represents the die-hard generation that fought the war and experienced defeat and dishonor. Led by Jefferson Davis, and especially by the prototypical unreconstructed rebel, Gen. Jubal Early, these former Confederate leaders created veterans' organizations, wrote partisan confederate histories, built monuments, made Robert E. Lee into a romantic icon, and desperately sought justification for their cause and explanations for their defeat. The Confederacy, argued the diehards, was never defeated; rather, it was overwhelmed by numbers and betrayed by certain generals at pivotal battles (namely James Longstreet at Gettysburg). The activities of the initial Lost

Cause advocates have been compared to the Ghost Dance of the Plains Indians of the late nineteenth century. As mystics, they remained "captivated by a dream," writes Gaines Foster, "a dream of a return to an undefeated confederacy." The "inner" Lost Cause was not, however, merely a band of bitter, aging, mystical soldiers. During the 1870s and 1880s they forged an organized movement in print, oratory, and granite, and their influence persisted until World War I.[16]

The "national" Lost Cause took hold during the 1880s primarily as a literary phenomenon propagated by mass market magazines and welcomed by a burgeoning northern readership. Avoiding the defensive tone and self-pity of earlier Lost Cause writers, successful local colorist John Esten Cooke found a vast and vulnerable audience for his stories of the genteel and romantic heritage of old Virginia. Cooke and other writers such as Thomas Nelson Page and Sara Pryor did not write about a defeated South or the Confederate cause. They wrote about the Old South, about the chivalry and romance of antebellum plantation life, about black "servants" and a happy, loyal slave culture, remembered as a source of laughter and music. They wrote about colonial Virginia—the Old Dominion—as the source of revolutionary heritage and the birthplace of several American presidents. Northern readers were treated to an exotic South, a premodern, preindustrial model of grace. These writers sought, not to vindicate the Confederacy, but to intrigue Yankee readers. Northern readers were not asked to reconcile Jefferson's Virginia with the rebel yell at the unveiling of a Confederate monument. They were only asked to recognize the South's place in national heritage.[17]

The conditioning of the northern mind in popular literature had its counterpart in veterans' reunions, which in the 1880s and 1890s became increasingly intersectional. Celebration of manly valor on both sides and the mutual respect of Union and Confederate soldiers fostered a kind of veterans' culture that gave the Lost Cause a place in national memory. The war became essentially a conflict between white men; both sides fought well, Americans against Americans, and there was glory enough to go around. Celebrating the soldiers' experience buttressed the nonideological memory of the war. The great issues of the conflict—slavery, secession, emancipation, black equality, even disloyalty and treason—faded from national consciousness as the nation celebrated reunion and ultimately confronted war with Spain in 1898. Many southerners became pragmatic about the memory of the war; they wanted to remember what was best in their past, but most important, they embraced the reunionism implicit in the concept of a "New South" and demanded respect from northerners. To most southerners, the Lost Cause came to represent this crucial double meaning: reunion and respect. Late in life Frederick Douglass rarely found it possible to concede the South both aspects of the national Lost Cause sentiment; at times he could acknowledge neither reunion nor respect on the terms that popular consciousness demanded. Inwardly, Douglass clung to a Victorious Cause of his own, resisting and wishing away Jim Crow, lynching, and the ongoing

[16] Connelly and Bellows, *God and General Longstreet*, 2–38; Foster, *Ghosts of the Confederacy*, 47, 60.
[17] See Connelly and Bellows, *God and General Longstreet*, 39–72.

betrayal of his people. And Douglass often took his version of the Victorious Cause to the public forum, demanding justice in the present, the arena of competing and rival memories.[18]

There were ghosts to be called up on all sides. White southerners were finding a balm for defeat and bereavement, autonomy in their own region, and a new place in the Union. Southern memory of the war had begun the long process of achieving resolution; southern ghosts could be purged. For blacks, however, many ghosts were not purged in the late nineteenth century and, indeed, they remain unpurged even today. Some twentieth-century black writers portray the burden of memory much as Douglass did. In August Wilson's recent play, *Joe Turner's Come and Gone*, the hero, Herald Loomis, a former sharecropper who has come north to Pittsburgh in 1911, is haunted by the memory of his seven years' unjust imprisonment on a chain gang. Loomis was kidnapped by a turn-of-the-century slave catcher (Joe Turner) who believed that emancipation was the worst thing that ever happened to the South. As he searches for his wife and a new start in life, Loomis is tormented not only by the memory of chains but also by visions of white bones rising out of the ocean, a clear and powerful image of the slave trade. In the dramatization of Herald Loomis's struggle to reemerge from a second slavery, we can find echoes of Douglass's challenge to America to "never forget" its responsibilities to the freed people. Wilson's use of history on stage transmits black cultural memory as a weapon, a source of spirit that enables people to grapple with their historical ghosts in an ever-sovereign present. Similarly, in Toni Morrison's novel *Beloved*, Sethe, a freed-woman living in Ohio during Reconstruction, confronts the return of the living ghost of her daughter, a child she had killed in infancy rather than permit her imminent return to slavery. The ghost, "Beloved," is a metaphor for all the haunting horror of slavery that the freed people have carried with them into their new lives. Beloved is memory itself, all-consuming, overwhelming, forcing Sethe to face each "day's serious work of beating back the past." At the end of the book Morrison suggests that to the characters in this wrenching story, "remembering seemed unwise." But she also reminds us as readers — as a people — to beware of the path left by Beloved as she vanished: "Down by the stream in back of 124 [Sethe's house] her [Beloved's] footprints come and go, come and go. They are so familiar. Should a child, an adult place his feet in them, they will fit. Take them out and they disappear again as though nobody ever walked there."[19] Collective historical memory, like the

---

[18] Foster, *Ghosts of the Confederacy*, 66–75. On the New South, see Woodward, *Origins*, especially 142–74. On the generational impact of the war in southern memory and on generational change in general, see David Herbert Donald, "A Generation of Defeat," in *From the Old South to the New: Essays in the Transitional South*, ed. Walter J. Fraser and Winfred B. Moore, Jr. (Westport, 1978), 3–20; and Werner Sollors, *Beyond Ethnicity: Consent and Descent in American Culture* (New York, 1986), 208–36.

[19] August Wilson, *Joe Turner's Come and Gone*. At this writing there is no published version of the play. It had its world premiere at the Yale Repertory Theatre, May 2, 1986. I viewed the play in May 1988 in New York City. Toni Morrison, *Beloved* (New York, 1987), 274–75. Another excellent example from the recent Afro-American literary tradition showing the power of historical memory over life in the present is David Bradley, *The Chaneysville Incident* (New York, 1981). On Bradley and black novelists' use of history, see Klaus Ensslen, "Fictionalizing History: David Bradley's 'The Chaneysville Incident,' " *Callaloo*, 11 (Spring 1988), 280–95.

deepest personal memories, can overwhelm and control us as do the ghosts in the work of Wilson and Morrison. But historical memory is also a matter of choice, a question of will. As a culture, we choose which footprints from the past will best help us walk in the present.

In the midst of Reconstruction, Douglass began to realize the potential power of the Lost Cause sentiment. Indignant at the universal amnesty afforded ex-Confederates, and appalled by the national veneration of Robert E. Lee, Douglass attacked the emerging Lost Cause. "The spirit of secession is stronger today than ever . . . ," Douglass warned in 1871. "It is now a deeply rooted, devoutly cherished sentiment, inseparably identified with the 'lost cause,' which the half measures of the Government towards the traitors have helped to cultivate and strengthen." He was disgusted by the outpouring of admiration for Lee in the wake of the general's death in 1870. "Is it not about time that this bombastic laudation of the rebel chief should cease?" Douglass wrote. "We can scarcely take up a newspaper . . . that is not filled with *nauseating* flatteries of the late Robert E. Lee." At this early stage in the debate over the memory of the war, Douglass had no interest in honoring the former enemy. "It would seem from this," he asserted, "that the soldier who kills the most men in battle, even in a bad cause, is the greatest Christian, and entitled to the highest place in heaven." Douglass's harsh reactions to the veneration of Lee are a revealing measure of his enduring attitudes toward the South, as well as his conception of the meaning of the war. He seemed to relish the opportunity to lecture his readers about their former enemies. "The South has a past not to be contemplated with pleasure, but with a shudder," Douglass cautioned in 1870. "She has been selling agony, trading in blood and in the souls of men. If her past has any lesson, it is one of repentance and thorough reformation."[20]

As for proposed monuments to Lee, Douglass considered them an insult to his people and to the Union. He feared that such monument building would only "reawaken the confederacy." Moreover, in a remark that would prove more ironic with time, Douglass declared in 1870 that "monuments to the Lost Cause will prove monuments of folly." As the Lost Cause myth sank deeper into southern and national consciousness, Douglass would find that he was losing ground in the battle for the memory of the Civil War.[21]

Douglass never precisely clarified just how much southern "repentance" or "reformation" he deemed necessary before he could personally extend forgiveness. He merely demanded "justice," based on adherence to the Civil War amendments and to the civil rights acts. Given the strength of his nationalism and his own southern roots, Douglass's vindictiveness toward the South probably would have softened

---

[20] [Frederick Douglass], "Wasted Magnanimity," *New National Era*, Aug. 10, 1871; [Frederick Douglass], "Bombast," *ibid.*, Nov. 10, 1870.

[21] [Frederick Douglass], "The Survivor's Meeting—A Soldier's Tribute to a Soldier," *ibid.*, Dec. 1, 1870; [Frederick Douglass], "Monuments of Folly," *ibid.* Douglass was also outraged by southerners' attempts to write the Lost Cause outlook into American history textbooks. "They have taken to making rebel schoolbooks and teaching secession and disloyalty in their primary schools," Douglass reported. See [Frederick Douglass], "Still Firing the Southern Heart," *ibid.*, Feb. 23, 1871.

more with time had not the resurgent racism of the 1880s and 1890s fueled the spirit of sectional reunion. "A spirit of evil has been revived," Douglass declared in a eulogy to William Lloyd Garrison in 1879, "doctrines are proclaimed . . . which were, as we thought, all extinguished by the iron logic of cannon balls." In the political victories of the southern Democrats and in the increasing oppression of the freedmen, Douglass saw a "conflict between the semi-barbarous past and the higher civilization which has logically and legally taken its place." He lamented the passing of so many of the old abolitionists like Garrison whose services would be needed in what Douglass called "this second battle for liberty and nation."[22]

From his position as a stalwart Republican, Douglass's condemnations of resurgent racism often seemed in stark contradiction to his support of the party that increasingly abandoned blacks. His allegiance to, and criticism of, the Republican party could emerge in bewildering extremes. Campaigning for Alonzo B. Cornell, Republican candidate for governor of New York in 1879, Douglass charged that too many Republicans had caved in to the charms of sectional reunion. The issues of the current election, he asserted, were "precisely those old questions which gave rise to our late civil war." Such rhetoric did not square with the realities of American politics during the Hayes administration. Like an angry revivalist wishing for a reawakening in his fellow party members, Douglass chastised "this tender forbearance, this amazing mercy, and generous oblivion to the past." Yet in an 1880 speech commemorating emancipation, Douglass declared: "Of the Republican party . . . it is the same as during and before the war; the same enlightened, loyal, liberal and progressive party that it was. It is the party of Lincoln, Grant, Wade, Seward, and Sumner; the part to which today we are indebted for the salvation of the country, and today it is well represented in its character and composition by James A. Garfield and Chester A. Arthur." Over the course of the 1880s his rhetoric shifted to harsher and more realistic assessments as Douglass faced the bitter truth about his party. In an 1888 speech he accused the Republicans of treating the freedman as "a deserted, a defrauded, a swindled outcast; in law, free; in fact, a slave; in law, a citizen; in fact, an alien; in law, a voter; in fact, a disfranchised man." Douglass pleaded with Republicans not to rest on their laurels and demanded that they convert their original values into a creative force for the new era. "I am a Republican, I believe in the Republican party . . . ," he asserted. "But . . . I dare to tell that party the truth. In my judgment, it can no longer repose on the history of its grand and magnificent achievements. It must not only stand abreast with the times, but must create the times."[23]

---

[22] Frederick Douglass, "Speech on the Death of William Lloyd Garrison," June 2, 1879, reel 15, Douglass Papers. The emergence of the New South in the 1880s caused great uncertainty among old abolitionists. They shared some of the optimism of the new era, but they also lamented the demise of Reconstruction and feared the control an autonomous South could wield over race relations. See McPherson, *Abolitionist Legacy*, 107–20; and Woodward, *Origins*, 107–74.

[23] Frederick Douglass, "Campaign Speech on Behalf of Alonzo B. Cornell," 1879, reel 15, Douglass Papers; Frederick Douglass, "Emancipation," Aug. 4, 1880, *ibid.*; Frederick Douglass, "Address Delivered on the Twenty-Sixth Anniversary of the Abolition of Slavery in the District of Columbia," April 16, 1888, reel 16, *ibid.*

Douglass's ambivalence toward the Republicans late in life stemmed from more than two decades of loyalty to the party. The party had been the primary vehicle through which he pursued his political ambitions, developed his political conscious- ness, and exercised some influence in the federal government. Beginning in 1877, when President Rutherford B. Hayes appointed him marshall for the District of Columbia, and through subsequent appointments as recorder of deeds for the Dis- trict of Columbia (1881–1886) and minister to Haiti (1889–1891), Douglass achieved a place, albeit largely emblematic, in Washington officialdom. But aside from per- sonal ambition, he had always imbued the Republican party with deeper, historical meanings. He saw it as the vessel of progress and as the institutional custodian of the Civil War's legacy. During the Grant years (1869–1877), he had stumped for the Republicans with an almost desperate zeal, as if only through the party could eman- cipation and the triumphs of Radical Reconstruction be preserved. An element of wish fulfillment no doubt both sustained his support of the Republicans and in- spired his later attacks on the party. But Douglass's Republican loyalty is best under- stood as part of his quest to realize a secure, abolitionist memory of the war. He continued to use the Republican party to demand that the nation confront its recent history, not run from it. What Douglass most wanted was not national reunion; he wanted racial justice, promised in law, demonstrated in practice, and preserved in memory.[24]

Whatever he thought of the Republican party, though, the aging Douglass never wavered in his critique of racism. "The tide of popular prejudice" against blacks, Douglass said in 1884, had "swollen by a thousand streams" since the war. Every- where, he lamented, blacks were "stamped" with racist expectations. Douglass ex- pressed the pain of being black in America: wherever a black man aspired to a profession, "the presumption of incompetence confronts him, and he must either run, fight, or fall before it." The alleged rapes by black men of white women were to Douglass manifestations of the South's invention of a new "crime" to replace their old fear of "insurrection." Lynching, therefore, represented a white, southern inven- tion of new means to exercise racial power and oppression. In a speech in 1884, com- memorating the rescue of fugitive slaves in the 1850s, Douglass chastised his Syra- cuse audience for preferring sectional peace over racial justice. "It is weak and foolish to cry PEACE when there is no peace," he cried. "In America, as elsewhere, injustice must cease before peace can prevail."[25]

The fourth source of Douglass's arguments in the debate over the memory of the Civil War was his conviction that the country had been seduced into "national for- getfulness," a peculiar American condition of historical amnesia. In his numerous retrospective speeches in the 1880s, Douglass discussed the limitations of memory. He knew that memory was fickle and that people must embrace an "ever-changing . . . present." Even his own "slave life," he admitted, had "lost much of its horror,

---

[24] See Quarles, *Frederick Douglass*, 252–82; and Waldo E. Martin, *The Mind of Frederick Douglass* (Chapel Hill, 1984), 79–91.
[25] Douglass, "Speech at the Thirty-Third Anniversary of the Jerry Rescue."

and sleeps in . . . memory like the dim outlines of a half-forgotten dream." But Douglass's greater concern was with collective memory, not merely with personal recollection. Douglass was rowing upstream against a strong current in American thought. As a people, Americans had always tended to reject the past and embrace newness. The overweening force of individualism in an expanding country had ever made Americans a future-oriented people, a culture unburdened with memory and tradition. Douglass was learning to appreciate one of Alexis de Tocqueville's great observations about American society: in America, each generation is a new people, and "no one cares for what occurred before his time." The discovery Tocqueville made in 1831 would ring only more true in the climate of laissez-faire government and social Darwinism of the Gilded Age. American individualism, wrote Tocqueville, makes "every man forget his ancestors . . . hides his descendants and separates his contemporaries from him; it throws him back forever upon himself alone and threatens in the end to confine him entirely within the solitude of his own heart."[26] To Douglass, the individualism that bred indifference and the racism that bred oppression were the twin enemies undercutting efforts to preserve an abolitionist memory of the Civil War.

Indeed, one of the ambiguities in Douglass's postwar thought is that while attacking the surging individualistic indifference of northerners who wished to forget the war issues, to forgive ex-Confederates, and to abandon the freed people, he was also an outspoken proponent of laissez-faire individualism, a celebrator of "self-made men."[27] There was perhaps no other solution for a black leader who had to preach self-reliance to his people while demanding national commitments from the government and from society at large. Moreover, Douglass was one of Tocqueville's Americans, trapped between the country's historic racism and his own embrace of individualism.

Most assuredly, though, Douglass was not one of those Americans who rejected the past. His laments about historical amnesia often echoed Tocqueville's prescience. He believed that individualism could coexist with social justice, that getting on in the world released no one from the weight of history. "Well it may be said that Americans have no memories," Douglass said in 1888. "We look over the House of Representatives and see the Solid South enthroned there; we listen with calmness to eulogies of the South and of traitors and forget Andersonville. . . . We see colored citizens shot down and driven from the ballot box, and forget the services rendered by the colored troops in the late war for the Union." More revealing still was Douglass's contempt for northern sympathy with the Lost Cause. He believed

---

[26] Frederick Douglass, "Thoughts and Recollections of the Antislavery Conflict," undated speech, reel 19, Douglass Papers; Alexis de Tocqueville, *Democracy in America*, ed. Thomas Bender (New York, 1981), 115, 397. On the significance of Tocqueville in understanding American individualism and the rejection of the past, see Robert Bellah et al., *Habits of the Heart: Individualism and Commitment in American Life* (New York, 1985), 27–51, 255–307.

[27] Frederick Douglass, "Self-Made Men," reel 18, Douglass Papers. Beginning in 1874 or earlier, Douglass delivered this speech during numerous lecture tours. On Douglass's conception of self-made men, see Martin, *Mind of Frederick Douglass*, 253–78.

northern forgiveness toward the South shamed the memory of the war. "Rebel graves are decked with loyal flowers," Douglass declared, "though no loyal grave is ever adorned by rebel hands. Loyal men are building homes for rebel soldiers; but where is the home for Union veterans, builded by rebel hands?" Douglass had never really wanted a Carthaginian peace. But he felt left out of the nation's happy reunion; the deep grievances of his people—both historic and current—were no longer to be heard. At the very least, Douglass demanded that the power to forgive should be reserved for those most wronged.[28]

The debate over the meaning of the war was not merely a question of remembering or forgetting. Douglass worried about historical amnesia because his version of the war, his memory, faltered next to the rival memories that resonated more deeply with the white majority in both North and South. Douglass may never have fully appreciated the complexity of the experience of the Civil War and Reconstruction for whites. The overwhelming number of white northerners who voted against black suffrage shared a bond of white supremacy with southerners who rejected the racial egalitarianism of Radical Reconstruction. The thousands of white Union veterans who remembered the war as a transforming personal experience, but not as the crucible of emancipation for four million slaves, had much in common with white Georgians who had found themselves in the path of Gen. William T. Sherman's march to the sea. There were many rival memories of the war and its aftermath, and there was much need for forgetting and healing. As Friedrich Nietzsche suggested, personal happiness often requires a degree of forgetting the past. "Forgetting is essential to action of any kind," wrote Nietzsche. "Thus: it is possible to live almost without memory . . . but it is altogether impossible to live at all without forgetting . . . there is a degree of the historical sense which is harmful and ultimately fatal to the living thing, whether this living thing be a man or a people or a culture." Nietzsche captured elements of both truth and danger in human nature. Douglass focused his efforts on the dangers of collective forgetting, not on its personal or cultural necessity. Douglass knew that his people, confined to minority status and living at the margins of society, could rarely afford the luxury of forgetting. Although he may not have thoroughly discriminated between the rival memories he confronted, he became fully aware of their power and their threat. Thus, with ever fewer sympathetic listeners by the late 1880s, Douglass was left with his lament that "slavery has always had a better memory than freedom, and was always a better hater."[29]

Those were not merely words of nostalgic yearning for a vanished past uttered

[28] Douglass, "Address Delivered on the Twenty-Sixth Anniversary of Abolition in the District of Columbia." On Confederate veterans' homes funded by the Grand Army of the Republic, see Foster, *Ghosts of the Confederacy*, 94.

[29] Friedrich Nietzsche, "On the Uses and Disadvantages of History for Life" [1874], in Friedrich Nietzsche, *Untimely Meditations*, trans. by R. J. Hollingdale (New York, 1983), 62; Douglass, "Thoughts and Recollections of the Antislavery Conflict." On the concept of historical forgetting, see Lowenthal, *The Past Is a Foreign Country*, 204–6. On northerners and black suffrage, see C. Vann Woodward, *American Counterpoint: Slavery and Racism in the North-South Dialogue* (Boston, 1964), 173–83.

The Robert G. Shaw–Fifty-fourth Massachusetts Monument was unveiled
May 31, 1898, in Boston Common as a memorial to the white commander and
black soldiers who died at the Battle of Fort Wagner, South Carolina, July 18, 1863.
Douglass's two sons served in the regiment.
Courtesy Boston Athenaeum.

by a man out of touch with changing times. In a sense, Douglass was living in the
past during the last part of his life; for him, the Civil War and Reconstruction were
the reference points for the black experience in the nineteenth century. All questions of meaning, of a sense of place, of a sense of future for blacks in America drew
upon the era of emancipation. Hence, the fifth source of Douglass's pledge to "never
forget": a tremendous emotional and psychological investment in his own conception of the legacy of the conflict. As an intellectual, Douglass had grown up with
the abolition movement, the war, and its historical transformations. His career and
his very personality had been shaped by those events. So, quite literally, Douglass's
effort to preserve the memory of the Civil War was a quest to save the freedom of
his people and the meaning of his own life.

Douglass embraced his role in preserving an abolitionist memory of the war with
a sense of moral duty. In an 1883 speech in his old hometown of Rochester, New
York, he was emphatic on that point.

You will already have perceived that I am not of that school of thinkers which teaches us to let bygones be bygones; to let the dead past bury its dead. In my view there are no bygones in the world, and the past is not dead and cannot die. The evil as well as the good that men do lives after them. . . . The duty of keeping in memory the great deeds of the past, and of transmitting the same from generation to generation is implied in the mental and moral constitution of man.[30]

But what of a society that did not widely share the same sense of history and preferred a different version of the past? Douglass's answer was to resist the Lost Cause by arguing for an opposite and, he hoped, deeper cultural myth—the abolitionist conception of the Civil War, black emancipation as the source of national regeneration.

In trying to forge an alternative to the Lost Cause, Douglass drew on America's reform tradition and constantly appealed to the Constitution and to the rule of law. Moreover, reversing a central tenet of the Lost Cause—the memory of defeat— Douglass emphasized the memory of victory, the sacrifices of the Union dead, and the historical progress he believed inherent in emancipation. This is what Douglass meant in an 1878 Memorial Day speech in Madison Square in New York, when he declared that "there was a right side and a wrong side in the late war which no sentiment ought to cause us to forget."[31]

In some of his postwar rhetoric Douglass undoubtedly contributed to what Robert Penn Warren has called the myth of the "Treasury of Virtue." He did sometimes imbue Union victory with an air of righteousness that skewed the facts. His insistence on the "moral" character of the war often neglected the complex, reluctant manner in which emancipation became the goal of the Union war effort. In structuring historical memory, Douglass could be as selective as his Lost Cause adversaries. His persistent defense of the Republican party after Reconstruction caused him to walk a thin line of hypocrisy. Indeed, Douglass's millennialist interpretation of the war forever caused him to see the conflict as a cleansing tragedy, wherein the nation had been redeemed of its evil by lasting grace.[32] Douglass knew that black freedom had emerged *from* history more than from policy deliberately created by human agents. Moreover, he knew that emancipation had resulted largely from slaves' own massive self-liberation. But winning the battle over the legacy of the Civil War, Douglass knew, demanded deep cultural myths that would resonate widely in society. He knew that the struggle over memory was always, in part, a debate over

[30] Douglass, "Speech on Emancipation Day."

[31] Douglass, "Speech in Madison Square."

[32] Warren, *Legacy of the Civil War*, 59–76. Warren illuminates the ambiguities and contradictions in the dual development of the "Lost Cause" and the "Treasury of Virtue." For Douglass's discussion of "The National Lincoln Monument Association," see *New National Era*, Oct. 27, 1870. This monument, never constructed as planned, was to be seventy feet high and contain many statues of Civil War military and political personalities and allegorical figures. In his editorial, Douglass seemed flushed with excitement. He saw the monument as "an eternal sentinel guarding the era of emancipation; an immortal herald proclaiming to all the races of men the nation's great civil and moral reforms. . . . In a word, a splendid bronze and granite portraiture of the final triumph of liberty and equality on American soil." *Ibid.* On later efforts for a monument to black soldiers (also unsuccessful), see John Hope Franklin, *George Washington Williams: A Biography* (Chicago, 1987), 171–74.

the present. In his view, emancipation and black equality under law were the great results of the war. Hence, while urging old abolitionists not to give up their labors in 1875, Douglass contended that "every effort should now be made to save the result of this stupendous moral and physical contest." Moreover, nine years later Douglass warned that unless an abolitionist conception of the war were steadfastly preserved, America would "thus lose to after coming generations a vast motive power and inspiration to high and virtuous endeavor." Douglass labored to shape the memory of the Civil War, then, as a skillful propagandist, as a black leader confident of the virtue of his cause, and as an individual determined to protect his own identity.[33]

In his book *The Unwritten War: American Writers and the Civil War*, Daniel Aaron observes that very few writers in the late nineteenth century "appreciated the Negro's literal or symbolic role in the war." Black invisibility in the massive Civil War fictional literature—the absence of fully realized black characters, even in Mark Twain or William Faulkner—is yet another striking illustration that emancipation and the challenge of racial equality overwhelmed the American imagination in the postwar decades. Slavery, the war's deepest cause, and black freedom, the war's most fundamental result, remain the most conspicuous missing elements in the American literature inspired by the Civil War. Black invisibility in America's cultural memory is precisely what Douglass struggled against during the last two decades of his life. Obviously, Douglass was no novelist himself and was not about to write the great Civil War book. But memories and understandings of great events, especially apocalyptic wars, live in our consciousness like monuments in the mind. The aging Douglass's rhetoric was an eloquent attempt to forge a place on that monument for those he deemed the principal characters in the drama of emancipation: the abolitionist, the black soldier, and the freed people. Perhaps the best reason the Civil War remained, in Aaron's words, "vivid but ungraspable" to literary imagination was that most American writers avoided, or were confounded by, slavery and race, the deepest moral issues in the conflict.[34]

The late nineteenth century was an age when white supremacy flourished amid vast industrial and social change. The nation increasingly embraced sectional reunion, sanctioned Jim Crow, dreamed about technology, and defined itself by the assumptions of commerce. Near the end of his monumental work, *Black Reconstruction* (1935), W. E. B. Du Bois declared himself "aghast" at the way historians had suppressed the significance of slavery and the black quest for freedom in the literature on the Civil War and Reconstruction era. "One is astonished in the study of

[33] Frederick Douglass, "Address at the Centennial Celebration of the Abolition Society of Pennsylvania," reel 15, Douglass Papers; Douglass, "Speech at the Thirty-Third Anniversary of the Jerry Rescue."

[34] Aaron, *Unwritten War*, 332–33, xviii, 340. On fiction and the Civil War, see also Robert A. Lively, *Fiction Fights the Civil War: An Unfinished Chapter in the Literary History of the American People* (Chapel Hill, 1957); and Joyce Appleby, "Reconciliation and the Northern Novelist, 1865–1880," *Civil War History*, 10 (June 1964), 117–29. On black literary activity and memory in the nineteenth and early twentieth centuries, see Arlene A. Elder, *The "Hindered Hand": Cultural Implications of Early African-American Fiction* (Westport, 1978). For the power of war over the imagination, especially in literary forms, see Paul Fussell, *The Great War and Modern Memory* (New York, 1975), 310–35.

history," wrote Du Bois, "at the recurrence of the idea that evil must be forgotten, distorted, skimmed over. . . . The difficulty, of course, with this philosophy is that history loses its value as an incentive and example; it paints perfect men and noble nations, but it does not tell the truth." As Du Bois acknowledged, it was just such a use of history as "incentive and example" for which Douglass had labored.[35]

Although his jeremiads against the Lost Cause myth and his efforts to preserve an abolitionist memory of the conflict took on a strained quality, Douglass never lost hope in the regenerative meaning of the Civil War. It was such a great divide, such a compelling reference point, that the nation would, in time, have to face its meaning and consequences. In an 1884 speech, Douglass drew hope from a biblical metaphor of death and rebirth—the story of Jesus' raising Lazarus from the dead. "The assumption that the cause of the Negro is a dead issue," Douglass declared, "is an utter delusion. For the moment he may be buried under the dust and rubbish of endless discussion concerning civil service, tariff and free trade, labor and capital . . . , but our Lazarus is not dead. He only sleeps."[36]

Douglass's use of such a metaphor was perhaps a recognition of temporary defeat in the struggle for the memory of the Civil War. But it also represented his belief that, though the struggle would outlast his own life, it could still be won. Douglass gave one of his last public addresses on the final Memorial Day of his life (May 1894) at Mount Hope Cemetery in Rochester, were he would himself be buried some nine months later. The seventy-six-year-old orator angrily disavowed the sectional recon-ciliation that had swept the country. He feared that Decoration Day would become an event merely of "anachronisms, empty forms and superstitions." One wonders if the largely white audience in Rochester on that pleasant spring afternoon thought of Douglass himself as somewhat of an anachronism. In a country reeling from an economic depression in 1893, worried by massive immigration, the farmers' revolt, and the disorder of growing cities, Douglass's listeners (even in his old hometown) may not have looked beyond the symbolic trappings of the occasion. One wonders how willing they were to cultivate their thirty-year-old memory of the war and all its sacrifice, to face the deeper meanings Douglass demanded. The aged Douglass could still soar to oratorical heights on such occasions. He asked his audience to reflect with him about their "common memory." "I seem even now to hear and feel the effects of the sights and the sounds of that dreadful period," Douglass said. "I see the flags from the windows and housetops fluttering in the breeze. I see and hear the steady tramp of armed men in blue uniforms. . . . I see the recruiting ser-geant with drum and fife . . . calling for men, young men and strong, to go to the front and fill up the gaps made by rebel powder and pestilence. I hear the piercing sound of trumpets." These were more than Whitmanesque pictures of bygone peril and glory. In a nation that now acquiesced in the frequent lynching of his people, that shattered their hopes with disfranchisement and segregation, Douglass ap-pealed to history, to what for him was authentic experience, to the recognition

[35] W. E. B. Du Bois, *Black Reconstruction in America, 1860–1880*, (New York, 1935), 725, 722, 715.
[36] Douglass, "Speech at the Thirty-Third Anniversary of the Jerry Rescue."

scenes that formed personal and national identity. On an ideological level, where Douglass did his best work, he was still fighting the war. By 1894 he was as harsh as ever in his refusal to concede the Confederate dead any equal place in Memorial Day celebrations. "Death has no power to change moral qualities," he argued. "What was bad before the war, and during the war, has not been made good since the war." A tone of desperation entered Douglass's language toward the end of his speech. Again and again he pleaded with his audience not to believe the arguments of the Lost Cause advocates, however alluring their "disguises" might seem. He insisted that slavery had caused the war, that Americans should never forget that the South fought "to bind with chains millions of the human race."[37]

No amount of nationalism, individualism, or compassion could ever change Douglass's conception of the memory and meaning of the Civil War. His pledge to "never forget" was both a personal and a partisan act. It was an assertion of the power of memory to inform, to inspire, and to compel action. Douglass was one of those nineteenth-century thinkers who by education, by temperament, and especially by experience believed that history was something living and useful. Even in the twilight of his life, there was no greater voice for the old shibboleth that the Civil War had been a struggle for union *and* liberty. "Whatever else I may forget," Douglass told those assembled at Mount Hope Cemetery, "I shall never forget the difference between those who fought for liberty and those who fought for slavery; between those who fought to save the Republic and those who fought to destroy it." The jubilee of black freedom in America had been achieved by heroic action, through forces in history, through a tragic war, and by faith. Among Douglass's final public acts, therefore, was to fight—using the power of language and historical imagination—to preserve that jubilee in memory and in reality. In a Rochester cemetery, he stood with the Union dead, waved the last bloody shirts of a former slave, a black leader, and a Yankee partisan, and anticipated the dulling effects of time and the poet Robert Lowell's vision of "the stone statues of the abstract Union soldier" adorning New England town greens, where "they doze over muskets and muse through their sideburns."[38]

[37]"Decoration Day," May 1894, reel 17, Douglass Papers.
[38] *Ibid.*, 9; Robert Lowell, "For the Union Dead" [1964], in *Norton Anthology of American Literature: Shorter Edition*, ed. Ronald Gottesman et al. (New York, 1980), 1842.

Rescripting a Troubled Past: John Brown's Family and the Harpers Ferry Conspiracy

Robert E. McGlone

The John Brown family was unique among famous nineteenth-century American families: it owed its public reputation largely to a single dramatic civil disturbance — the Harpers Ferry crisis. That desperate effort to free the slaves cost the lives of John's sons Watson and Oliver and nearly that of their half brother, Owen, who escaped Virginia's justice. John Brown's raid, his trial, and his execution on December 2, 1859, gave his wife and children a notoriety reborn with each new tale of the Old Man's fanaticism and daring.[1] But the Browns remained in the public eye only as witnesses to his deeds, defenders of his cause, and bearers of his legacy. None of John Brown's eight surviving children or his score of grandchildren gained public attention in his or her own right. Unlike such celebrated American families as the Adamses, Byrds, Harrimans, Roosevelts, and Winthrops, the Browns could boast neither wealth nor learning nor conspicuous careers, apart from the brief tenure of John himself as a guerrilla leader. And whereas the histories of other well-known families begin with the success stories of the founders, the Browns' fame was rooted in spectacular failure. In a profound sense, the family was born anew in the heroic gesture that ended with the hanging of its founder.

It is not the family's modest achievements, but its rebirth — a remarkable mutation of consciousness — that commends Brown's heirs to our attention. That transformation emerged gradually in their long struggle to come to terms with the troubled legacy of Harpers Ferry. It set new emotional and social parameters for their lives. To be sure, children of the famous must often learn to live with burdensome family traditions. But John Brown's sons were adults when their father suddenly became a martyr to the antislavery cause. All of them, and one of Brown's daughters, had played some part in his "war against slavery." The need to justify their own roles

Robert E. McGlone is assistant professor of history at the University of Hawaii at Manoa. An earlier version of this essay was presented at the biennial meeting of Phi Alpha Theta in New York City, December 29, 1985. The author wishes to thank Richard Immerman, Carroll and Leslie Johnson, Marion McGlone, James Mohr, Idus Newby, Fritz Rehbock, Herb Roitblat, George Simson, Bertram Wyatt-Brown, and Dave Thelen, Susan Armeny, and the referees of the *Journal of American History* for valuable comments and suggestions.

[1] The best scholarly account of the John Brown raid is Stephen B. Oates, *To Purge This Land with Blood: A Biography of John Brown* (New York, 1970).

Watson Brown, who died at Harpers Ferry of a gunshot wound at age twenty-four.
Courtesy Kansas State Historical Society.

complicated their efforts to interpret the past. Their father's public image, moreover, was profoundly ambiguous, reflecting sectional and ideological divisions within the nation and ambivalence about the use of violence to effect reform.

As heirs of Old Osawatomie, the surviving Browns shared the adulation and hostility his memory inspired. They were invisibly scarred stigmatics, privately but perennially reworking their own relationships with "Father" while bearing public witness to the purity of his motives. Bound by allegiances shaped in childhood, pressed by public disclosures of the family's alleged misdeeds, they could neither dismiss nor merely romanticize the past. In recurring efforts to justify themselves and defend their honor, they introduced wholesale, if unrecognized, distortions into their family history. In so doing they refocused their own identities and reconceived the family's past in obedience to their father's legend.

At the heart of the process was a profound restructuring of memories of crucial events in their lives. Its achievement entailed unwitting distortions of those distant episodes. A selective memory of the conspiracy permitted them to reinterpret — or forget — events not in the new scenario. A telescoping of memories excised discordant details. Such simplifications tended to separate memories from their actual contexts, substituting general for specific circumstances and highlighting the symbolic and moral significance of those events. The scenario resulting from that serendipitous reworking of the past gave morally unambiguous and psychologically self-affirming roles to the children of Old John Brown, bonding them to one another in the memory of their "martyred" father and painting them into a heroic canvas.

Something profound was at work in the Browns' reconstruction of their roles in the Harpers Ferry conspiracy. In their troubled search for collective vindication, they ultimately shared in the evocation of a portentous childhood event — a solemn family oath to make war on slavery — that had either been forgotten for nearly half a century or had never occurred. Convinced that the sacred oath explained the history of the John Brown family, they infused an invented memory with mythic significance.

The Browns' evocation of a partially factitious family past raises an issue of perennial interest to scholars: How can sincere people be convinced of the truth of memories that the researcher knows cannot be accurate representations of past events? How can they call up images of episodes that did not happen? The answers to these questions are logically prior to any assessment of personal memories. Yet historians have neglected the remarkable body of research on memory produced by experimental psychologists in the past two decades. Preferring to borrow from "dynamic psychology" (psychoanalysis), many have short-circuited processes such as learning, perception, and memory in assessing the sources of the behavior of historical figures. Irrational impulses do influence history. But if cognitive processes are driven in part by unconscious motives, they also enjoy considerable autonomy. Thus, to understand conduct, historians must take account of memory's influence. Memory is the compass of our actions.

Today experimental, cognitive psychologists are asking questions and establishing principles pertinent to historical inquiry. Beginning in the 1880s, most psychologists interested in memory worked in laboratories, seeking to establish the principles by which associations of words, ideas, and other verbal or sensory data are formed, coded, and recalled from memory. Recognizing the limitations of stimulus-response theories of memory, cognitive psychologists have recently focused on the strategies people employ in mastering information and in retaining a sense of the meaning or gist of the knowledge stored in memory. Increasingly, they have forsaken the laboratory to study memory in "natural contexts." They conclude that memories are not mere copies of the past, but "reconstructions" serving our present needs.[2]

These reconstructions are made possible by unconscious knowledge structures that help preserve memories and general knowledge over an entire life-span. Variously termed "scripts," "schemata," and occasionally "frames," the structures provide the conceptual frameworks we use to perform, encode, and later to remember our activities. Scripts are "standardized generalized episodes" against which actual episodes are understood and through which the essence of particular experiences is encoded. Scripts facilitate the deep processing of important events that would otherwise be retained only momentarily. Scripts are not scenarios or accounts of particular events, but codifications of the rules by which everyday experiences are understood and remembered. They provide us a sense of the appropriate reasons for undertaking an activity, the conditions and "props" necessary to complete it, and the roles and human actions ordinarily required to carry it out. The many scripts we learn inform our daily lives with orderly expectations and structure our recall of experiences otherwise lost to us.[3]

Researchers in the growing subfield of autobiographical memory have used the notion of scripts to explain puzzling phenomena akin to the Browns' restructuring of their past. Cognitive psychologists agree that autobiographical memory provides our sense of continuity and personal identity. But it is not a wholly faithful account of the past. Autobiographical memories may fuse and blend as repetitious events lose detail when scripted for long-term recall. Craig Barclay observes that "events" that did not happen but merely resemble "what one expects from prior recurring experiences may be incorrectly identified as happening in the past." The tendency of autobiographical memories to reflect a "self-schema"—a "cognitive structure that contains generic knowledge about the self"—helps explain how personal memories are distorted, changed, and lost over time.[4]

By *rescripting*, I mean, therefore, not a deliberate rewriting of the past, but a transformation in the controlling expectations and logic of life situations that finally reorders autobiographical memories. In rescripting, the script-driven processing of

---

[2] See, for example, Ulric Neisser, "John Dean's Memory: A Case Study," *Cognition*, 9 (Feb. 1981), 1–22. The best introduction to recent research on long-term memory is Ulric Neisser, ed., *Memory Observed: Remembering in Natural Contexts* (New York, 1982). An attempt at a synthesis of recent thinking about memory is Israel Rosenfield, *The Invention of Memory: A New View of the Brain* (New York, 1988).

[3] The first systematic discussion of scripts appeared in Roger C. Schank and Robert P. Abelson, *Scripts, Plans, Goals, and Understanding* (Hillsdale, N. J., 1977). On conceptual issues relating to scripts, see Roger C. Schank, *Dynamic Memory: A Theory of Reminding and Learning in Computers and People* (Cambridge, Mass., 1982). On the rules for structuring conceptual elements within a narrative, see Perry W. Thorndyke, "Cognitive Structures in Comprehension and Memory of Narrative Discourse," *Cognitive Psychology*, 9 (Jan. 1977), 77–110; and Jean M. Mandler and Nancy S. Johnson, "Remembrance of Things Parsed: Story Structure and Recall," *ibid.*, 111–51. Inspired by advances in brain physiology and computer modeling, a new interdisciplinary field called parallel distributed processing (PDP) has developed. See David E. Rumelhart and James L. McClelland, eds., *Parallel Distributed Processing: Explorations in the Microstructure of Cognition* (2 vols., Cambridge, Mass., 1986).

[4] Craig R. Barclay, "Schematization of Autobiographical Memory," in *Autobiographical Memory*, ed. David C. Rubin (Cambridge, Eng., 1986), 89; William F. Brewer, "What Is Autobiographical Memory?" *ibid.*, 25–49, esp. 27, 30–32.

personal memories refocuses an individual's self-schema, deleting incongruous experiences and validating false memories as authentic. Rescripting adds or takes away information to make a life story coherent and believable at a particular time. By creating false events in personal memory, it also helps to prompt new strategies of recall and hence to elicit newly accessible memories of actual events.

The rescripting of the Browns' family identity can be understood in part as an unconscious strategy to accommodate to the losses they suffered at Harpers Ferry and to recurring attacks on their character and reputation. Harpers Ferry was a watershed event in the family's history. While growing up, the sons and oldest daughters of John Brown had known their father as a pious, industrious farmer, tanner, and wool merchant who belonged to the large antislavery clan of land-rich "Squire" Owen Brown of Hudson, Ohio. For many years their young lives were centered in the orderly farming towns of the Western Reserve, where Grandfather Owen maintained what they later called their "ancestral home." Confident, proud, and ambitious, the sons of John Brown rejected their father's "old-fashioned" religious beliefs and eventually determined to make their future in Kansas without him. A half century later they saw themselves as survivors of a historic crisis inspired by their father's fanaticism. Creatures of his legend, they feared privately that his bloodline destined them to lives of episodic mental instability and poverty.[5] His deeds bequeathed them only a perpetual, ambiguous celebrity and a distant fellowship with New England's "holy warriors." Whipsawed by perennial controversy, the Browns now saw themselves paradoxically, as unique yet undistinguished, heroic yet insignificant, exalted yet despised.

The crucible of this complex transformation was their father's legend.

The initial impetus for the Browns' rescripting of their past was the failure and consequent exposure of their conspiracy against slavery. The Harpers Ferry raid left John Brown a captive facing swift and certain execution, and for more than a generation it held his family hostage to unwanted notoriety and private misgivings. Pride in being the family of Old Brown was tempered by realization that even among abolitionists their father had been a zealot, a self-anointed apostle of righteous violence—"an instrument in the hands of God," as he had often said. Yet the family was proud of his courage and untutored eloquence at his Virginia trial and in his serenity while awaiting the hangman. Their spirits rallied at his assurances that he died "for God's eternal truth and for suffering humanity on the scaffold."[6] To them, not he, but Virginia was on trial. If, to others, John Brown seemed the apotheosis

[5] See, for example, Jason Brown interview by Katherine Mayo, Dec. 13–14, 1908, Oswald Garrison Villard Collection (Rare Book and Manuscript Library, Butler Library, Columbia University, New York, N.Y.). For an assessment of the evidence of mental disorder in the Brown family, see Robert E. McGlone, "The 'Madness' of Old John Brown: The Problem of Psychiatric Diagnosis in History," paper presented at the annual meeting of the American Studies Association, Miami Beach, Oct. 30, 1988, esp. 30–31 (in Robert E. McGlone's possession).

[6] John Brown to "Dear Children, All," Nov. 22, 1859, Boyd B. Stutler Collection (West Virginia Department of Culture and History, Charleston).

of abolitionist extremism, to his wife and children—as to a wider circle of kinsmen, friends, and advocates of "forcible means"—his humanitarian motives and personal sacrifices sanctified the killings at Harpers Ferry.

After the Civil War, Brown's martyrdom seemed less perfect. Even admirers often remembered him as a figure of moral ambiguity or doubtful sanity. Forty years after the raid, Thomas Wentworth Higginson, once a member of the secret committee of six that financed Brown's army, conceded offhandedly that by the time of Harpers Ferry the "delicate balance of [Brown's] zealot's mind" had become "somewhat disturbed." Thus, if emancipation had vindicated Brown's ends, even to northern sympathizers his means came to seem questionable. The political storm seeded by his brief capture of the federal arsenal at Harpers Ferry was widely judged to have been a cause of the Civil War. His prophecy that "the crimes of this *guilty, land: will* never be purged *away*; but with Blood" echoed stridently through the Gilded Age. To many Americans in the twilight of Reconstruction, John Brown had been a prophet of chaos and bloodshed, not liberation.[7]

As the radicalism of his generation receded, moreover, a profound ambiguity in Brown's role emerged. Having given his life to free the slaves, Brown was a symbol of racial acceptance in a time of growing racial intolerance. Paradoxically, he was divisive for his very effort to unite black and white. He had appealed to the tenets of an American creed, but his raid polarized sentiment over slavery. He had proclaimed the brotherhood of man yet helped to cut away the fragile sutures of trust and political fellowship that bound the nation together. Using the language of the Declaration of Independence, he had denounced the principle of government by and for whites alone. Thus, he had helped shatter the moral compromises that sustained a precarious armistice between North and South. And, implicitly, he challenged the principles of white supremacy and local self-rule on which the next generation restored the Union.

Inevitably, his heirs were honored for his idealism and scorned for his fanaticism. While other ex-abolitionists found vindication in the past, the Browns had to defend the family's war against slavery. In light of the raid's disastrous end, they could not celebrate the triumph over slavery without sorrow. For them the anniversary, not of Jubilee, but of their father's "murder" by the state of Virginia marked the passing years. "It brings sad recollections," wrote Brown's daughter Ruth in 1892, "yet we rejoice that our precious father went to the scaffold joyfully, and with a forgiving smile on his lips."[8]

Changing public perceptions of their father and themselves thus bound them to a crisis that had been at once political, cultural, and moral. Popular legends and a growing body of polemical literature about John Brown opened new fronts in the

---

[7] Thomas Wentworth Higginson, *Cheerful Yesterdays* (Boston, 1900), 223. On his way to the gallows, John Brown, gave this handwritten statement to a bystander. John Brown, statement, Dec. 2, 1859, John Brown, Jr., Papers (Ohio Historical Society, Columbus).

[8] Ruth Brown Thompson to Frank G. Logan, Dec. 2, 1892, Frank G. Logan Collection (Chicago Historical Society, Chicago, Ill.).

family's ancient war against slavery and pressed Brown's children to explore their
own understandings of the crusade. Reminiscent accounts of events in Kansas and
at Harpers Ferry published by old adversaries and false claimants to a share of their
glory required the Browns to search their memories and their fading, precious letters
from the Old Man to set the record straight. For the Browns recollections of even
trivial events in their antislavery days might symbolize the cause and family honor.[9]

The character of the witnesses called against the Browns and their own understanding of the audiences they addressed decisively shaped their efforts to rekindle
past loyalties and confound their critics. As memory researchers have shown,
different kinds of cues or prompts dictate distinct "search strategies" and consequently elicit different "memory contents" for the same events.[10] Threatening disclosures, for example, might inspire elaborate rehearsals or recountings. In December 1879 the *Lawrence Daily Journal* published the "confession" of James
Townsley, who in 1856 had been part of a free-state raiding party that had killed
five proslavery men near Pottawatomie Creek following the sack of Lawrence by a
proslavery posse. Townsley's story compelled the Browns to admit that Old Brown
had ordered the "executions" and led the party. But they assiduously marshaled
fading memory fragments to vindicate the deed. Hadn't the free-state leadership
assigned John Brown to "sweep" the Pottawatomie? Weren't the slain men members
of the "bogus" proslavery court that had wrongly indicted the Browns? Hadn't the
victims themselves publicly threatened the Browns? In the end, hadn't John Brown's
blow stopped the killing of free-state settlers and frightened slaveholders into
leaving the territory?[11]

On many occasions, by contrast, friendly local newspapers sent reporters to the
homes of John Brown's aging sons and daughters to recount familiar tales of their
heroic past. Those interviews prompted casual and pleasant rehearsals of what were
by then heavily scripted episodes. The efforts of John Brown's sons and daughters
to provide sympathetic biographers with assurances about the Old Man's character
initiated searches of their childhood memories of their father. Controversies in
magazines like the *Nation* and the *Andover Review* cued searches for memories to

---

[9] Ulric Neisser has coined the term "repisodes" for a single, mistaken recollection that actually represents a
set of repeated experiences or related events. Neisser, "John Dean's Memory," 20.

[10] See, for example, Brian J. Reiser, John B. Black, and Peter Kalamarides, "Strategic Memory Search Processes,"
in *Autobiographical Memory*, ed. Rubin, 100–121. The methodological rigor and interview techniques of oral
historians might be enhanced by exposure to this research. See John A. Neuenschwander, "Remembrance of Things
Past: Oral Historians and Long-Term Memory," *Oral History Review*, 5 (1978), 45–53; and Trevor Lummis, "Structure and Validity in Oral Evidence," *International Journal of Oral History*, 2 (June 1981), 109–20.

[11] See, for example, notes of interviews with Owen and Salmon Brown, both participants in the Pottawatomie
killings. Owen Brown interview by Franklin B. Sanborn, June 27, 1880, Franklin B. Sanborn Folder (Houghton
Library, Harvard University, Cambridge, Mass.). Salmon Brown interview by Sanborn, Nov. 17, 1911, Stutler Collection. In a letter to an abolitionist in Vermont, Salmon declared in 1859 that his father was not "a participator"
in the Pottawatomie killings. Salmon affirmed nonetheless that the deed "was all that saved the territory from being
over run with drunken land pirates from the Southern States." See Salmon Brown to Rev. Joshua Young, Dec. 27,
1859, in James T. Malin, *John Brown and the Legend of Fifty-Six* (Philadelphia, 1942), 267. Salmon later justified
this and other denials of complicity in the killings on the grounds of loyalty to the others and the danger of prosecu-
tion. Salmon Brown to Sanborn, Aug. 8, 1909, Stutler Collection. Salmon condemned James Townsley as a coward
and a liar. Salmon Brown to William E. Connelly, May 28, 1913, *ibid.*

vindicate the family's literary champions. Over the years, the family's diverse audiences and unbidden critics helped them fashion a new sense of who they were and what it meant to be a Brown.

In this rescripting of the family's troubled past, the surviving Browns found new meaning for their lives in altered memories of their roles in the conspiracy to overthrow slavery.

In a final letter to his family from Charlestown prison, where he awaited execution, the Old Man exulted "that so many of you as have had the opportunity; have given full proof of your fidelity to the great family of man."[12] Family legend and early partisan biographers have persuaded modern writers to accept that appraisal of the family's loyalty. But Brown knew the truth was quite different. In fact, Brown's wife, three of his six sons, and his son-in-law had remained at home during the raid, and all the Browns were ambivalent about his campaign in Virginia. Even the three sons who joined that campaign were dismayed when they learned that he intended to seize the federal arsenal and armory at Harpers Ferry. Yet in later years the surviving Browns endlessly reaffirmed their loyalty to "Father" and to the private war in which he, three of his sons, and two young kinsmen died. The family's unacknowledged effort to reconcile old doubts with later professions of unqualified support led them to reshape their past.

In deserting from the Old Man's war against slavery, the sons did not repudiate the cause. Their reluctance to fight was rooted in their bitter experiences in Kansas. Five of Brown's sons had settled on claims near Osawatomie in the spring of 1855, only to be swept into the conflict between free-state and proslavery factions. The guerrilla war that finally brought their father to national attention for a time shattered their morale. The three older sons surviving from John's first marriage lost their youngest brother, Frederick, killed at Osawatomie by a proslavery posse. Held for months by territorial authorities, burned out of his home, deserted by his rifle company, the eldest son, John, Jr., suffered more than a year from sleeplessness, a "foreboding of danger," and an "absolute inability to prevent shedding tears no matter how trivial the cause." The second son, Jason, was also despondent and feared that he too would have a "crazy spell." Both men abandoned their claims and took their wives and children back to Ohio. The third son, Owen, who fled Kansas with his father, was afflicted with "nervous fever" and lameness from an accidental gunshot wound. "Sick of fighting and trouble" like his brothers, Owen became hysterical with remorse for his part in the Pottawatomie killings, and guilt haunted him long afterwards. At a family Christmas gathering back in Ohio, John's sons told their uncle, Jeremiah Root Brown, they did not support their father's scheme to "carry the war into Africa," as abolitionists often called the South. Returning to the family

---

[12] John Brown to "My Dearly beloved Wife, Sons: & Daughters, *every one*," Nov. 30, 1859, John Brown Collection (Kansas State Historical Society, Topeka). The town where Brown was imprisoned is now known as Charles Town, West Virginia.

farm in the Adirondacks, Brown's sons Salmon and Oliver informed their mother, Mary Ann Day Brown, that all the sons had resolved to fight no more. Thus, the Kansas years unsettled filial ties and undercut Brown's paternal authority. [13]

The sons' resolution was a crippling blow to John Brown, and it was more than a year before he gained a recruit — Owen — among his sons. In a sense, Owen's enlistment not only saved John's dream, but in later years it validated Owen's brothers' interpretation of events leading to Harpers Ferry: Owen was their witness. Although in 1859 John Brown's recruits reprimanded Owen because he disputed John "in any & everything," the son nonetheless sustained his father through periods of doubt and depression. When Brown's company balked on learning the Old Man's plan to capture the arsenal at Harpers Ferry, Owen and his half brothers finally relented and persuaded the doubters to accept a modified version of the "invasion." Owen was thus a bridge between his father and the hesitant young men in the company. For two years he personified the fraternity that kept the tiny army together while the Old Man scratched for funds and weapons. After the raid Owen was a living monument to the family's sacrifices. A dreamer with a crippled arm, he lived for years in a shack behind the comfortable home of John, Jr., then as a caretaker on the nearby estate of Jay Cooke, and in the years before his death in 1889 as a virtual hermit on "Brown's Peak" above Pasadena, California. A frail, kindly old man, he drifted through the years asking little of the present and dwelling much in the heroic past he helped his family relive. In the rescripting of the family's identity, Owen personified the commitment and trust in the Old Man the others wished they had shown.[14]

Unlike Owen, Brown's other sons were or would soon be married when, in January 1858, John wrote home to ask for recruits for his Virginia campaign. Their responses depended in part on the wishes of the women in the family. Indeed, Brown's letter was not so much a summons as a plea directed chiefly to his wife Mary and his daughter Ruth, who had married a "staunch" abolitionist neighbor, Henry Thompson.[15]

Not even John's week-long visit in March persuaded Ruth that Henry, who had been shot in a skirmish in Kansas, would survive a campaign in slavery's very citadel. Protesting her loyalty to the cause and insisting that Henry had made his own deci-

[13] John Brown, Jr., to Gen. [Edward B.] Whitman, Feb. 26, 1858, *ibid.* Jason Brown interview; Henry Thompson interview by Mayo, Aug. 22–Sept. 1, 1908, *ibid.* Wealthy Hotchkiss Brown to Ruth Brown Thompson and Henry Thompson, Jan 4, 1857, Brown-Clark Collection (Hudson Library and Historical Society, Hudson, Ohio); John Brown to "Dear Wife," March 31, 1857, Stutler Collection, John Brown to Sanborn, Aug. 13, 1857, quoted in Franklin B. Sanborn, *The Life and Letters of John Brown, Liberator of Kansas, and Martyr of Virginia* (1885; reprint, New York, 1969), 412–14.

[14] Owen Brown Diary, Feb. 17, 1859, Horatio Nelson Rust Collection (Henry E. Huntington Library and Art Gallery, San Marino, California); Owen Brown to John Brown, July 12, 1858, Villard Collection; Owen Brown to John Brown, May 2, 1859, Ferdinand J. Dreer Collection (Historical Society of Pennsylvania, Philadelphia); [Owen Brown] to "Dear Sir," Aug. 18, 1859, *ibid.* A neglected account of the "mutiny" is Charles Plummer Tidd to Thomas Wentworth Higginson, Feb. 10, 1860, Thomas Wentworth Higginson Papers (Boston Public Library, Boston, Mass.) Owen's later years may be traced in the correspondence of his brothers, John, Jr., and Jason. His death is reported in Jason Brown to "Dear Family," Jan. 14, 188[9], Clarence S. Gee Collection (Hudson Library and Historical Society). See also *Sandusky Daily Register*, Jan. 25, 1889, p. 1.

[15] Nelson Hawkins [John Brown] to "My Dear Wife & children every one," Jan. 30, 1858, Villard Collection.

sion, Ruth told her father that Henry could not be spared to fight. Ruth wanted desperately to help, and in the years after Harpers Ferry, she testified again and again that John was not the cruel patriarch depicted by his enemies, but a "tender, loving father" of whom she sought only to be worthy. In the family's emerging image of itself, Ruth softened and domesticated her warrior-father.[16]

Mary Brown also played a crucial role in the transformation of the family. The daughter of a struggling blacksmith with too many children to support, she was seventeen when she married John, a sober, respected widower twice her age and already the father of six children. A large, strong woman, she bore twelve children in the next fourteen years and a thirteenth six years later. All but six of her children died in infancy or childhood. Reserved, pious, and largely unschooled, she rarely defied her husband. Yet she refused to join him in Kansas, and plagued by "anxious forebodings," she tried to persuade her sons to come home even before the fighting there threatened them.[17]

The reluctant, anxious woman who emerges from the Brown family letters is not the resolute Mary Brown portrayed in historical literature. That Mary was created by abolitionists determined to provide their martyr with a worthy mate. In fact, abolitionists consciously tutored Mary in the role they wanted her to play, persuading her to attempt to visit her husband in jail, presenting her at public meetings and private receptions in Boston and Philadelphia, even writing letters for publication in her name.[18] John Brown's early biographers gave literary sanction to the abolitionists' image of an obedient, stoical Mary. So compelling did this tradition become that modern scholars have affirmed that Mary "subordinated herself completely" to her husband's will, enduring every hardship in silence.[19]

But the evidence points to a different conclusion. Mary was no more willing to send her sons to Virginia than to Kansas. She concealed her opposition until July 1859, when John sent Oliver home with an urgent request that she come south herself. John needed her to keep house and to quiet suspicions about his actions among

[16] Ruth Brown Thompson to John Brown, April 21, 1858, John Brown Collection (Kansas State Historical Society); Ruth Brown Thompson, "Reminiscences of John Brown of Kansas and Harper's Ferry," Dec. 2, 1882, p. 14, Rust Collection.

[17] Oliver Brown to "Dear Mother, Brother, & Sisters," Feb. 4, 1856, Villard Collection.

[18] Mary's ghostwriters were Mrs. Marcus (Rebecca) Spring and the Philadelphia abolitionist, Dr. William H. Furness. Evidence of their authorship is in J. Miller McKim to John Brown, Nov. 23, 1859, Villard Collection; McKim to Higginson, Nov. 23, 1859, Higginson Papers; McKim to William Lloyd Garrison, Nov. 25, 1859, Gee Collection. Furness assisted with Mary A. Brown to Henry A. Wise, Nov. 21, 1859, Dreer Collection; Spring with Mary A. Brown to John Brown, Nov. 13, 1859, Villard Collection; and Mary A. Brown to John Brown, Nov. 24, 1859, *ibid.*

[19] Early depictions of a stoical Mary Brown include James Redpath, *The Public Life of Captain John Brown* (Boston, 1860), 7, 46–47, 66; Sanborn, *Life and Letters of John Brown*, 496–99; Richard J. Hinton, *John Brown and His Men* (London, 1894), 443–44; William Edward Burghardt Du Bois, *John Brown* (1909; reprint, New York, 1962), 39, 96, 104; Oswald Garrison Villard, *John Brown, 1800–1859: A Biography Fifty Years After* (1910; reprint, Gloucester, Mass., 1965), 24–25; John Newton, *Captain John Brown of Harper's Ferry: A Preliminary Incident to the Great Civil War, of America* (New York, 1902), esp. 30–31. On Mary's "subordination," see Oates, *To Purge This Land with Blood*, 26. The abolitionists' martyr is discernible in Benjamin Quarles, *Allies for Freedom: Blacks and John Brown* (New York, 1974), 168; Albert Fried, *John Brown's Journey: Notes and Reflections on His America and Mine* (Garden City, 1978), 33–34; Barrie Stavis, *John Brown: The Sword and the Word* (South Brunswick, 1970), 26, 29. Writers hostile to Brown depict Mary as "the woman he had wronged." Hill Peebles Wilson, *John Brown, Soldier of Fortune: A Critique* (Lawrence, Kans., 1913), 381.

neighbors around the Maryland farmhouse he had leased to conceal his weapons and his growing "army." "I dont see how we can get along without [you]," Brown wrote. "I would not have you fail to come on by any means . . . I want you to come right off."[20]

Mary refused. She sent no reply. She even did "everything in her power" to prevent her impetuous, moody, fifteen-year-old daughter, Annie, and Oliver's frail, sixteen-year-old wife, Martha Brewster Brown, from going in her place. To conceal the "real truth" from John, Annie and the others agreed to make excuses for Mary. But Mary's failure to come to the Kennedy farm was "a sorry disappointment" to her husband, who suspected the deception and Mary's unspoken opposition to the enterprise that had become his obsession. Mary never publicly acknowledged her disapproval of John's scheme. Bound by public belief in her partnership with her martyred husband and dependent on the financial assistance of his abolitionist friends, she sustained the family's conspiracy of silence about the Browns' past sins of disloyalty and disbelief. Her silence permitted the others to refashion the history of the family as their own needs dictated.[21]

By the summer of 1859 three of Brown's sons had agreed to fight beside their father. But like Henry Thompson, the other three sons had not, and in October 1859 they were far from the tragic scene at Harpers Ferry. John, Jr., found other ways to busy himself, while Jason and Salmon flatly refused their father's appeal. All three paid an emotional price for their choices. In later years they struggled to reconcile their avowal of the cause with their absence from the ranks of the "immortal twenty-one."[22] That inner conflict clouded their perceptions of the past and energized the rescripting of the family's history.

The Old Man had hoped to win over Mary's second "boy," Salmon, a big-boned, husky twenty-two year old. As a child Salmon had been a perpetual trial to his mother and to his father, whose strict "Sunday-school rules" of conduct and frequent absences tempted his youngest sons "to carry on pretty high." A stubborn, sometimes pugnacious youth, Salmon had gone to Kansas in the spring of 1855 feeling "more like a fight now, than I ever did before." Like Owen and Henry Thompson, he was wounded in Kansas, yet he later returned, hoping to avenge the

---

[20] John Brown assured Mary she would face "no more exposure here than at North Elba." See John Brown to Mary A. Brown, July 5, 1859, in Villard, *John Brown*, 404–5.

[21] Annie Brown Adams, statement to Franklin B. Sanborn, Nov. 1886, Logan Collection. The story of the several funds raised to support Mary Brown and her children has not been fully told. In March 1857 John Brown wrote to several abolitionist friends to ask that $1000 be raised to provide for his wife in the event of his death. See William Lawrence, *Life of Amos A. Lawrence* (Boston, 1899), 126–27; and Sanborn, *Life and Letters of John Brown*, 408. Substantial sums were given. Trustees of that fund disbursed sums to other members of the Brown family and to widows of several of Brown's volunteers who died in the raid. See William Lloyd Garrison, Jr., to John Brown, Jr., Jan. 6, 1890, John Brown, Jr., Papers (Rutherford B. Hayes Library, Fremont, Ohio). See the list of the contributors and beneficiaries to the Mary Brown Relief Fund, unsigned, n. d., Stutler Collection. See also Villard, *John Brown*, 280–81.

[22] This phrase first appeared in a resolution adopted at a public gathering at John Brown's graveside on July 4, 1860. *Liberator*, July 27, 1860, pp. 117–18.

death of his half brother Frederick. By the time his father appealed to him to go to Virginia, Salmon had married Abbie Hinckley, who, like other wives in the family, opposed her husband's going to make war against slavery. "She dominated him," one of Salmon's sisters later remembered, "and actually prevented his going to say goodbye to his brothers when they set out from North Elba . . . for fear that at the last moment he would join them."[23]

Salmon never admitted that his failure to go with his brothers was influenced by his bride's entreaties. But the explanations he offered in later years betrayed a wish to excuse his absence. At times he attributed his refusal to prescience. "I said to the boys before they left," Salmon told a well-informed researcher fifty years after the raid, " 'You know father. You know he will *dally* till he is trapped.' " At other times Salmon offered other explanations. In a newspaper interview given two years before the account just cited, he stated that "none of us expected the movement to result fatally, and so [father's] going away at that time was no different from other occasions. In this version, Salmon shook hands with his father as John left. " 'I wish you could go along,' he said to me, 'but someone has to stay and take care of things at home.' " Thus, it was not foresight but "only . . . chance" that Salmon did not go to Harpers Ferry.[24]

The latter explanation implies that Salmon would have been at Harpers Ferry had his father not assigned him other responsibilities. If that were so, his conscience might have been satisfied. Salmon was too deeply committed to the memory of his father and his family's antislavery tradition to renounce the raid in principle. In 1867 he even made a public demand that an anonymous critic of his father come forward. In 1909, at age seventy-three, he insisted that the Browns' ancient struggle against slavery was his "chief interest" in life. Ten years later, paralyzed from the waist down and suffering from arthritis and long sieges of pneumonia, he killed himself with his old Kansas pistol after celebrating his father's birthday. The last of John Brown's sons to die, he never expressed remorse for his part in the killings on Pottawatomie Creek. For six decades he kept faith with his father's memory. But only in his imagined and contradictory accounts of his refusal to go to Harpers Ferry had his father provided the absolution he needed.[25]

The only son of John Brown with more than a common school education, John, Jr., traveled for a time as a lecturer on phrenology. Accepting his role as the oldest son, in 1854 he persuaded his brothers to leave their parched Ohio farms for more promising homesteads in Kansas. There he served as vice-president of a free-state convention at Lawrence and a member of the Topeka legislature's executive com-

[23] Salmon Brown interview by Mayo, Oct. 11–13, 1908, Villard Collection; Salmon Brown to John Brown, May 21, 1855, Sanborn Folder; Sarah Brown interview by Mayo, Sept. 16–20, 1908, Villard Collection.

[24] Salmon Brown interview by Mayo, Villard Collection; Salmon Brown interview by W. C. Whit, 1906, quoted in *Akron Beacon Journal*, Nov. 2, 1975, sec. F, p. 1. In yet another version, Salmon declared that his father "urged and reasoned and regretted my determination to stay at home, perhaps as he had never regretted the act of any of his children." Salmon Brown, "My Father, John Brown," in *A John Brown Reader*, ed. Louis Ruchames (London, 1959), 182–89, esp. 188.

[25] *Red Bluff* [California] *Independent*, Oct. 16, 1867, p. 2; Salmon Brown interview by Mayo, Villard Collection; Salmon Brown, "My Father, John Brown," 184–85.

mittee. In the latter role, he sponsored a resolution urging free-state settlers to form militia companies, and as captain of a newly organized militia company, briefly freed two slaves. It was John, Jr.'s appeal for weapons that first brought his father to the territory.[26]

It is not surprising that John, Jr., later spoke proudly of his contributions to the Harpers Ferry raid. He played an active part in the conspiracy, raising funds among sympathizers in the Northeast, arranging places of refuge in western Pennsylvania for freed blacks, recruiting among black fugitives in Canada. He shipped weapons, labeled as mining equipment, to his father's man in Chambersburg, Pennsylvania, for overland haul to John's leased Maryland farm. A trusted agent, John, Jr., was to be his father's channel of communication with allies and family once the fighting in Virginia began.[27]

It is a measure of the extent to which participation in the raid became symbolic of commitment and manhood that in his later years John, Jr., had to justify his absence from Harpers Ferry. Speaking to sympathetic audiences, he invariably stated that he was "not looking for [the blow] so soon, and was in Canada, or otherwise I would probably have been captured or killed with the rest." Those statements invited skepticism. His half sister Sarah recalled that the other sons "found it conspicuous that he always managed to keep out of danger." His plea of ignorance about the timing of the raid might excuse his absence, but it implied that he was only a marginal participant or a negligent agent. In 1910 John Brown's first scholarly biographer, Oswald Garrison Villard, expressed contempt for John, Jr.'s repeated claim that the raid had taken him "completely by surprise." Even John, Jr.'s old ally, Richard J. Hinton, who had also been one of the Old Man's absent volunteers, concluded that the son's "misapprehension, if such it was, seems to have been the cause of delays" among his Canada recruits.[28]

John Jr.'s critics were right and wrong. In fact, John, Jr., had returned from Canada six weeks before the raid, and he was alerted that the first action was not far off. But his father did not ask him to cancel plans to make a recruiting trip to Cleveland at the end of September, and word that anyone reaching Chambersburg would not find the road open "for some time to come" reached John, Jr., too late for him to join the company. He had asked several times that his name be added to the company muster, and as he left for Cleveland he pledged, "You will have me with you just as soon as I am satisfied I can do more and be of more use there than where I am." The projected foray had been delayed more than a year, and John, Jr., like his contact in Chambersburg, expected a long campaign affording other op-

[26] On John Brown, Jr.'s career as a lecturer and in Kansas, see Richard O. Boyer, *The Legend of John Brown: A Biography and a History* (New York, 1973), 142–43, 447–53, 511–13; and Diary of John Brown, Jr., Sol Feinstone Collection (George Arents Research Library, Syracuse University, Syracuse, N.Y.). On the appeal, see John Brown, Jr., to John Brown, June 29, July 2, 1855, Sanborn Folder.

[27] John Brown to "Dear Wife & Children All," Oct. 1, 1859, James W. Eldridge Collection (Huntington Library); John Brown to "Dear Wife; & Children *All*," Oct. 8, 1859, Stutler Collection.

[28] *Sandusky Daily Register*, Feb. 27, 1888, p. 1. See also *ibid.*, Mar. 9, 1888, p. 4; *ibid.*, Mar. 19, 1888, p. 1; Sarah Brown interview; Villard, *John Brown*, 406–7, 414, 422–23; Hinton, *John Brown and His Men*, 263, 269.

portunities to fight. Yet John, Jr., had not been on "detached duty" in Canada when his father struck; he was at home in Ohio writing letters to allies, caring for his livestock, and enjoying a busy but comfortable life with his wife and friends. If his absence from the raid reflected no lack of courage or dedication to the cause, he might still have been present had he gone to Chambersburg instead of Cleveland.[29]

The tragic end of the conspiracy removed the burdensome question whether to join his father in Virginia and enabled John, Jr., to conquer his fears and misgivings. He never wavered thereafter in his public avowal of the cause. Only months after Harpers Ferry, he accepted a commission from the Haitian government to persuade fugitive slaves in Canada to take up land grants in the black republic. After the Union defeat at the first battle of Bull Run, he recruited a company of antislavery men to fight "for the freedom of all." Long after the war, he appealed for public support for "colored refugees" in Kansas, sent boxes of grapes to the Haymarket anarchists, and otherwise tried to remain "faithful to [his] highest sense of duty."[30]

He could not speak of Harpers Ferry without emotion. He filled his home with memorabilia of Kansas and his father. On his parlor wall a large portrait of his father hung just above his own, inviting comparison. He responded sharply to public attacks on his father's character, flying off rebuttals to newspapers and offering testimony to his father's scholarly defenders. To the faithful he sent "relics" of his father and photos of himself. Until his death of heart failure at seventy-three in 1895, he cherished his role as his father's namesake, coconspirator, and fellow defender of the "cause of truth."[31]

That John, Jr., believed his public explanations of his role in the raid is probable; frequent "rehearsal" of his memories might by then have scripted the new scenario. But it is significant nonetheless that he needed an excuse for his absence that left no question about his courage or commitment. Even his service to the Union could not, symbolically, transcend his failure to join in that final act of sacrifice in his father's cause. Nor could it insure John, Jr.'s primacy in the inner circle of the faithful who claimed recognition for their readiness for martyrdom at Harpers Ferry.

Even his position within the family was at issue. The story of Owen's loyalty to his father and of his escape from Harpers Ferry was well known. Watson and Oliver had died in the fighting, and Frederick had been killed in Kansas. Even Salmon and Henry Thompson, who had both refused to fight in Virginia, bore scars received in the service of Old John Brown. John, Jr., the bearer of his father's name, could

---

[29] John Brown, Jr., to John Henry Kagi, July 25, Aug. 27, 1859, Dreer Collection; John Brown, Jr., to Kagi, Oct. 1, 1859, quoted in the *New York Journal of Commerce*, Oct. 27, 1859.

[30] John Brown, Jr.'s work in behalf of the Haitian Emigration Bureau is evident in John Brown, Jr., Diary, John Brown, Jr., Papers (Ohio Historical Society). See also Wills D. Boyd, "James Redpath and American Negro Colonization in Haiti, 1860–1862," *The Americas*, 12 (Oct. 1955), 169–82. On John, Jr.'s plan to aid the black "refugees," see John Brown, Jr., to Horatio N. Rust, Apr. 30, June 20, 1879, Rust Collection. On his journey to Kansas and his dispatch of funds to aid the "emigrants," see John Brown, Jr., Diary, July 7, July 24, Nov. 11, 1879, Feinstone Collection. On his support for the Chicago anarchists, see John Brown, Jr., to Sanborn, Nov. 11, 1887, Stutler Collection.

[31] See John Brown, Jr., to editor, *Chagrin Falls* [Ohio] *Exponent*, Dec. 12, 1883, typed copy, Stutler Collection; *Akron Beacon*, Jan. 1881, typed copy, Stutler Collection.

not be less a Brown than his brothers. The security of his place in the family thus demanded that since he had not been at Harpers Ferry, he prove he could not have been there. His closely ordered but mistaken memories accomplished that purpose and thus gave him permission to speak for the martyrs. On some level, his selective evocation of the past satisfied his need to affirm himself not only a hero of Harpers Ferry but also first among his father's sons.

In rescuing his self-esteem, John, Jr., furthered the reconstruction of his family's past. His brother, Jason, eighteen months his junior, however, threatened to make the family's heroic reappraisal of its past a charade. Jason was a doubter, a Brown unwilling to kill for the cause. For a time his misgivings jeopardized his sense of belonging to the family.[32] But like the others he was captive to his father's legend, and he judged himself severely. In his view he proved his kinship with the others only in possessing the family's deficiencies and failings. "It is a Brown trait to be migratory, sanguine about what they think they can do, to speculate, to go into debt, and to make a good many failures," he explained fifty years after Harpers Ferry. "If I hadn't inherited it, I might have been worth something more than nothing now." For Jason as for the other children of John Brown, the family had become a projection of John's historical image. But unlike the others, "Jay" felt diminished and compromised by that image. He was unable to write an autobiographical essay for Ruth's projected family history and had not "the courage to try again," he wrote to Franklin B. Sanborn in 1892. As a symbol of the Browns, he felt unworthy.[33]

To an outsider, Jason's condemnation of the Pottawatomie killings and his refusal to go to Harpers Ferry might seem acts of courage. But those dissents belied the contention that all the Browns had been willing to sacrifice their lives for the cause. Thus Jason threatened to inhibit the rescripting of his family's past, and his apostasy had to be denied. Hence his brothers and sister explained that he had been too "tender" to fight but denied he had opposed the war against slavery. Even Jason's father had never rebuked him. Indeed, from his prison cell, the Old Man had written a friend praising Jason as "a most tender, loving, and steadfast friend," who, although "bashful and retiring," was "right" about most things, was "both morally and physically brave," and would not "deny his principles to save his life."[34]

Ultimately, Jason was assimilated into the Browns' new self-image and embraced

---

[32] Jason repeatedly questioned the wisdom of taking the war into Virginia, only to repent. See Jason Brown to John Brown, Feb. 8, 1858, Villard Collection; Jason Brown to John Brown, Apr. 25, 1858, Dreer Collection; Jason Brown to John Brown, May 2, 1859, Villard Collection. In May 1859, his brother Owen wrote their father that Jason "*at this late hour wishes to be considered one of us.*'" Owen Brown to John Brown, May 2, 1859, Dreer Collection. Yet in late June Jason refused his father directly, pleading, he later remembered, his "horror of war," his inability to kill "anything," and the fragile health of his pregnant wife, Ellen Sherbondy Brown. Jason Brown to Sanborn, July 13, 1892, Stutler Collection.

[33] Jason Brown interview, Villard Collection; Jason Brown to Sanborn, July 13, 1892, Stutler Collection.

[34] The Pottawatomie killings are condemned in Jason Brown to Mary, Watson, Oliver, Annie, Sarah, and Ellen Brown, Aug. 13, 1856, Villard Collection. Jason later accepted his brothers' view that the killings had been necessary. See Katherine Mayo, notes of interview with Jason Brown, Dec. 13–14, 1908; Villard Collection; Henry Thompson interview, Villard Collection; Salmon Brown to Connelly, May 28, 1913, Stutler Collection; and Jason Brown, statement to Franklin G. Adams, Apr. 2, 1884, John Brown Collection (Kansas State Historical Society). John Brown to Rebecca Spring, Nov. 24, 1859, quoted in Sanborn, *Life and Letters of John Brown*, 600.

its ethos. But at a cost. To him the tragedy at Harpers Ferry vindicated, not his common sense or his notion of his duty to his wife, but his father's heedless faith in his own destiny. Not John himself, but the legend scorned Jason. If, as the Browns came to believe, the family had been dedicated, self-sacrificing, even recklessly valorous in upholding the cause, Jason could conclude he was but a poor Brown. "I have always considered myself the greatest coward, moral & physical, in our family," he told a researcher repeatedly in 1908. In a sense, Jason was a casualty of the war he had refused to fight. But his harsh appraisal of himself served to confirm the outlines of the family's rescripted past.[35]

Thus, the once reluctant conspirators closed ranks against the family's widening circle of critics. Gradually, in searching the past for the origins of their crusade, they redefined the family's ethos — its guiding beliefs and sentiments — and reconstituted its image. Finally, in a climactic step in the rescripting of the family's history, they found a sanction for their fateful embrace of "forcible means."

Of course they had grown up in an antislavery family. Their paternal grandfather, Squire Owen, a first settler and prominent landowner in Hudson, had been a leader of the separatist antislavery movements that established a new Free Congregational church in Hudson and Oberlin College. The children of John's first wife, Dianthe Lusk Brown, who died in childbed in 1832, had listened to hushed reports of fugitives in the neighborhood and sometimes watched as their father, their uncles, and Grandfather Owen concealed runaway slaves in their homes and barns. The three oldest boys had heartily approved their father's proposals to adopt a slave child and to found a school for black children. In 1849 John moved his second wife, Mary, and their nine children to North Elba, New York, so he might assist a colony of black families settled on land donated by the wealthy abolitionist, Gerrit Smith. Thus, like her stepchildren, Mary's own youngsters grew up with blacks as neighbors, houseguests, and family friends.[36]

According to the family tradition forged in the rescripting of the family's history, the antislavery sentiments of the oldest sons — Dianthe's boys — were transformed into a sacred pledge in the late 1830s when their father conducted an impromptu lesson that culminated in a prayer and a formal oath of allegiance to the cause. As John, Jr., remembered the event, his father, stepmother, and the three oldest boys, then in their teens, had gathered in the kitchen of the Haymaker farmhouse in Franklin (now Kent), Ohio. Their father declared it "his settled conviction" that American slaves would not become free "except through force." With profound seriousness, John, Jr., remembered, his father asked each son individually if he were willing to help free the slaves. After kneeling to pray, "we all rose and with right

---

[35] Jason Brown interview, Villard Collection.
[36] On the Browns' work on the Underground Railroad, see Boyer, *Legend of John Brown*, esp. 401–5; Oates, *To Purge This Land with Blood*, 63–64. On John's 1834 proposal to adopt "at least one" black child, see Sanborn, *Life and Letters of John Brown*, 40–41.

John Brown, Jr., as a student at Grand River Institute in
Austinburg, Ohio, in the early 1840s.
Courtesy Boyd B. Stutler Collection, West Virginia Department of Culture and History.

hands raised, took upon us an obligation of secrecy, of fidelity and devotion to the work of a forcible resistance to slavery in our country."[37]

The story of the Family Oath or Family Compact, as Brown biographers have variously called it, seemed plausible. But was it true? How reliable was the evidence? Although John, Jr., left at least two accounts of the family oath, we have no direct statement from his brothers. We know only that Jason gave a somewhat different version of the event to Franklin B. Sanborn, John Brown's most assiduous literary defender, and that John, Jr., consulted Owen's recollections in preparing his own initial story. As Villard pointed out in 1910, the accounts that John, Jr., and Jason provided Sanborn of this dramatic incident conflicted on key points.[38] But the story is questionable for more weighty reasons. First, John, Jr., did not actually mention the Family Oath until 1885, nearly half a century after the supposed compact and a quarter century after the Harpers Ferry raid. Any plausible reason to keep his vow of secrecy about the oath had vanished with the execution of his father and the emancipation of the slaves. John, Jr., offered his account to Sanborn, a close friend who was then preparing his *Life and Letters of John Brown*. By then the full story of the Browns' crimes during the Kansas border war of 1856 and their conspiracy of silence had become public. Both their father's image as a devoutly religious man martyred for the cause and the family's integrity were being challenged by hostile writers and former Kansas allies. The old accusation that John had conceived his plan to attack Harpers Ferry only after his son, Frederick, had been killed in Kansas—that the Old Man was either mad or vengeful—had gained credibility with those new revelations. The story of the Family Oath, which placed the origins of the plan to attack slavery two decades before the Browns went to Kansas, served to refute the charge that John sought vengeance at Harpers Ferry and to restore his credibility as a rational, deeply religious man, prophetically inspired to see that slavery could be destroyed only by force of arms.[39]

The most serious difficulty with the story of the Family Oath is that no contemporary evidence can be found to support it. John's notebook for 1838–1844 affords no hint that he was then thinking of an attack on slavery or that he had pledged his family to oppose it. Nor did John Brown mention the oath in letters to members of his immediate family or to his father, who had witnessed with deep satisfaction his son's pledge to oppose slavery at an 1837 meeting in Hudson called to mourn the slain abolitionist printer, Elijah Lovejoy. John made no reference to the Family

[37] John Brown, Jr., to Sanborn, Feb. 16, 1885, Anthony Collection (New York Public Library, New York, N.Y.).

[38] Villard, *John Brown*, 45–47. Stephen B. Oates is also skeptical about the story. Oates, *To Purge This Land with Blood*, 369n17. Richard O. Boyer accepts it uncritically. Boyer, *Legend of John Brown*, 332–33. See also Quarles, *Allies for Freedom*, 17–18, 203n7.

[39] On at least two likely occasions, John, Jr., failed to mention the oath. See John Brown, Jr., testimony to federal commissioner in Gerrit Smith's suit against the *Chicago Tribune*, July 19, 1867, Villard Collection; and John Brown, Jr., to Gen. John C. Cochrane, Feb. 23, 1878, *ibid.* Sanborn's jousting with Wendell Phillips Garrison, a son of William Lloyd Garrison, and Edwin Lawrence Godkin, who pronounced Sanborn's claims of Brown's early commitment to use force against slavery a "legend," may be followed in Wendell Phillips Garrison, "The Preludes of Harper's Ferry," *Andover Review*, 14 (Dec. 1890), 578–87; Wendell Phillips Garrison, "The Preludes of Harper's Ferry," *ibid.*, 15 (Jan. 1891), 55–66; Franklin B. Sanborn to editor, *ibid.* (March 1891), 309–11; [E. L. Godkin], "Notes," *Nation*, Dec. 4, 1890, p. 443; and Sanborn, "John Brown's Family Compact," *ibid.*, Dec. 25, 1890, p. 500.

Oath or to any implied covenant when he asked Mary and his sons to aid him in
his Virginia campaign. He failed to tell of such a compact in his unfinished history
of the Brown family in Kansas, even though he hoped to use the history to raise
money for the cause. Twice in writing to his wife, moreover, John denied responsibility for inspiring his sons' fighting in Kansas. If he had indeed persuaded Mary
and his oldest sons to take a sacred oath to make war against slavery, he could hardly
have claimed to be blameless.[40]

Thus it is difficult to escape the conclusion that the Family Oath either had little
significance for the Browns until long after Harpers Ferry or that the event had not
really occurred as John, Jr., and Jason variously remembered it. Perhaps, beleaguered by their critics, the sons had reminisced one evening about their childhood and had remembered their father's oath at the Lovejoy meeting in Hudson.
Had their father not asked them to join him in warring against slavery? Somehow,
sometime, a solemn family commitment to fight slavery had surely been born. In
calling up memories of the scene in the old Haymaker house in Franklin, John, Jr.,
Jason, and Owen perhaps unconsciously devised a sanction for their violence in
Kansas and brought the moral authority of their father's public vow to the aid of
their own threatened self-esteem. In evoking the story of the Family Compact, John
Brown's eldest sons gave form to an inchoate process that had shaped their early
lives. They anchored the family's antislavery tradition in a specific, seemingly transcendent event and established the purity of their motives. In doing so, they created
a family myth.

But the myth of the oath to fight slavery was more than a moral sanction for the
Browns' crimes in Kansas and their roles — real or imagined — in the Harpers Ferry
conspiracy. Whatever its basis in experience, since the oath gained its imprimatur
only many years later, we must ask what implicit functions its rediscovery — or
invention — served at that time. The answer is clear. By suppressing the ambivalence
and doubt the Browns had felt about the Virginia campaign, the myth redefined
their roles and bonded them together afresh. It expressed not so much their convic-
tions about the cause as their shared loyalty to their father's memory.

But the story was a false memory created by rescripting. Three sorts of evidence
betray its scripted origins. First, the sons' accounts differed on points that reflected
their individual life histories. John, Jr., insisted that his father had pledged the boys
to the use of arms, but Jason recalled only that they were sworn to "do all in their
power to abolish slavery," which to him did not mean using force. Second, scripting
is suggested in casual "rehearsals" of the oath story. Speaking to a reporter from
a friendly local newspaper in 1889, for example, John, Jr., recited the now familiar
story — this time placing the oath in 1842 and including the younger children in

---

[40] John Brown's Memorandum Book, Dec. 3, 1838–Nov. 6, 1844 (Department of Rare Books and Manuscripts,
Boston Public Library); John Brown, "A Brief History of John Brown Otherwise (Old Brown) & His family: As
Connected with Kansas; by One Who Knows," c. July 1858, Dreer Collection; John Brown to "Dear Wife," Mar.
31, 1857, Stutler Collection; Nelson Hawkins [John Brown] to "My Dear Wife & children every one," Jan. 30, 1858,
Villard Collection.

the scene. "The whole family joined [Father] in the compact and there was never any wavering in our allegiance" from that date, he said.[41] Such accounts lacked the precision demanded by the Browns' earlier need to provide Sanborn with evidence of their father's steadfast purpose. In their initial accounts of the oath, the sons had used inductive strategies and devices such as easily remembered "marker events" to place the oath in the chronology of their lives. In reminiscing for a local newsman, they felt details were of no importance.

Third, an actual episode of such significance and emotional appeal might have survived in vivid detail for many years as a "flashbulb" memory.[42] Yet the boys' own responses to their father's questions, as reported in old age, seem predictable and unconvincing. The oath taking left too few traces of the surrounding situation in the old Haymaker house to be considered a flashbulb event. Clearly, the story draws heavily on memories scripted in childhood — generic memories of family gatherings before the hearth and of the ritual oaths beloved of childhood. In the growing national climate of conspiracy, treason, and civil war that shaped their adult lives, the Browns' perceptions of oaths must have changed. But if public oaths in that turbulent era might be used to coerce, secret oaths remained investitures in the true faith. Thus, driven by self-schemata in which loyalty to the cause had become the final measure of manhood, the aging sons of John Brown unknowingly fused scripts of family routines with scripts of private oaths to retrieve the false memory of the Family Oath.

Such mistakes of memory are frequent occurrences. Autobiographical memory is not an archive from which we may call up "time capsules" of unaltered experience. In fact, psychologists have shown that in controlled experiments subjects frequently identify deliberately fabricated "nonevents" as events that have occurred in their own lives. The tendency to accept nonevents as authentic memories, writes Craig Barclay, will "vary directly with the conceptual similarity between nonevents and what one expects to have occurred in one's life."[43] The Browns' retrieval of the oath is remarkable, not because of the story's scripted, conventionalized contents, but because the three sons each found a measure of personal redemption in the same factitious episode.

Thus, without conscious intent, the sons had provided a historical explanation of the origins of the John Brown family. Implicitly, the myth of the oath not only defined the Browns' relationship to the world at large, but it distinguished John's descendants from earlier generations of Browns and the collateral kin with whom,

---

[41] Sanborn, *Life and Letters of John Brown*, 138; *Sandusky Daily Register*, May 31, 1889, p. 2.

[42] A jarring experience, such as learning the news of the assassination of President John F. Kennedy, can produce a "flashbulb memory" preserving vividly the circumstances in which someone experienced the event. But even flashbulb memories may acquire mistaken details. See Roger Brown and James Kulik, "Flashbulb Memories," in *Memory Observed*, ed. Neisser, 23–40; Brewer, "What Is Autobiographical Memory?" 35–36; Ulric Neisser, "Nested Structure in Autobiographical Memory," in *Autobiographical Memory*, ed. Rubin, 71–81, esp. 79.

[43] Barclay, "Schematization of Autobiographical Memory," 92.

in biological terms, they were inseparably linked. After the oath John's immediate family constituted an elect even among the fiercely antislavery clan that Squire Owen had fathered in Ohio. To the family inheritance transmitted through the "blood" and through the nurturing family neighborhood, the myth of the oath added a religiously inspired covenant between the Browns and God. It codified many of the complex psychological changes in the survivors that the glorious failure of the Harpers Ferry conspiracy had triggered. And it bore witness to the emergence of the John Brown family.

With the revelation of the oath in 1885, the process of rescripting that began with the spectacular failure at Harpers Ferry reached a culmination in John Brown's family. The Browns had at last joined their father morally and spiritually in his war to free the slaves. They had embraced his ambiguous legacy. A mutation of consciousness had occurred. A half century earlier they had numbered themselves readily among the three score descendants of Owen Brown of Hudson. They had stood in relation to the Brown past much as their father had. Indeed, in their early lives, it had not been their father, but their "aged" grandfather who symbolized the family's militant opposition to slavery. When five of John's sons determined to emigrate to the Kansas Territory in 1854, it was the old squire, not their father, who sent them off with the admonition never to show the "white feather" of cowardice.[44] But Owen had expressed his indignation over slavery through local and state antislavery societies and the church. He had sanctioned violence only in self-defense. A leading citizen of Hudson for fifty-one years, he had sunk his spiritual roots deep into the Ohio soil he farmed.

A quarter century after Harpers Ferry, John Brown's heirs had lost sight of Squire Owen's heritage. The martyr's children now saw themselves as bearers of a legacy uniquely their own. They were possessed by the memory of their father. It was renewed by endless requests from morbid well-wishers for relics of the martyr, by grotesque newspaper stories about the remains of the brothers who fell at Harpers Ferry, by promoters' degrading commercial schemes to exploit their father's name, and by ceaseless and bitter controversies over his character and motives. Their image of themselves now reflected the public perception of Old Osawatomie. When, after years of silence on public questions, John, Jr., appealed for funds to promote a worthy cause, he conceded that his proposal, "considering that it comes from one of the John Brown family, bears with it perhaps, an odor of fanaticism." Then he added: "Besides, what have I done thus far in my life to gain public confidence?"[45] The appeal was a paradigm of the Browns' problem: the very legend that defined their public identity also dwarfed their accomplishments and convinced them of their own insignificance. The family's acknowledged history of extremism, violence,

---

[44] Salmon Brown to Sanborn, Nov. 17, 1911, Stutler Collection. Although this challenging send-off is mentioned in a reminiscent account, Grandfather Owen Brown continued to give John's sons advice and money to aid them in Kansas. See, for example, John Brown, Jr., and Wealthy H. Brown to "Dear Grand Parents," March 20, 1856, Gee Collection.

[45] *Cleveland Leader*, Apr. 22, 1877, Stutler Collection.

poverty, and mental instability—and their guilt for the Pottawatomie "massacre"— all burdened John Brown's children.

Thus their final affirmation of the war against slavery symbolized more than an effort to refute their enemies. By enlisting at last unreservedly in their father's vanished army, they placed their failings in the context of a higher morality. If they were not, as John, Jr., admitted, "oppressed with the burdens of this world's goods," they had sacrificed much for the blacks.[46] If they had advocated violence, in their view "forcible means" had been required to free the slaves. If their father had been a fanatic, they had all sworn an oath to God to devote their lives to making freedom a reality for the oppressed. And if Harpers Ferry had severed the Union, it had purged the Republic of its greatest evil. Thus in calling up the Family Oath, John Brown's sons affirmed their commitment not just to the Browns' ancient opposition to slavery but also to the moral fanaticism their father had made holy. In that cove-. nant, they found the courage to face their enemies, to vanquish doubt, and to declare themselves the righteous children of Old John Brown.

False memories like the Browns' may teach us much. We edit our memories. A "totalitarian ego," as Anthony G. Greenwald puts it, unconsciously introduces "revisions" and "fabrications" into our personal histories.[47] But our false memories are not arbitrary creations. They are plausible scenarios, meeting rational tests. The nonevents we use to fill in our personal histories are expressions of the same processes that induce us to infer the missing pieces in the plot of a novel. Our autobiographical memories are governed by a logic of events that has its own integrity. Memories of nonevents are flags warning the historian to look for controlling scripts that belong to deep-rooted self-schemata. Thus when historians learn to "read" the underlying meaning of our errors in memory as shrewdly as they now interpret deliberate falsehoods, they will open a window to the self. And when scholars of the family discover the logic of false family memories, they will unlock the matrices of family identities.

[46] John Brown, Jr., to Sanborn, Apr. 12, 1875, Dreer Collection.
[47] Anthony G. Greenwald, "The Totalitarian Ego: Fabrication and Revision of Personal History," *American Psychologist*, 35 (July 1980), 603–18.

Power and Memory in Oral History: Workers and Managers at Studebaker

John Bodnar

No one who has conducted oral history interviews has escaped the question, "But how do you know it is true?" The issue of veracity remains important for anyone interested in analyzing oral expressions of memory in historical research. Obviously, memories are limited, and a complete reconstruction of the past through memory (or any other means) is not possible. Oral historians have generally combined the memories they recorded with other kinds of records or cross-checked their interview material with data gathered from other interviews. Their work has yielded extremely valuable insights into particular historical questions, but it has not eliminated the need to think carefully about what people actually remember about their past.

An analysis of the memories revealed in oral interviews with men and women who formerly worked at the Studebaker Corporation automobile plant in South Bend, Indiana, offers suggestions about the nature or "truth" of the memories captured in oral interviews. This material, recorded mostly between 1984 and 1985, allows not only a partial reconstruction of the traditional history of labor and management at the plant, but, more importantly for our purposes, a partial reconsideration of the social construction of memory: the interviews can be read not only to discover what people remembered but also to discover how they went about the process of organizing and creating their memories in the first place.

David Lowenthal has written that the "contingent and discontinuous facts of the past become intelligible only when woven together as stories." Indeed, what appears most compelling about the Studebaker memories is not the details of life in the plant, which was much like life in other auto plants, but the "narrative structures" or central plots in which individual memories and discrete bits of evidence were placed. Those plots actually reveal the way in which workers and managers at Studebaker gave meaning to their experiences; they organized the past for both the historical actor and the interviewer who attempted to understand it.[1]

John Bodnar is professor of history at Indiana University. Research for this article was supported in part by a grant from the National Endowment for the Humanities.

[1] David Lowenthal, *The Past Is a Foreign Country* (Cambridge, Eng., 1985), 218; Edward M. Bruner, "Ethnography as Narrative," in *The Anthropology of Experience*, ed. Victor W. Turner and Edward M. Bruner (Urbana, 1986), 143–49.

Memories of work and life at Studebaker were neatly arranged by workers and managers into three major plots, all corresponding roughly to the structure of power in a given period. Memory was a cognitive device by which historical actors sought to interpret the reality they had lived — and, it appears, they could never do so alone, without reference to a social context. I mean that the details they recalled were varied, but the themes to which they linked those details often represented the interests of powerful institutions as much as they did the interpretations of ordinary people. The memories of Studebaker workers and managers, in other words, tend to confirm Edward M. Bruner's assertion that narratives are not only structures of meaning but structures of power as well.[2]

In recounting the first plot, which corresponded approximately to the two decades prior to World War II, individuals tended to describe a relatively stable and orderly world where tension and conflict were acknowledged but subjugated. In this story powerful institutions — the company and the union — cooperated to keep Studebaker solvent during the difficult days of the 1930s.

In the second plot, however, which described events and experiences from World War II to the closing of the plant in 1963, the dominant narrative stressed disorder and tension, rather than stability. Almost everyone remembered that period as a direct contrast to the prewar era. In their story, the symbiotic prewar relationship between the company and the union weakened considerably, and workers appeared divided in their loyalties between the two institutions. Disorder was more characteristic of the structure of power and, therefore, the structure of memory.

In recounting a final plot, covering the period from 1963 until the arrival of oral historians in the 1980s, people recalled the coexistence of order and disorder. Unlike the stories of the two earlier eras, which were interlaced by events at the workplace, accounts of the last period revealed more of people's personal lives. In this instance, revealed memory was more layered, more expressive of varied public and private experiences, and less dominated by the fate and viewpoints of powerful institutions.

The discovery that memories from the Studebaker project were tied intimately to structures of power and that individual memory was heavily influenced by positions and interpretations stated in public is crucial to this essay. In the first place, those findings suggest that individuals did not remember alone; they discussed the events of their experience and formulated explanations of what had occurred in their lives with other people. In this paper I refer to that discussion and formulation as *social discourse*. In the second place, the tying of discrete pieces of personal experience and memory to larger plots or narrative structures suggests that in the past powerful forces had attempted to influence, shape, and order the meaning of events, and, by implication, the way in which they would be remembered. Institutions that usually operated at the level of the political entered the personal level and influenced people's thoughts and memories. It is that relationship between the individual experience as encountered and retold and the individual's confrontation

---

[2] Bruner, "Ethnography as Narrative," 144.

with dominant institutions and perspectives that this essay examines in order to explore the process of creating memory that can enter oral historical accounts.

The possibility that much material transmitted in oral history has been previously discussed and that such recollections contain complex bits of private, collective, and hegemonic perspectives has already been suggested by scholars in other disciplines who use memory as a source. As the anthropologist Judith Modell noted, scholars who rely on field interviews have come to realize that orally transmitted data has been shaped over a long period of time through considerable thought and discussion. In a similar way Samuel Schrager, a folklorist, concluded after interviewing pioneer settlers and lumber workers in Idaho that his subjects were drawing on prior conversations they had with one another. Schrager felt his interviews provided a new context for telling "preexistent narratives."[3]

If oral histories contain mostly stories that have previously been told before or subjected to public discourse, some historical agents may have exerted more influence on the shaping of a given story than others. This point is suggested by a number of scholars who have relied on memory. Jan Vansina, studying oral traditions in Africa, concluded that all "traditions" could be divided into official and private. He believed that dominant groups created official versions of the past, for instance, that were basically canonical and served as obstacles to establishing memories or traditions that could undermine the existing structure of order or authority.[4]

Sociologists who have studied working-class populations in France have also noted the ties between official versions of the past, social and political discourse, and what ordinary individuals remember. "One only ever remembers," Nathan Wachtel wrote, "as a member of a social group." He goes on to say that the "irreducible originality of personal recollections are in fact produced by the criss-crossing of several series of memories" that correspond to groups such as the community or work unit to which one belongs. Wachtel found that in advanced industrial societies official traditions or historical accounts designed to explain the legitimacy of existing institutions and leaders not only kept the accounts of ordinary people off the historical record but apparently infiltrated people's private memories and consciousness as well. He discovered personal and official histories intertwined in oral histories he gathered among French workers.[5]

Ultimately the interview material from Studebaker reveals threads or layers of experience. Dominant plots from the earlier eras were heavily infiltrated by versions of experience that served the needs of powerful institutions; personal memories were

[3] Judith Modell, "Stories and Strategies: The Use of Personal Statements," *International Journal of Oral History*, 4 (Feb. 1983), 4–11; Samuel Schrager, "What Is Social in Oral History?" *ibid*. (June 1983), 76–78.

[4] Jan Vansina, *Oral Tradition as History* (Madison, 1985), 98–99, 120; Dan Ben-Amos, "The Strands of Tradition: Varieties in Its Meaning in American Folklore Studies," *Journal of Folklore Research*, 21 (May–Dec. 1984), 105; Lowenthal, *The Past Is a Foreign Country*, 327.

[5] Nathan Wachtel, "Memory and History, Introduction," *History and Anthropology*, 2 (Oct. 1986), 2–11; Barbara Allen, "In the Thick of Things: Texture in Orally Communicated History," *International Journal of Oral History*, 6 (June 1985), 93–96.

more evident when powerful institutions ceased to exert much force on the construction of meaning and memory.

But the interviews were not originally planned to explore the social shaping of
memory. They were designed to probe the nature of labor-management relationships in a rather straightforward manner. A questionnaire was designed to guide
the narrator through the interviewees' life cycles: childhood, adolescence, and work
life before Studebaker, at Studebaker, and after the plant had closed. Clearly, the
intended focus was on work at the auto plant, on the line or as a manager, but the
hope existed that those interviewed would place their work experiences in the context of their individual lives.

To some extent the resulting interviews produced what had been sought. They
contained thousands of bits of information about life and work inside the company
and elsewhere as well. But they also produced evidence of structures of memory that
were unanticipated and did not seem to be a product of any scholarly planning.
The time structure of the questionnaire was based on the individual life course, but
the dominant time structure emerging in the interviews was based on changes in
the pattern of institutional power and social order that existed in the past. Those
changes defined the era of union and company cooperation, the era of union and
company disagreement, and the era without a strong union or company. This is not
to say that the questions asked made no difference. If we had asked questions about
leisure activities, we might have discovered a different structure. But that is not the
point. Regardless of the questions, respondents would have produced narrative plots
of some kind that had been influenced by agents powerful in the social space under
examination.[6]

The Era of Stability

If one simply listened to Studebaker memories for the period before 1945, it would
be easy to conclude that social discourse and individual reflection had produced
consensus. Individuals described a past in which the automobile company was a very
good place to work, in part because of the vast networks of kin that toiled together
within its walls. This theme was repeated in a manner that generally lacked originality and reflected to a great extent the power and the ability of dominant institutions to create an interpretation of reality and reproduce it in the minds of many
others. There is no denying the existence of a large number of kin networks within
the plant or the fact that some workers derived satisfaction from their employment.
At times this positive image, however, superseded all others and was described almost automatically.

The image of Studebaker as a "friendly factory" populated by generations of

[6] Copies of most interviews cited in this study are on file at the Indiana University Oral History Research Center
in Bloomington. Individuals who worked on the project included Gary Bailey, Robert Thomas King, Naomi
Lichtenburg, John Wolford, and Robin Zeff. A few taped recordings concerning Studebaker, made in 1979 by Janet
Weaver in a separate project, were consulted in research for this paper. The Weaver interviews are located at Discovery Hall, South Bend, Indiana.

proud and related craftsmen producing cars of incomparable quality existed throughout this century but was crystallized during World War II. Taking fragments of reality, Paul Hoffman, the corporation president, launched a national advertising campaign in 1945 and 1946 lauding the "miracle of American war production" at his company and citing reasons why it was such a "complete success." Central to his explanation was the argument that Studebaker possessed "the finest group in any industry—fathers, sons, and grandsons, saturated with a great tradition." Seeking to gain a large share of postwar consumer spending, Hoffman assured Americans and his own work force that Studebaker was building the "best passenger cars and trucks your money can buy." In those proclamations the company helped to produce a symbolic picture of the workplace and worker-management relations that persisted past the company's demise in 1963. In the 1980s some customers and employees recalled the image of the "friendly factory" producing goods of superior quality in comparison to the mass-produced autos of Detroit. That was exactly the image Hoffman had intended to convey.[7]

Although evidence exists that Studebaker had achieved a reputation as a good place to work and as a company filled with proud families by the 1920s, Harold Churchill, president of the company from 1956 to 1961, explained that systematic advertisement of that image began in the 1930s. According to Churchill, the company nearly went bankrupt in 1933 and attempted to rely on "Madison Avenue advertising" to tell the public and its employees that they could have faith in the firm because of its "strong, underlying father-son heritage." Elmer Danch, who was employed in the corporation's public relations office, recalled working during World War II on advertisements that showed fathers at Studebaker building planes that might be piloted by their sons. Advertisements proclaimed that the company was just waiting for "that boy to get back so he could be with his father." Such symbols were important not only to promote worker morale and patriotism but also to keep Studebaker competitive in a labor market marked by shortages. After the war, even with the infusion of thousands of new workers from outside the South Bend area, company publications such as the *Wheel* still featured family pictures prominently. Histories of the companies published in 1942 and 1952 as well as national periodicals contain numerous photographs of Studebaker fathers and sons.[8]

[7] Paul G. Hoffman, "Why Was Studebaker Chosen for Such Critical War Tasks?" *Life*, Nov. 26, 1945, p. 69. On Hoffman at Studebaker, see Alan Raucher, *Paul G. Hoffman: Architect of Foreign Aid* (Lexington, Ky., 1985), 1–43. A sociologist has found that no longitudinal data on kinship ties in the plant survives. The same study also suggests that, although the company promoted an image of fathers and sons working as skilled craftsmen to build cars, the father-son relationship was not common in the plant and few workers learned skilled tasks at Studebaker. See Elisabeth Klaus, "A Family of Families: When Family Relations Are Work Relations" (Ph.D. diss., Notre Dame University, 1986), 123–24, 250–52, 379–80.

[8] Raucher, *Paul G. Hoffman*, 16–17; Harold Churchill interview by Robert Thomas King, Feb. 28–29, 1980, (Indiana University Oral History Research Center, Bloomington); Elmer Danch interview by John Wolford, Sept. 25, 1984, *ibid*; George Hupp interview by King, Feb. 19, 1980, *ibid*; Theodore Zenzinger interview by Wolford, July 24, 1984, *ibid*. Frederick H. Harbison and Robert Dubin, *Patterns of Union-Management Relations* (Chicago, 1947), emphasized the "father-son" aspect of the Studebaker work force. It was also described in popular histories of the company including Stephen Longstreet, *A Century of Wheels* (New York, 1952), 103; and K. S. Smallzried and Dorothy James Roberts, *More Than You Promise: A Business at Work in Society* (New York, 1942), 309.

Actual testimony based on oral interviews with Studebaker workers confirms the existence of widespread kinship networks throughout the plant, although such arrangements did not make Studebaker unique among American factories. Family members were especially important in providing entrée into the plant for young workers, but such associations were also a source of pride and comfort. Memories offered evidence, moreover, that the idealized version of the "friendly factory" was shared by many of the rank and file. Steve Megyesi entered the plant in 1942 because his father and brother were already there. His desire to follow them was so strong that he took "shop courses" in high school to prepare for his eventual arrival at Studebaker. Once in the plant he even requested a transfer to work with a relative. He synthesized his experience in a way that would have made the public relations department proud:

> Studebaker used to be known as a father and son team. And it was like working with a family. It really was. . . . There was a job to be done, and there was no animosity among people in different departments. They just helped each other to get the job done. It was a terrific place to work.[9]

Ray Burnett indicated that Studebaker meant a lot to his grandfather because it was "a way of life; it wasn't just an automobile company." Burnett himself, who worked on the final assembly, remembered that he had looked at the water tower near the plant as a child and "kind of felt he would be working there." He distinctly recalled his father talking of the effort that all workers felt they had to exert during the war. For Burnett it was a "kind of togetherness." He claimed that it would not be easy to put into words but "we more or less felt as a team." And Harry Poulin, who began working for the company in 1940, both invoked and defended the positive image.

> But Studebaker had just a fantastic family picture. Families worked together to build a car, and there would be so much pride in it. . . . It was advertised in *Life Magazine*, for instance, you would have a whole page of a family of Studebaker workers . . . building automobiles and this was true. And they may have gotten a little lazy during the war but this came back, and when we were building cars again their workmanship showed.[10]

Memories of the period prior to World War II revealed a reality more complex than the image of a "friendly factory" of friends and neighbors building quality cars.

[9] Steve Megyesi and Doris Megyesi interview by Robin Zeff, Aug. 23, 1985 (Indiana University Oral History Research Center).

[10] Ray Burnett interview by Wolford, Sept. 25, 1984, *ibid.*; Dale Wiand and Alice Wiand interview by John Bodnar, May 23, 1984, *ibid.*; Robert Hagenbush interview by Wolford, July 24, 1984, *ibid.*; Harry Poulin interview by Wolford, July 25, 1984, *ibid.* The issue of worker loyalty to the company became divisive in the early 1950s. In 1953 the company suspended nineteen employees for purchasing new model cars from other companies, after workers initiated work stoppages to protest such purchases by their fellow employees. See "Decision and Order before the NLRB," box 23, UAW Local 5 Papers (Archives of Labor History and Urban Affairs, Wayne State University, Detroit, Mich.); *South Bend Tribune*, Feb. 8, 1954, p. 8; Mary Schoonaert interview by Zeff, July 25, 1985, (Indiana University Oral History Research Center); B. A. Ewing interview by Wolford, Aug. 27, 1984, *ibid.*; Megyesi interview.

Those who had experienced the earlier years described a tough, no-nonsense approach to production. But the crucial point was that there was little disagreement among the workers interviewed. Nearly everyone who remembered the era described the coexistence of tough discipline on the production line and the positive image Studebaker had as a place to work. That alliance was necessary because it was precisely during the pre–World War II era that the other great institution competing for worker loyalty emerged—Local 5 of the United Automobile Workers of America (UAW). Tough discipline could easily be recalled not only because it existed but also because it served as a background that explained why the union local had to come into being in the first place. Tough discipline and the "friendly factory" could coexist in the layered memories of the prewar period because they both served centers of power—the company and the union—in an era when both institutions prided themselves on getting along and taking credit for Studebaker's survival and success. No doubt such discipline was enforced because workers were often reluctant to meet company production schedules, but when they recalled the workplace Studebaker employees talked about the issue of discipline in a different way.

To the extent that people remembered work relationships in the 1920s and 1930s, they recalled raw authority and discipline on the part of foremen. Individuals worked at an unrelenting pace when they were not laid off, and foremen hired and fired arbitrarily. In reminiscences and discussion afterwards workers had fashioned a fairly uniform view on this point by the time oral interviews were conducted. Dale Wiand began in the early 1930s by sinking holes in crankshafts. He claimed that he had "to work like mad" to keep his drill sharp so it would not "chatter." "They'd really get mad at you if you left 'chatter marks' on the crankshafts," he recalled. Harry Brodzinski's father actually left the plant in 1933 and returned to farming near South Bend because work at the plant was difficult and sporadic. Casmer Paskiet complained that foremen were unfair and demoted people they did not like to "penalty jobs." He elaborated: "See, in the twenties the company had the final word on everything. You was subjugated to do whatever he'd [foreman] tell you and that's it . . . or else." George Hupp explained that if you fell behind on the assembly line, two or three foremen "would be right on your neck wanting to know why."[11]

Interviewees generally discussed discipline in the prewar period before discussing their recollections of the origins of the union. The establishment of an auto workers union local at Studebaker in the 1930s was certainly not an unique event for the times, but the local probably achieved a more secure status than many of its counterparts elsewhere. The formation of Local 5, UAW, took place between 1934 and 1937 in a relatively peaceful fashion, without massive strikes or violent confrontations with management. It was all the more surprising because an important sit-down strike took place at the Bendix Products Corporation plant in South Bend in 1936

[11] Wiand interview; Harry Brodzinski interview by Wolford, Aug. 8, 1984 (Indiana University Oral History Research Center); Casmer Paskiet interview by Wolford, Sept. 24, 1984, *ibid.*; Hupp interview, *ibid.* Similar events are described in Joe Kuminecz interview by Wolford, July 23, 1984, *ibid.*; and Otto Klausmeyer interview by Bodnar, May 22, 1984, *ibid.*

when Local 9, UAW, was established. Indeed, during that sit-down Studebaker workers contributed cash to the Bendix workers and exchanged wage information with their fellow auto workers, but they never moved against their own employer.[12]

The few accounts that discuss unionization at Studebaker during the depression decade emphasize workers' reluctance to strike against the firm because it had come close to bankruptcy in 1933 and because its officials, including Paul Hoffman, agreed not to resist unionization in return for continued production and labor peace. Some people actually credited Hoffman with launching the union, so powerful was his image as a friend of the average worker. Walter Nowicki claimed that "when he said get organized, we did."[13]

Hoffman was clearly not that powerful, and unionization at Studebaker, as elsewhere, ultimately originated in the dissatisfaction produced by arbitrary foremen, the growing fear of joblessness, and the national organizing drives of the 1930s. Brodzinski explained that "things were rough" by 1932. "We'd go to work for one hour, and they would send us home," he complained. It was the rank and file, influenced by men who brought union traditions from midwestern coalfields and who were willing to risk foremen's retribution for passing union information throughout the plant, not Paul Hoffman, who generated the organizing impulse at Studebaker. The union, moreover, introduced a system of stewards to settle grievances, hear worker disputes, and weaken the authority of the foremen many had come to despise. As Studebaker entered the era of World War II, the union now stood alongside Hoffman and the company as a partner of somewhat equal stature. Both laid claims to worker loyalty and took responsibility for Studebaker's survival during the 1930s. Hoffman and top management took steps necessary to avoid bankruptcy in the 1930s and facilitated the emergence of the union. The union, for its part, refrained from striking and putting the company in jeopardy and was able to improve conditions in the plant. It all appealed to everyone's sense of logic and facilitated the development of stable memories of an era that certainly had tensions and appeared stable only when contrasted with the era following World War II.[14]

An Era of Instability

Memories of Studebaker in the period after World War II described a world that was not nearly so ordered as the prewar world. The major institutions of power—the company and the union—did not get along, and they tended to compete for worker loyalty rather than to create an appearance that everyone cooperated in one large "friendly factory." The disordered plot dominating recollections of the era was rein-

[12] See "Cash Contributions to Bendix Local 9," box 2, UAW Local 9 Papers (Archives of Labor History and Urban Affairs). Joe Kuminecz recalled a weekly collection for the Bendix workers of "a buck a man"; Kuminecz interview.
[13] Walter Nowicki interview by Janet Weaver, March 2, 1979 (Discovery Hall, South Bend, Ind.).
[14] Nowicki interview; L. R. Richardson interview by Weaver, Sept. 5, 1979, Oct. 31, 1979, (Discovery Hall); Burnett interview; Brodzinski interview; Raucher, *Paul G. Hoffman*, 25–28; J. D. Hill, *A Brief History of the Labor Movement of Studebaker Local No. 5, U.A.W.-C.I.O.* (South Bend, 1953).

Mary Nowicki (middle) with co-workers in the sewing room, 1940s.
Courtesy Studebaker National Museum, South Bend, Indiana.

forced by the era's negative outcome. This second narrative was not a story of proud workers and company survival, but one of internal strife culminating in the closing of the plant. Expressions of dissent and disagreement were more explicit as workers were unsure of where to place their loyalty. Women workers felt the union betrayed them; their male counterparts resisted the implementation of time study by the company. Disordered social structures and contentious discourse, in other words, produced memories that were more varied and less neatly tied together. Little difference separated the disordered plot from the disordered past.

Memories in this second era did agree on one point: wartime experience had changed the tenor of labor-management relations at Studebaker and, thus, the balance of power. The existence of cost-plus contracts, many felt, had weakened the company's ability to produce in the most efficient manner. The union, moreover, grew large and powerful because of the infusion of thousands of new workers during the war and perhaps because of a weakening of management's drive for economy. Harold Churchill recalled that the company never made the profit the public thought it did with cost-plus contracting. But, he claimed, that system produced a "state of mind" among workers that "the well would never run dry."[15]

---

[15] Harold Churchill interview by King, Feb. 23, 1980 (Indiana University Oral History Research Center); Hupp interview; Kuminecz interview; Brodzinski interview.

Workers and managers both recalled that after the war the union reigned supreme in the plant. Hoffman was apparently intent on preserving the image of a "friendly factory" where proud craftsmen toiled as a device to attract consumers.[16] Consequently, he and other top company officials were reluctant to impose stern discipline in the plant. Otto Klausmeyer, a middle-level supervisor, bristled at what he perceived to be the lax state of authority. He claimed that management was "soft" and did not care about labor costs as long as they could be added to the price of an automobile. After the war Klausmeyer personally checked on the manpower needs of the plant's sixth floor. He found 896 workers there when only about one-fourth that number was needed. He generalized in language that was somewhat symbolic: "They were throwing parts at each other, hanging out windows. They'd go away for a month's vacation and come back, and somebody would punch their clock in the meanwhile." A fellow supervisor on the final assembly line, Harry Brodzinski, felt that "people" respected the company prior to 1946. Afterward, he became disgusted with men who were sabotaging production. He claimed that union leaders were defending jobs "on the line" that were unnecessary. And he lamented that "top management told you to take it easy" and "don't muddy the water" because they were afraid of work stoppages.[17]

Cliff MacMillan, who eventually became a company vice-president, came to Studebaker for the first time in 1948 as part of a survey team investigating industrial relations. After only two days in the plant, he concluded that Studebaker had a reputation for no (authorized) strikes because formal strike actions were unnecessary, since management always compromised with worker demands. MacMillan provided a glimpse into management's thinking when he recounted a meeting between the company president and a key production official who wanted to conduct time studies. MacMillan explained Studebaker management's view that if the union stewards objected, the program should be stopped. "Don't do anything to get those people upset," the president had cautioned. MacMillan recalled men in the stamping division working from morning until noon to reach their quotas and sitting around, telling stories and reading newspapers the rest of the afternoon.[18]

The situation described by MacMillan and other plant officials probably explains the profile of the Studebaker work force presented in the unpublished study MacMillan and his survey team produced. Compiled in 1949, the report found a relatively satisfied group of workers. When asked how they liked working at Studebaker, 98 percent of the foreman, 95 percent of the stewards, and 98 percent of the rank

---

[16] Raucher, *Paul G. Hoffman*, 35. For confirmation of union power in the postwar plant, see Robert M. Mac-Donald, *Collective Bargaining in the Automobile Industry* (New Haven, 1963), 259–84; and Harbison and Dubin, *Patterns of Union-Management Relations*, 206. Local 5 revealed newfound vigor after the war by attempting to build a cooperative housing development for its members and demanding wage increases that workers at General Motors received. It also raised funds to help striking workers at the Oliver Corporation in South Bend in 1946. See *South Bend Tribune*, Jan. 21, 1949, p. 1.

[17] At Studebaker the subassembly lines produced component parts of automobiles and fed the final line that assembled the vehicles. It was in final assembly that management later sought to establish efficiency standards for the entire plant, provoking much turmoil. Klausmeyer interview; Brodzinski interview.

[18] Cliff MacMillan interview by Bodnar, May 11, 1984 (Indiana University Oral History Research Center).

and file claimed they were either "well-satisfied" or liked it "very much." The basis for such satisfaction was generally given as either "confidence in management" or "material satisfaction." Some disagreement existed in response, however, to a question that touched on an obvious sore point. When asked, "are men producing the right amount of work?" only 51 percent of the foremen answered affirmatively, whereas about 80 percent of the stewards and workers did. The overwhelming majority, however, felt union and "top management" got along at Studebaker and nearly everyone selected "good times" over "labor trouble" or "over-production" as a summary of what would happen at Studebaker "in the next couple of years."[19]

The view of undisciplined labor relations described by managers was generally shared by the rank and file. In this case memories may have produced a more accurate picture than the contemporary survey, since the 1949 document only hinted at a possible lack of consensus and satisfaction in the plant. George Hupp recalled the era after the war as a time when people came to work drunk and the union forced the company into concessions it should not have made. Odell Newburn's reconstruction of conditions in the foundry where he worked at that time differed widely from the image of a "friendly factory." He described a place where fumes and gases constantly kept men irritable and recalled a high accident rate caused by workers who hurried to meet their quotas, especially when summer heat became oppressive. And John Piechowiak remembered that after the war he saw a lot that was not "right." He told of people "dogging it on the job" and "just putting in their time."[20] Besides prompting disobedience, discontent infiltrated memories. In the tension-filled atmosphere of the postwar factory, women especially seethed under what they recalled as unfair treatment, despite their significant contributions to production during the war. They were very reluctant to return to the household. They recalled considerable resentment in both the plant and the union at their postwar demand for equal seniority rights. They wanted to protect their ability to work by acquiring the right to "bump" into mens' jobs as well as those traditionally held by women if they could perform the tasks. (The bumping system permitted workers who lost their jobs to displace fellow workers in other job classifications who had less seniority.) Women packed the union hall and forced consideration of a motion to abolish separate seniority lists by gender but were defeated by the union's huge male majority.

Women were especially upset because they thought the union played favorites, recalling laid-off male workers sooner than laid-off females after the war. Mary Van Daele claimed that she told Paul Hoffman himself that she deserved to be called back ahead of others who had already returned. Mary Nowicki claimed "you had to fight for your seniority." She claimed that females had worked at sewing upholstery and inspecting engines during the war and were angry at being laid off once the war ended. Insult was added to injury during the bumping or laying-off process

    [19] Survey Research Center, University of Michigan, "The Studebaker Study," 1949, pp. 2, 8, 36, 215–17, 270, 311, 371, 377–78 (in John Bodnar's possession).
    [20] Hupp interview; Odell Newburn interview by Wolford, July 10, 1984 (Indiana University Oral History Research Center); John Piechowiak interview by Wolford, Oct. 8, 1984, *ibid.*; Mary Nowicki interview by Zeff, July 25, 1985, *ibid.*

itself. Louise Dzierla recalled having to train the person who was going to replace her. In a summary statement of female dissatisfaction with the union Dzierla complained:

> There was no separate union for the ladies. And the women would never have a chance to go out on strike and be able to lead the way. So the only time we went on strike [was] when the men voted for it and we'd have to follow. . . . When we had grievances on anything, they'd talk about it but there was never nothing special done for the ladies.[21]

Both men and women were deeply troubled by the issue of bumping during the fifties. The practice appeared to increase, especially after the early 1950s, when management attempted to reduce the size of its huge work force, which had approached twenty thousand in 1948. Workers were not sure who was to blame for bumping, the union that allowed it or the company that caused it. Younger workers more susceptible to bumping came to resent older ones, and disunity in the work force was exacerbated. One employee, Donald Handley, took a job as a utility man who moved around the plant filling in for absent workers because he felt he would be less likely to be bumped from that job.[22]

Workers at Studebaker also had a clear recollection that absenteeism was a persistent problem during the era of uncertainty. Men described workers punching the time clock for buddies who decided to take off work or held other jobs. A number of those interviewed operated auto repair and auto painting businesses on the side and a very large number operated small farms outside South Bend.[23]

No issue dominated the memory of conflict in the plant during the turbulent fifties more than time study. The strong sales record and postwar prosperity that had perpetuated laxity on the part of both labor and management after the war came to an abrupt halt in 1954. During that year Studebaker saw its share of the auto market drop from 3.8 to 2.8 percent. Studebaker laid off many workers and reduced working hours for others. Heightened levels of tension resulted as management initiated bold moves to cut costs and increase productivity. Managers' most controversial move was to end the incentive or quota system, which paid the worker a full day's wage for meeting a daily quota. Company officials now claimed that because production quotas were too low, workers reached them easily each day and spent too much time loafing—a point on which some worker memories agreed.

---

[21] Mary Van Daele interview by Zeff, July 25, 1985, *ibid.*; Mary Nowicki interview; Schoonaert interview; Louise Dzierla interview by Zeff, July 7, 1985 (Indiana University Oral History Research Center). Women were particularly threatened after the war by men with high seniority in Studebaker's aviation division who bumped into the automotive division. See *South Bend Tribune*, Feb. 4, 1945, p. 1; *ibid.*, June 3, 1945, p. 1.

[22] Donald Handley interview by Wolford, Oct 7, 1984 (Indiana University Oral History Research Center); Marion Zielinski interview by Wolford, Oct. 7, 1984, *ibid.* John Piechowiak took a lower paying job because he felt that a less desirable position would not attract workers looking for someone to bump; Piechowiak interview. Klausmeyer interview; Hupp interview; Alice Speeks interview by Zeff, July 28, 1985 (Indiana University Oral History Research Center); Paskiet interview.

[23] Handley interview; Zielinski interview; Paskiet interview; Piechowiak interview; Hagenbush interview; Charles Wolfram interview by Bodnar, May 23, 1984 (Indiana University Oral History Research Center).

Studebaker wanted to move to a straight hourly wage system in order to keep workers busy all day and increase production, although the net result would be a reduction in workers' income. When the union rank and file initially rejected the plan in the summer of 1954 and threatened a walkout, anxious company officials got union leaders to call a mass rally and explain that wages would still be higher than the industry average. Because the company's claim was accurate, workers finally approved the plan. Worker approval was gained in part by strong appeals from the union leadership, but the intensity of the leaders' effort revealed the degree of dissension within the ranks. Competing recollections reflect the discord. Joe Kuminecz recalled that the workers would have been willing to work for scrip if that were needed to save the company, but Robert Hagenbush called the plan a "wage cut" that hurt the incomes of many workers. Dale Wiand recalled that he did not like the idea at all and was reluctant to accept it.[24]

After eliminating the incentive plan and reducing income, the company continued its offensive by increasing time studies on various jobs and establishing minimum levels of output per task. Those efforts evoked additional resentment. Mary Van Daele remembered times when "they would come around with a piece of paper and pencil and they'd want you to work like a robot. You never did enough." Harry Brodzinski recalled that when workers realized that industrial engineers were going to go up and down the line checking jobs "the shit hit the fan."[25]

The rank and file voted to accept the end of the incentive system in 1954, but their memories suggest that they continued to feel and to vent displeasure at its abolition. Determined resistance to time-motion studies increased. Workers recalled sabotage in the "friendly factory," with cushions ripped out of car seats at final assembly, water put in gas tanks, and soda bottles placed in door pockets. Such practices disturbed some workers and further fractured the world of workers at Studebaker. Walkouts proliferated, especially in the final assembly, an area under close company (and time-motion) scrutiny. But even the walkouts divided the work force. Workers who drove long distances to work in South Bend everyday resented them immensely and blamed them on "radical [union] stewards."[26]

Throughout the 1950s, employee memories indicated, the struggle to make sense out of the turmoil and contention at Studebaker continued. The very forms the recollections of these historical actors took provide an account of what it was like

---

[24] Les Fox interview by Janet Weaver, March 5, 1979 (Discovery Hall). Studebaker wages as a whole averaged thirty-six cents an hour above the industry average. See "Can a Union Have It Too Good?" *U.S. News*, Aug. 20, 1954, p. 9; *South Bend Tribune*, Jan. 11, 1954, sec. 2, p. 1; *ibid.*, Jan. 13, 1954, p. 1; *ibid.*, March 12, 1954, p. 31; and *ibid.*, April 23, 1954, sec. 2, p. 1. Kuminecz interview; Hagenbush interview; Wiand interview.

[25] Van Daele interview; Brodzinski interview. The process of time study of jobs accelerated after 1956 when Studebaker temporarily merged with the Packard Car Company and the labor process came under the influence of Packard officials.

[26] Hagenbush interview; Wolfram interview. Union stewards at Studebaker remained powerful until the company went out of business. Elsewhere in the auto industry they were replaced by union committeemen who serviced larger numbers of workers and became less susceptible to direct influence from plant workers and more to influence from union officials. See Nelson Lichtenstein, "Auto Worker Militancy and the Structure of Factory Life, 1937–1955," *Journal of American History*, 67 (Sept. 1980), 335–53, esp. 350.

to experience those times. They suggest that the actors' loyalties and consciousness were divided not simply because they were involved in a class struggle but also because the traditional sources of authority in the plant, the company and the union, no longer worked in unison to command their loyalty. Real events had tarnished the image and memories of a "friendly factory" and of the earlier alliance between workers and the company. During the four years preceding the closing of the plant in 1963, controversy was continuous. Workers performed tasks more slowly than usual during time studies and walked off their jobs frequently. The "nineteen-day strike" of 1959 was recalled by nearly everyone because of its unprecedented length and because by then workers felt they could make no more concessions to the company. Union and management were so divided by 1963 that Cliff MacMillan, now in charge of industrial relations, told the company president not to make any agreement with "those bastards now because they [the union] don't stay with anything." In a final strike during the year the plant closed, workers prevented the car of the company president — a Mercedes-Benz — from leaving the plant and accused him of "smuggling stuff out." He could not smuggle out anything of consequence, but by that time, he symbolized an insensitive company. Worker resentment had become so strong by the 1960s that Joe Nagy won election as president of the local union by running on a platform that claimed Studebaker was not a "friendly factory," but a "sweatshop" where people worked too hard and work standards were not subject to arbitration.[27]

The Era of Adjustment

The last few weeks of 1963 remain fixed in the minds of many former Studebaker employees for two reasons. They will never forget the announcement on December 9 of the decision to end automobile production in South Bend and close the plant. Many also vividly recall the fact that the American flag at the plant flew at half-staff in honor of President John F. Kennedy, who had been recently assassinated and who had been considered a friend of the auto workers. To many Studebaker workers, Kennedy apparently represented a hope that the troubled condition of their workplace would be corrected. In a sense Kennedy stood as a new authority symbol that would now solve problems in South Bend that neither the company nor the union appeared capable of solving. Robert Hagenbush, a union steward, stated: "we set our sights highly on Kennedy, you know. They liked what he was doing and that was a blow to the people. And then it wasn't long after that we got the blow of closing the place down."[28]

At Studebaker life was dominated by the interests and influence of the company and the union. When the interests of those two powerful agents coincided,

[27] MacMillan interview; Hagenbush interview; Wolfram interview; MacDonald, *Collective Bargaining in the Automobile Industry*, 284. On the stopping of the president's car, see MacMillan interview. Hagenbush interview; Frank Nemeth interview by Wolford, Oct. 8, 1984 (Indiana University Oral History Research Center).

[28] Hagenbush interview.

Amid striking workers, Studebaker's president leaves the plant in
a black Mercedes-Benz, January 1962.
Courtesy Studebaker National Museum, South Bend, Indiana.

memories about life at the plant were generally ordered and conflict was relegated
to a subtheme. When the interests of powerful institutions were at odds and when
workers were less certain of where to direct their loyalties, memories revealed a place
that was in greater disorder and conflict. Cultural construction, in other words, mir-
rored social reality. The closing of the plant eliminated as sources of power not only
the company but eventually the union as well.[29] Individual lives were suddenly
released from the grip of those institutions and their claims for loyalty. Memories
too were freed. Expressions of personal feeling and descriptions of individual life
patterns became more numerous, as attention was diverted from preoccupation
with the struggle for power and control that had become all-consuming by the
1950s.

The plant closing certainly did little for the economic well-being of employees.

---

[29] Although Studebaker closed, Local 5, UAW, survived the demise of the auto plant by increasing its representation in other companies in the South Bend area.

Robert Hagenbush putting tie rod on chassis (about 1946).
Courtesy Studebaker National Museum, South Bend, Indiana.

The Studebaker pension fund was 80 percent underfunded, and workers younger than forty received no benefits. Those between forty and sixty received severance pay in lump sums that averaged under six hundred dollars, and those over sixty got extremely modest monthly retirement checks. Mary Schoonaert's husband, for instance, who had worked at the plant for thirty-four years, received a monthly check of one hundred dollars.[30]

Before 1963, Les Fox recalled, if you predicted that the plant would close workers would "laugh in your face" and "call you a company stooge." But the reality of closing brought an unexpected dose of shock and concern. Alice Wiand "felt sorry" for her displaced husband and worried about his future prospects at age forty-nine, because he had not applied for a job in years. "It was scary," she explained, "because you don't know what's going to happen . . . or where you'll have to go." Harry Brodzinski never thought Studebaker would close because the plant had survived so many crises before. For Charles Wolfram the closing was like learning that a family member had an illness "that you knew is going to terminate in death." Robert Hagenbush recalled the reaction to the announcement by men on his line. "Everybody was bawling and crying," he related, "especially old-timers because they couldn't get jobs anywhere else."[31]

Recollections of the plant closing are remarkable not only because they reveal a sense of surprise on the part of workers but also because they suggest that a certain amount of discourse took place after 1963 as Studebaker employees attempted to

[30] Charles Craypo, "The Deindustrialization of a Factory Town: Plant Closings and Phasedowns in South Bend, Indiana," Nov. 1983, p. 26. (in Bodnar's possession); Schoonaert interview.

[31] Fox interview; Wiand interview; Brodzinski interview; Wolfram interview; Hagenbush interview; Nemeth interview. For a discussion of worker acceptance and rejection of plant shutdowns, see Staughton Lynd, *The Fight against Shutdowns: Youngstown's Steel Mill Closings* (San Pedro, 1980).

Banner headline announces plant closing, December 10, 1963.

understand the cause of the shutdown. In an effort to interpret something beyond the realm of personal experience and with no dominant institution left to offer explanations of reality, ordinary people forged their own complex set of interpretations. They did not focus so much on the labor strife that everyone recalled vividly and experienced personally as on the complicated nature of the automobile market and the decisions of a board of directors that by the 1960s met in New York City. It was as if the class conflict that Studebaker employees described in their recollections of the fifties had never existed. Some managers, such as Otto Klausmeyer, did blame union excesses for the company's demise, and some workers faulted management's decision not to build a new plant in the 1950s to replace the antiquated six-story structure in downtown South Bend. But such assertions were not dominant in memories. Workers and managers alike talked more of the difficulties of competing with the large auto manufacturers in Detroit, the poor quality of Studebaker's dealership system, and the board of directors' ignorance of auto production—many directors were bankers. Such information had apparently circulated in South Bend and could be found in the memories of ordinary workers, union officials, and former company executives. It seemed, in other words, to emanate from a communitywide discussion. That process may account for the explanation's tendency to revolve around multiple factors, rather than one simple reason.

When social discourse was heavily influenced by powerful institutions, as in the Studebaker employees' recollections of the period before 1963, formulations of reality such as the "friendly factory" or the competing charges over issues such as time study tended to "assist" individuals in forging interpretations in the present and memories of the past. When communication between South Bend residents became less "distorted," discourse produced more complex and less tidy explanations of what was going on. Thus, most explanations for the closing roughly paralleled Brodzinski's. His answer was complex, and probably grounded in shared discourse, rather than simply personal encounters. He explained: "Well, I would say that we had a lot of reasons. I'm not saying that labor was the number one reason, no way. I think we had some bad engineering and bad dealers."[32]

When individuals were asked to describe their own adjustments after losing their jobs at Studebaker, something they could do only by relying on private experience, they revealed how acutely sensitive they were to their place within a community and a group. They invariably made a distinction between their own historical experience and that of others with whom they had worked. In other words, they were incapable of providing answers that did not draw on both personal experience and shared discourse. To put it another way, the expression of the personal could now be made in clearer terms and was no longer subjugated by the views of dominant institutions. Individual respondents basically survived the transition to new lives in reasonably good terms but recalled real suffering and turmoil in the lives of others. In effect, such memories acknowledged a sense of both individual survival and community devastation in the aftermath of the plant closing. The "others" who suffered were symbolic representations of the devastation that all of them had felt. The reality of some making transitions to other jobs softened the impact over time but did not eliminate the need to convey devastation somehow.

Personal narratives almost always described a reasonably successful transition by the narrators themselves. Wolfram got a job with the Jeep Corporation, which took over an old Studebaker war plant near South Bend. A number of workers were recruited immediately by other auto manufactures. Wiand went to a General Motors plant in Illinois where he did not like having to fix his own machinery. He eventually returned to Bendix because his family did not want to leave South Bend. Megyesi found work in Kalamazoo, Michigan, immediately after Studebaker closed but also returned to South Bend eventually as a purchasing agent. A number of men went to Gary, Indiana, to make windshield wipers. Others got jobs with the state of Indiana as corrections officers or toll collectors on the turnpike.[33]

[32] On communication and its distortion, see Anthony Giddens, *Central Problems in Social Theory: Action, Structure, and Contradiction in Social Analysis* (London, 1979), 175–80. Brodzinski interview; Klausmeyer interview; Wolfram interview; Piechowiak interview; Burnett interview; Handley interview; Zielinski interview; James Kowalski interview by Wolford, Sept. 11, 1984 (Indiana University Oral History Research Center).

[33] Wolfram interview, Brodzinski interview; Wiand interview; Megyesi interview; Hagenbush interview; Handley interview; Zielinski interview; Danch interview; MacMillan interview; Kuminecz interview; Eugene

Pain and suffering were nearly always located in the lives of others. Some people were alleged to have taken their own lives while others were able to put the experience temporarily behind them and go fishing in Michigan. Schoonaert generalized for the Studebaker working class: "Lots of people shot themselves or they took poison because they couldn't take it." Paskiet said that most workers in his department were older and got pensions on which to survive. "But the other departments were really hit hard," he asserted, "because some people just had a couple of years to go [until retirement]." Handley claimed that there were suicides and divorces over the closing involving "guys who did not have the ability to get other jobs." He explained that he did have the ability, however, because he had learned a trade at Studebaker "but a lot of guys never try to learn."[34]

Conclusion

The crucial point about the Studebaker interviews is not the facts they presented, but the dominant plots into which the facts were fitted. The material is revealing not so much for what was remembered or said as for the manner in which memory was organized. Apparently, historical participants, like historians, place conceptual frameworks upon past events. In the material recounted here memories were basically grouped around the themes of the rise of the union and the survival of a company that was a good place to work, the tensions of an era that led to the destruction of the factory as both a good place to work and an entity, and the adjustment to disorder that included personal survival and communal devastation.

The dominant theme emerging from recollections of the first era served the needs of dominant institutions as much as, or more than, those of individuals. That is to say, positive things were said about the union and the company; both had a hand in allowing the factory to remain open in the 1930s and creating a good place to work. In a sense, the memory of that era was explicitly hegemonic; consequently, class conflict was described but relegated to a minor position in the sequence of historical events. The consciousness of workers as they recalled the prewar period revealed something of a world that was actually repressive and tightly controlled by the company and the union, but that repression was submerged in memory because it had been suppressed in the past and because the overall era seemed to produce a more orderly world than the one that followed.

Memories of the 1950s served the needs of dominant institutions less because

Cyrnes interview by Zeff, Aug. 25, 1985 (Indiana University Oral History Research Center). Craypo, "Deindustrialization of a Factory Town," 26, claimed that about one-third of Studebaker workers were without jobs eight months after the plant closed. The rest either found work or retired.

[34] Schoonaert interview; Paskiet interview; Handley interview; Zielinski interview; MacMillan interview; Newburn interview; Fox interview; Wolfram interview. Barry Bluestone and Bennett Harrison, *The Deindustrialization of America: Plant Closings, Community Abandonment, and the Dismantling of Basic Industry* (New York, 1982), 65, cites national data indicating increases in cardiovascular disorders, suicides, and homicides due to plant closings. A 1% increase in unemployment over a six-year period can result in 920 suicides and 20,000 cardiovascular deaths.

those institutions were unable to exert the same amount of influence over consciousness. Discourse was contentious, and little agreement was produced. Not only were workers divided in their loyalties between the company and the union; factionalism characterized the union itself. Most workers disliked time study initiatives by the company, but some did not agree with their fellow toilers who periodically disrupted production. Order and authority were weaker in the decade, and, consequently, they were less able to mute the existence of class conflict in memory. A decade of disagreement and decline left people confused and uncertain of what had happened. Charges and countercharges between the union and the company and between the union and its workers had left discourse unstable and consciousness exposed to a greater variety of contradictions. The repression and control of the prewar era were replaced by debate and uncertainty.

After 1963 the traditional institutions that dominated consciousness and discourse in the community were gone or weakened and, therefore, the complex layers of memory were more exposed. Narrative structures were not inevitably hegemonic. By that I mean that the personal was revealed in a more exact way and was not so intertwined with the political, although they never were entirely separate. Discourse over the political—the closing of the plant—emerged in the interviews in a form that suggested a more open process of communication. The dominant plot to the memories of the era revolved around the personal and the communal because the familiar centers of authority that had helped shape convenient explanations of historical events and social change were no longer operating: the company was gone, and the union was weak. Individuals were able to make distinctions between personal adjustment and community devastation. That ability suggests that they may have recognized that their lives and their memories were in their own hands and less dependent upon hegemonic institutions.

The dominant plots in the Studebaker memories, in other words, were grounded largely in the structure of power that surrounded these workers and managers but also in the individual search for order and meaning. When powerful institutions existed, commanded loyalty, and were united, the discrete facts of individual memory were placed within a theme of order and unity. When powerful institutions existed but were at odds, the dominant narrative was one of contention and conflict, with sides drawn between the followers of the two dominant institutions. Those institutions strongly influenced the nature of social discourse in both the prewar and postwar periods. Their ability to determine the arguments or political positions articulated during discourse was such that it was almost impossible to find memories that deviated from the dominant plots that had been worked out for given eras. Almost no one really felt the era before the war was disorderly or contentious and almost no one saw the fifties as harmonious, in interesting contrast to the way in which the two periods are generally portrayed by scholars. In part that was so because of the actual features of the two eras. But clearly the times were never as completely ordered or as completely disordered as they appeared in the Studebaker employees' recollections.

When the dominant institutions that so affected consciousness and memory—

but did not eradicate the facts of history—crumbled after 1963, memory became
less political. Personal experience was revealed in more detail, and descriptions of
reality—such as those concerning the plant closing—were constructed in more complex terms. The plot was still layered and included the personal and the political,
but it was less infiltrated by hegemonic institutions, because they were absent, and
more directly shaped by individual assertions. When expressed more clearly, individual memory revealed something of a desire for order. Devastation and disorder
were subjugated or placed within the lives of others. This was similar to the subordination of class conflict to the theme of order in memories of the period prior to
World War II, a process that served the interests and reputation of the company.
Disorder could not be muted in the memories of the 1950s because no power—
institutional or individual—was influential enough to do so. The Studebaker interviews conformed closely to Frederic C. Bartlett's point that there is a "social determination of remembering" that consistently establishes a "persistent framework" into
which recalled facts must fit.[35]

In all of this, the existence of social discourse and the conflict between the dominant and the subordinate, between institutional and individual perceptions, was
reaffirmed time and time again. Consciousness and memory were continually
influenced by what David Sabean has called the "arguments" over the common
things of everyday life.[36] By implication they could not be shaped entirely either
by elites or by ordinary people. At times dominant institutions appeared able to
control the interpretations of events—the formation of culture. At other times,
when power was more diffuse, so were the recollections and interpretations of the
past. Through all the complexity, personal recollections and historical facts survived.

These interviews, finally, suggest not only how memory was created but also when
it was created. Particular eras seem to have been defined and given dominant plots
to a great extent just after they were deemed by ordinary people to have been completed. Thus, memories plotted in the 1950s rendered the prewar era as more orderly than it actually was. The eventual return of settled lives and jobs by the 1970s
helped to make the decade leading to the plant closing entirely tumultuous. The
points of transitions between contrasting eras were real events—the war, the closing.
But while they may have meant something else to those outside the community,
to those inside they had peculiar meanings that could be learned only through oral
histories. The subjects of these interviews underscored David Carr's point that only
from the perspective of the end do the beginnings and middle of a narrative make
sense. If powerful institutions played a vital role in shaping the plot of some eras,
ordinary people retained the ability to decide where one chapter would end and
where another would begin.

[35] Frederic C. Bartlett, *Remembering: A Study in Experimental and Social Psychology* (Cambridge, Eng.,
1967), 293–97.
[36] On the need to look for "hidden levels of discourse" and ideology in oral history narratives, see Ronald J.
Grele, "A Surmisable Variety: Interdisciplinarity and Oral Testimony," *American Quarterly*, 23 (Aug. 1975), 29–32.
David Sabean, *Power in the Blood: Popular Culture and Village Discourse in Early Modern Germany* (Cambridge,
Eng., 1984); T. J. Jackson Lears, "The Concept of Cultural Hegemony: Problems and Possibilities," *American Historical Review*, 99 (June 1985), 567–93, esp. 569–71.

Remembering the Discovery of the Watergate Tapes

Introduction

David Thelen

On Friday, the thirteenth of July 1973, in the ornate Senate Caucus Room, the Senate Watergate Committee was completing two months of televised hearings into illegal campaign activities during the 1972 election. The faces of the seven senators and the leading counsels had become familiar to Americans, who were growing increasingly troubled by the revelations and charges that appeared on the news each night. Only two weeks earlier former White House counsel John Dean had testified in exquisite detail about elaborate steps taken by the administration of Richard M. Nixon to hide its connections to illegal activities. Nixon denied Dean's charges. Who, everyone wondered, was telling the truth? How would the truth be determined?

Across the street on that same afternoon five little-recognized people headed for an appointment in the basement of the Dirksen Senate Office Building in room G-334. None of them expected that the meeting was going to be much different from other preliminary interviews between Watergate Committee staffers and current and former White House employees. To the Democratic staffers, Scott Armstrong and Gene Boyce, the Republican staffer, Donald Sanders, and the stenographer, Marianne Brazer, the interview was just the latest in a crowded week of fishing for information that might reveal whether Richard Nixon or John Dean was telling the truth. To the witness, Alexander P. Butterfield, a former administrative aide at the White House, the interview was a distraction between his work that morning at the Federal Aviation Administration, where he was the chief, and a ceremonial function the next day at a new air traffic control center in New Hampshire, and, four days after that, an object of greater anticipation, his official visit to the Soviet Union. As they started the conversations around the green felt-covered table no one imagined that some four hours later the staffers would emerge with the way to determine who was telling the truth, that they were to discover something that would lead to the president's resignation.

What follows are the recollections of the three people who created the discovery that afternoon.

Scott Armstrong came to that interview as an investigator with a bent for advocacy and journalism. While a student at Harvard Law School, he had worked for a con-

Cartoonist Jim Berry gave this autographed drawing to
Alexander Butterfield after the Watergate Committee hearing.
Courtesy NEA, Inc.

sulting firm that investigated firms holding government contracts. Before coming to the Watergate Committee, he had been a car dealer and, most recently, deputy coordinator of the New England Correctional Council, a group that attempted to introduce new approaches to penology. Since high school he had been a good friend of the *Washington Post*'s Watergate investigator, Bob Woodward, who had helped him get the appointment as investigator for the Senate committee. His work for the Watergate Committee and particularly his questioning of Butterfield added to his reputation as an investigator. He went on to assist Woodward and Carl Bernstein with *The Final Days* and then to become an investigative reporter for the *Washington Post* from 1976 to 1984, with time off to coauthor an exposé of the Supreme Court, *The Brethren*, with Woodward. In 1985 he created the National Security Archive, which he currently directs, to assemble and disseminate "national security" information that it acquires from the United States government.

Donald Sanders had honed his investigative skills as a detective and legislative investigator. After graduating from the University of Missouri School of Law, doing legal work in the Marine Corps for two years, and practicing law (including as city attorney) in Columbia, Missouri, Sanders joined the Federal Bureau of Investigation (FBI) in 1959. For ten years he was an investigator and supervisor for the FBI. In 1969 he became chief counsel for the House Internal Security Committee (newly reformed from the notorious House Committee on Un-American Activities), which he served until he joined the Senate Watergate Committee. Although Nixon's friends never forgave him for asking the question that revealed the existence of the tapes, Sanders believes that his work in probing Watergate actually improved his career opportunities. He went on to investigate the security of nuclear plants for the Nuclear Regulatory Commission, to lobby senators for the Pentagon, and to direct investigations for the Subcommittee on Investigations of the Senate Intelligence Committee (1977–1979) and the Senate Ethics Committee (1979–1982). In 1983 he returned to Columbia, Missouri, to practice law.

Alexander Butterfield came to the White House in 1969 following a distinguished career in the air force. Although he loved flying planes (and was a much-decorated pilot), he had also served as an aide to leading military officials. He rose through the ranks of aides to become a White House military aide for the secretary of defense in the Johnson administration. His old classmate at the University of California, Los Angeles, H. R. Haldeman, chose him as his chief administrative aide in the Nixon administration. Haldeman's offer promised an important administrative challenge, as well as an opportunity for even better jobs after he left the White House. In March 1973 he was glad to move from the White House back to his original interest, aviation, becoming chief of the Federal Aviation Administration. What happened to him as a result of his revelations is part of the story he tells in the following conversation.

The participants concluded during the interview that Butterfield's revelation marked a "historical" moment and sensed that they would be asked to reconstruct it. Each went about the reconstruction a bit differently. Sanders kept detailed notes during the course of the interview. Almost immediately afterward, chief minority counsel Fred Thompson asked for his notes, and Sanders never saw them again. Three days after the interview he constructed a new account of the meeting itself, of his question, and of Butterfield's response. He has used that 1973 reconstruction as a basis for part of the account published here.

Armstrong acquired the notes taken during the interview by stenographer Marianne Brazer. Since Brazer did not take shorthand, her notes were not so much a verbatim transcript as a record of the questions and answers she thought significant recorded as accurately as she could write them down during the give-and-take. Armstrong used Brazer's notes as the basis for an account he wrote in December of 1974 for Bob Woodward and Carl Bernstein to include in *The Final Days*.[1] According to Armstrong, Woodward and Bernstein used much of this account in their book. Armstrong has drawn heavily on the 1974 memorandum, elaborating on the context, partisan setting, and his own role and perceptions in this account for the *Journal*.

Butterfield routinely made notes of his own activities. He examined Brazer's notes three weeks after the interview. As he began to think of writing a more formal account or giving an elaborate interview to a journalist, he arranged a discussion on May 31, 1974, in which he, Sanders, and Armstrong compared their memories of what had happened on July 13, 1973. In 1975 Butterfield did write an account that he envisioned as part of the introductory chapter of a book he hoped—and still hopes—to complete at some future point. He brought no notes to our meetings and said in 1988 that he did not use his notes and 1975 account as prompts for any of his recollections.

Historians concerned with what actually happened in room G-334 on that afternoon fifteen years ago may well be struck by the discrepancies and even occasional inaccuracies in the accounts that follow. Perhaps the most dramatic discrepancy in the accounts is that each of the major participants remembers differently "the" question that led a reluctant Butterfield to acknowledge the tapes' existence. There are also what appear to be errors of fact. In our conversations Butterfield recalled that it was H. R. Haldeman who had asked him to install the White House taping system, when it had actually been Lawrence Higby. Butterfield also recalled that he had received his summons to testify in public while he was at a barbershop in the Ritz-Carlton Hotel, when the hotel was actually called the Sheraton-Carlton. Although historians generally believe that such minor memory lapses are the natural result of the passage of time since the event being recalled, Scott Armstrong gave dramatic evidence that the workings of memory are far more complex. Within less than an hour after the interview ended he told chief majority counsel Sam Dash that he, not Don Sanders, had asked the question that led Butterfield to disclose the taping system. At stake was whether Butterfield would be a Democratic witness, with Democrats receiving the right to ask him to reveal the tapes in public session, or a Republican witness. "I literally was sure I'd asked that question," Armstrong recalls. For the next eighteen months he was positive that Sanders had "fabricated"

---

[1] Compare pages 105–15 of Armstrong's account in this volume with Bob Woodward and Carl Bernstein. *The Final Days* (New York, 1976), 54–57.

his claim to asking "the" question and that Dash had surrendered to a desire to maintain a nonpartisan aura when he accepted Sanders's account and allowed the minority (Republican) staff lawyer Thompson to ask Butterfield "the" question in public. Armstrong only concluded that his recollection was inaccurate eighteen months later when he examined Brazer's notes of the interview. Even to this day Armstrong believes that Butterfield was thinking about Armstrong's earlier question when he answered Sanders.

What is interesting for a conception of history that places memory close to its center is not that there are errors and discrepancies in accounts published fifteen years after an event, but how each of the participants has created a different narrative from the same original event in the years since 1973. Rather than our customary concern with what actually happened in room G-334, we can focus on which parts of the story each participant "forgot," "remembered," and reshaped, when and why. Since 1973 Armstrong has associated with people who value investigative skills and who also applauded the disclosure of the tapes and Nixon's resignation. As he has evolved the story, he likes to emphasize his overall strategy for interviewing witnesses and his use of a White House memo as the factors that led Butterfield to answer the question. He likes to see himself as the active creator of the disclosure. Most of Sanders's associates have likewise applauded his role. Butterfield, on the other hand, has associated with people who think that he toppled a great president and has paid a high price in his career for his disclosure. Not surprisingly, he has constructed a memory in which in 1973 he passively, even reluctantly, "remembered" and then disclosed the tapes in response to questions posed by others.

Even as each participant reshaped a story over time to meet different needs of the moment, each believed that the latest story was a vivid, unchanged, and accurate record of precisely what had occurred in room G-334. Armstrong's anger at Sanders and Dash for depriving him of the credit he positively remembered that he was entitled to was one example. As Butterfield reflected on one of my questions and prepared a written elaboration and modification of his original recollection six weeks later, he prefaced his new version with: "I have to tell you that my recollections have been and are very clear. They really are." The need to see memories as vivid and unchanging interacts with participants' constant testing and reshaping of memories in response to new needs and perceptions to make memory a creative process.

Chronology

June 17, 1972 — Five men arrested after breaking into the Democratic National Committee headquarters in the Watergate complex.[2]

June 22, 1972 — Nixon denies White House involvement.

September–October 1972 — *Washington Post* in many stories links Watergate defendants to White House and to the Committee for the Re-election of the President (CREEP).

[2] Chronology taken from Woodward and Bernstein, *Final Days*, 457–61; J. Anthony Lukas, *Nightmare: The Underside of the Nixon Years* (New York, 1976); and Congressional Quarterly, *Watergate: Chronology of a Crisis* (Washington, 1975).

January 8–30, 1973—Trial of seven men indicted for Watergate burglary. Five plead guilty. E. Howard Hunt and G. Gordon Liddy are convicted by jury.

February 7, 1973—Senate establishes select committee to investigate Watergate.

March 1973—Butterfield leaves White House to become administrator of Federal Aviation Administration.

March 23, 1973—Judge John Sirica reports that Watergate defendant James McCord charged he and other burglars were put under "political pressure" to plead guilty by higher-ups who approved the break-in and that perjury was committed in their trial.

April 30, 1973—Nixon announces resignations of H. R. Haldeman, John D. Ehrlichman, Attorney General Richard Kleindienst, and firing of White House Counsel John Dean.

May 17, 1973—Senate Watergate Committee begins nationally televised hearings.

May 18, 1973—Archibald Cox is named special prosecutor.

June 25–29, 1973—Dean testifies before Watergate Committee and accuses the president of participation in cover-up.

July 13–16, 1973—Butterfield reveals existence of White House tapes and testifies before Watergate Committee.

July 23, 1973—Cox subpoenas recordings of nine presidential conversations and meetings. Senate Watergate Committee subpoenas five tapes.

July 26, 1973—Nixon refuses to turn over subpoenaed tapes.

August 29, 1973—Judge Sirica rules Nixon must turn over tapes.

October 10–12, 1973—Vice President Spiro Agnew resigns, and Nixon nominates Gerald R. Ford as vice president.

October 12, 1973—U. S. Court of Appeals upholds Sirica's decision that Nixon must surrender tapes.

October 20, 1973—"Saturday Night Massacre" in which Cox is fired as special prosecutor and Attorney General Elliot Richardson and Deputy Attorney General William Ruckelshaus resign in protest.

October 23, 1973—White House announces that subpoenaed tapes will be turned over but soon reveals that some tapes were missing and others had been partially erased.

March 1, 1974—Grand jury indicts Haldeman, Ehrlichman, and five others in the cover-up. It names Nixon as "unindicted co-conspirator."

April 11, 1974—House Judiciary Committee subpoenas forty-two tapes as part of deliberations over possible impeachment of Nixon.

April 18, 1974—Special Prosecutor Leon Jaworski subpoenas an additional sixty-four tapes.

April 30, 1974—Nixon releases edited transcripts of tapes sought by Judiciary Committee but announces he will not release those sought by Jaworski.

July 24, 1974—U. S. Supreme Court rules that Nixon must turn over sixty-four tapes to Jaworksi.

July 27–30, 1974—Judiciary Committee passes three articles of impeachment.

August 9, 1974—Nixon resigns.

Watergate Reminiscences

Donald G. Sanders

Sixteen years have passed since the burglary of the Democratic National Committee headquarters in the Watergate Office Complex in Washington, D.C. The arrests of the burglars occurred in the very early hours of a Saturday morning, June 17, 1972. The Sunday edition of the *Columbia* (Missouri) *Tribune* had no report of the event. In the Monday *Tribune* there was a brief report at the bottom of page 1. Over the next week there was only one small follow-up story—on page 12. This initial treatment of the event by the press was not unusual. There was no immediate sense that this was the predicate for something very serious.

To view Watergate in perspective it is essential to remember that it occurred when presidential power was great—the weakening from Vietnam was still incipient. John F. Kennedy and Lyndon B. Johnson had been very powerful, dynamic executives. Richard M. Nixon's first term in office vastly consolidated power in the White House. I had already worked on the congressional staff for four years, and I specifically recall learning, in contrast to what I had been taught in high school civics, that the legislative branch was not nearly an equal to the executive branch. In such basic matters as congressional efforts to obtain executive branch witnesses for routine hearings or to gain access to even unclassified files, the executive branch response was cavalier. While Congress was already approving hundreds of millions of dollars for executive branch computers, for example, Congress itself was still in the Model A Ford category.

What I am leading to is the proposition that one did not then lightly contemplate serious battle with the White House nor lightly contemplate accusations of serious misconduct within the White House. And if one did, in contrast to the situation today, there was little expectation that access could be gained to White House documents, or that White House staff would not invoke executive privilege if called to testify. There was a very different aura about the infallibility and inaccessibility of the White House. The balloon had yet to be punctured.

I say this to underline how I felt, and to give you a sense of the pervasive disbelief that filled the room, soon after the Watergate Committee was organized. when Sen. Lowell Weicker (the Connecticut Republican on the committee) stated in a closed-door meeting that he felt culpability for the break-in could extend all the way to Bob Haldeman. Mind you, he wasn't even accusing the president—but to think that

---

Donald G. Sanders now practices law in Columbia, Missouri, with the firm of Shurtleff and Froeschner. He also serves as one of three commissioners on the governing body of Boone County, Missouri. This remembrance, in modified form, was originally prepared for delivery as an oral address.

Donald G. Sanders, deputy minority counsel, Sen. Howard Baker, and
Sen. Sam Ervin during Senate Watergate Committee hearings, June 1973.

he was virtually accusing the president's right-hand man. Most of us were in-
credulous.

After reading of the arrest of the burglars in the Democratic National Committee
office, I had a persistent feeling that it was more than a rogue operation. I thought
surely it would prove to be a conscious design of the Committee for the Re-election
of the President to gather political intelligence. I had absolutely no thought that
it might extend into the White House. It did not seem remarkable to me that one
campaign committee should try to collect data on another, but I was shocked that
it involved breaking and entering. As the months passed, it seemed strange that
the news accounts revealed no firm tie to the leaders of the reelection committee.

It was of paramount importance to the White House to keep the lid on until
the November election. The White House strategy was to present the appearance
that there was no one of higher rank than Gordon Liddy involved. In reality Liddy
had cleared his illegal activities, and his $200,000 budget, with the executive
director of the reelection committee, Jeb Magruder, and the attorney general of the
United States, John Mitchell — still in office, but serving as the de facto head of the
reelection committee. Moreover, before the break-in, Liddy's overall plan for covert
intelligence had been reported to Haldeman by John Dean.

And so, when the grand jury indictment of the burglars was made known in September 1972, with just fifty-two days to go to the election, the Department of Justice

made the phenomenal pronouncement that there was no evidence of higher-up culpability.

When I learned in January 1973 that the Senate was forming an investigative committee, I made application for a staff position. I had been in Washington nine years, five at the headquarters of the Federal Bureau of Investigation (FBI) and four working as chief counsel for Congressman Dick Ichord (a Missouri Democrat). Of course, I would have liked to become chief counsel for Sam Ervin or Howard Baker. That was not to be. But despite my previous service with a House Democrat, my employment record attracted Baker and his new Chief Counsel, Fred Thompson. My job was to be deputy minority counsel.

I was impressed by Howard Baker's earnest instructions at one of my earliest meetings with him that we were to turn over every possible stone and, in his precise words, "let the chips fall where they may." My admiration and respect for Baker continued to grow. In public his behavior is gentlemanly and statesmanlike; he is exactly the same in private. While he deeply hoped the Republican National Committee, a distinct entity from the reelection committee, was not involved in the illegal conduct (it was eventually proved that it was not), he nevertheless urged us on to get all the facts. Baker served a vital role as negotiator and mediator between the committee and the White House and in disputes in the Senate between the Republican and Democratic parties.

Staff work began around the first of March 1973. We started with only slightly more than had been in the press. While hiring went on, Fred Thompson and I spent nights reading news reports—piecing together a mosaic of what was already known and who the key players were. We compiled a list of leads to be investigated. Some work had been started by a Senate subcommittee headed by Edward M. Kennedy and the House Banking and Currency Committee under Wright Patman. They withdrew when we began. Our objective was to try to trace a line of authority upward from Liddy.

In 1987, as the Iran-Contra affair was revealed, there was news coverage about Lt. Col. Oliver North's secretary, Fawn Hall. It shouldn't come as any surprise where we chose to start. Sure, with Gordon Liddy's secretary. When the big fellows refuse to talk with you, there's usually a coterie of others around them without whom they couldn't function. I must say, however, that attitudes about the inviolability of a personal secretary's knowledge have changed some since then. There were never any legal constraints on what a secretary could disclose, except for classified information or possibly something specified by contract, but there may have once been an unwritten code of honor about secrets she knew. Liddy's secretary had a melodious name: Sally Harmony. I conducted the interview with Sally Harmony, but I felt secret twinges of conscience in asking her to reveal her boss's business. It seemed somewhat akin to invading the attorney-client relationship.

Several sessions were required with Harmony. She lied at first to protect Liddy. She was not quite as eager as Fawn Hall. Eventually, she revealed that Liddy gave her wiretapped recordings of telephone conversations to transcribe, and that he sent political intelligence information to Jeb Magruder. She told us that Liddy was under the supervision of Magruder and John Mitchell, although on paper Liddy was shown as legal counsel to the finance director. Liddy went to the trouble of ordering a special printing of stationery with brightly colored borders, emblazoned with his code word "Gemstone," which Harmony used to prepare reports of wiretapped conversations. The purpose of the stationery was to alert those to whom it was sent to be discreet in handling it. Harmony took the bill for this stationery directly to Magruder. He approved it but told Harmony to destroy the invoice. Bit by bit, the Watergate conspiracy was being pieced together.

As an aside, in speaking of Sally Harmony, I'm reminded of a rather unkind joke that circulated among staff and press concerning the way in which one committee senator questioned witnesses in the public hearings. As was customary, this senator had his staff assistant prepare questions for the senator to use in the hearings. Unfortunately, the senator had a habit of paying more attention to his questions than to the witness's answers. The story goes thus: "Now, Mrs. Harmony, tell me, did Gordon Liddy meet with John Mitchell on April 2, 1972?" Answer: "No, sir." Next question: "Well, then, tell me, Mrs. Harmony, what did they discuss?"

One other early witness is of interest. She was the secretary to Liddy before Harmony—in January and February 1972, in the crucial period when Liddy was presenting to the attorney general, in the very office of the attorney general, his elaborate plans for political kidnaping, mugging, bugging, burglary, and prostitution. The secretary told me she recalled Liddy carrying into his office a thick pack of poster boards of large dimension, perhaps three feet by four feet. These were the graphic aids he used in his presentation to the attorney general.

The big break in the case however was the letter of Jim McCord to Judge John Sirica. McCord, you will recall, had been the hands-on supervisor of the burglary crew. As a Central Intelligence Agency (CIA) veteran, he did not like the indications that the CIA was being blamed for the burglary. Neither did he relish an impending stiff sentence from Judge Sirica, nor the information he had been hearing that some other defendants were receiving financial assistance.

McCord had no firsthand knowledge of the involvement of Liddy's superiors, but he had hearsay helpful to investigators. He accused Magruder of perjury before the grand jury, and he alleged that Magruder, Mitchell, and Dean had participated in the planning for covert intelligence. McCord's letter generated an epidemic of nervousness in Washington, and several individuals started talking.

The most notable witness was John Dean, who had frequent contact with the president. He testified for several days. In one of his scenarios, he said that in a conversation with the president in one of the president's offices, the president drew him to a corner of the room and in a quiet voice told Dean that he, Nixon, had been foolish in discussing clemency for one of the burglars with Chuck Colson. Dean seemed to suspect that there was some White House recording capability, but the discovery of it did not occur until two weeks later—on Friday the thirteenth, July 13, 1973.

Senator Ervin's staff scheduled an interview with Alexander Butterfield at 2:00 P.M. on July 13. It was to be held in a small, secure, windowless room in the basement of the Dirksen Senate Office Building. The room was big enough for only a desk, a table, and several chairs. Butterfield was then head of the Federal Aviation Administration, but he had been an assistant to Haldeman, and as such he had occupied a very small office immediately adjoining the Oval Office. It was his job to control, absolutely, the president's schedule, that is, to make it work. If someone was due to see the President at 1:12 P.M., Butterfield was responsible for ushering the person in at 1:12 P.M. He was the pivot point for papers and persons going into and out of the Oval Office.

Butterfield had been scheduled for interview for two reasons: (1) he was one of a number of persons who had frequent contact with the president and key staff such as Haldeman, and (2) he could specifically provide insights to the White House methods for preserving on paper what transpired in the Oval Office.

I participated in the interview of Butterfield as Senator Baker's representative. Ervin's staff sent one attorney, an investigator, and a secretary. The investigator was Scott Armstrong, who later coauthored with Bob Woodward the best seller exposé of the United States Supreme Court entitled *The Brethren*. Bob Woodward was a very close friend of Armstrong. He was the *Washington Post* reporter who wrote *All the President's Men* with Carl Bernstein.

Scott Armstrong and the other attorney questioned Butterfield for about three hours concerning Nixon's office routine. Armstrong had a document from the White House containing some summaries of Dean's conversations with Nixon. It would be logical to question how they were constructed. Of course, they could have been put together immediately after a meeting by personal recollections and by reference to notes. But there was another dimension to the quality of those summaries, it seemed to me. I couldn't put my finger on it, but they had a measure of precision that went beyond those possibilities.

I had a fixed agreement with Ervin's staff; I would not interrupt or interfere with their conduct of an interview, and they were not to interfere with mine. Once they were finished, I would have whatever time I wanted for questioning. So, for three hours I simply listened and took notes, knowing that eventually it would be my turn.

As the minutes passed, I felt a growing certainty that the summaries had to have been made from a verbatim recording. I wondered whether Butterfield would be truthful if asked about a hidden recording system. I thought surely if such a system existed, the president would never have said anything incriminating on record. I wondered, if it existed, how it could therefore be of any value — remarks on it would be self-serving. Or, to consider it from a positive viewpoint, remarks on it would prove the president's innocence — in other words, contradict what John Dean was alleging. But if there were exculpatory recordings, why hadn't the president revealed the system and used it to his advantage? I was mystified that Ervin's staff hadn't asked Butterfield about tape recordings. I seriously considered the consequences of

Butterfield revealing, in answer to *my* question, that there were recordings. If they were incriminating, did I want on my shoulders the fate of the presidency? It all seemed quite enormous. But Baker had said to let the chips fall where they might. It occurred to me that Butterfield would soon walk out of the room and this opportunity might not repeat itself. No matter how limited the circle of persons who would know of a recording system, I was sure Butterfield had to be included.

There was one other factor in my reasoning. I had served five years in FBI headquarters, on the fourth floor of the Department of Justice building, just below J. Edgar Hoover's fifth-floor suite. For years I heard comments about a built-in recorder in Hoover's office for use on occasions when he needed to preserve what was said. It was inconceivable to me that the office of the president (via the Secret Service) hadn't availed itself of a technological process that the FBI had.

And so my time came. It was no "cool-hand Luke" at work. My heart was pounding and my breath was shortened as I began questioning. I had resolved to go through with it only minutes before. I decided, for some unknown reason, not to bluntly ask if there was a tape recording system. After a few preliminaries, I asked Butterfield if he knew of any reason why the president would take John Dean to a corner of a room and speak to him in a quiet voice, as Dean had testified. His reply was stunning; he said, "I was hoping you fellows wouldn't ask me that. I've wondered what I would say. I'm concerned about the effect my answer will have on national security and international affairs. But I suppose I have to assume that this is a formal, official interview in the same vein as if I were being questioned by the committee under oath." I said, "That's right." He continued, "Well, yes, there's a recording system in the White House." We were all thunderstruck. Butterfield said the president wanted this kept absolutely secret, but he felt he had no other choice.

The system had been installed, he said, on Nixon's instructions, probably for historical use. There were microphones in the Oval Office, the Cabinet Room, the president's office in the Executive Office Building, the Lincoln Sitting Room on the second floor of the White House, in Aspen Lodge at Camp David, and in the telephones in all those rooms except the Cabinet Room.

When Butterfield finished it was 6:30. Knowing Armstrong's reputation for leaks, I asked Ervin's staff for renewed promises of secrecy. I then tracked down Fred Thompson at the pub across the street. Naturally, he was having a beer with a newsman. If I had appeared excited, the reporter would have been alerted, so I ordered a beer and engaged in small talk for awhile. Eventually, I asked Fred to step outside. On the street corner I told him the story, and he ran to telephone Senator Baker. I went home, late again for dinner. Senator Baker called me at home on Sunday for a firsthand account because Butterfield wanted to meet with him.

On Monday, after first resisting a committee subpoena, Butterfield testified before the committee in public, and you saw him on television. I couldn't believe we had kept the story from the *Washington Post*. We hadn't. I heard later through the grapevine that the *Post* had the story, but not enough corroboration to print it.

The battle for access to the tapes, and their erasures and disappearances, is another story, as is the impeachment proceeding. But the process was now irreversible.

Friday the Thirteenth

Scott Armstrong

In May of 1973, a few members of the Democratic staff of the Senate Committee on Presidential Campaign Activities—Sam Dash, Jim Hamilton, Marc Lackritz, Terry Lenzner, and I—began interviewing John Dean in extensive (some as long as ten hours) secret sessions usually taking place in the recreation room of his Alexandria, Virginia, home. Dean had left the White House abruptly the month before, when it became apparent that he was likely to be made the scapegoat for the Watergate affair. His attorneys had sought and received a tentative agreement that in return for receiving from the committee immunity from the use of his congressional testimony against him in court, Dean would provide a complete account and documentation of his activities. To assure that Dean was willing to cooperate and that his story was credible and not self-serving, the staff interviewed him at length during mornings, afternoons, and evenings. Dean's account was extraordinary in both detail and scope and was often backed up by memoranda, particularly where Dean's account went into intelligence abuses not directly connected with the Watergate break-in. As Dean told his story in secret, the majority staff went out and interviewed other witnesses to corroborate it.

In late May, with the hearings already two weeks underway, Marc Lackritz and I insisted on taking Sam Dash to lunch at the Monocle restaurant next to the Dirksen Senate Office Building where we worked. We were deeply disturbed that the interviewing of possible corroborating witnesses was not systematic. Those interviewed were not being asked the full complement of relevant questions. Worse still, many important witnesses, such as secretaries, clerks, and functionaries, were being overlooked. We suggested to Dash that a template of standard questions be drawn up for every interview. I drew a chart (what we came later to call a "satellite chart") of the key witnesses who had come into contact with Dean and about whom Dean was to testify publicly. I then drew several sample charts of every individual we knew worked for, or was regularly in touch with, each satellite witness. We suggested that a systematic effort be made to identify everyone who could add something to confirm or refute Dean's testimony. Dash enthusiastically agreed.

Back in our office we started our investigative template with questions about each individual's daily routine and responsibilities, hoping to commit interviewees to

Scott Armstrong is executive director of the National Security Archive in Washington, D.C. He was principal assistant to Bob Woodward and Carl Bernstein in the research and writing of *The Final Days*, and some portions of the following article appear in that book. Those portions appear in *The Final Days*, copyright © 1976, by Bob Woodward and Carl Bernstein, reprinted by permission of Simon and Schuster.

Scott Armstrong

telling us what they would know about in the normal course of business before we posed the tougher questions. We developed chart after chart of prospective witnesses. As Dean's public testimony approached, scheduled for the end of July, the public hearings called on the key witnesses about whom Dean would testify. In preparation for each such witness, the staff met privately in a downstairs interview room with his staff, secretaries, and so forth, hoping to find clues to back or defeat Dean's story.

In general, the minority (Republican) staff was not told what Dean had told us beyond the summaries prepared for the full committee in order to get him granted immunity. This was primarily because of several incidents early on in which Sen. Howard Baker's staff had been caught leaking things back to the White House (one staff member was fired for it). Moreover, Dean had told the majority staff that when he was still in the White House he had worked out a deal with Baker himself to help the White House sabotage the hearings. The longer we held back what Dean had told us, the more anger the minority staff felt. But as we interviewed the satellite witnesses, the committee ruled that the majority staff must take along a member of the minority staff. Thus the minority staff was developing its own knowledge of Dean's forthcoming testimony.

As Dean's testimony approached, his credibility increased with the majority staff. Detail after detail that he had provided in secret sessions was confirmed. In one case, Dean's recollection of what the participants in a cover-up meeting at LaCosta County Club wore—two noncomplementary plaids for which Dean recalled not only the colors but also the names of the Scottish clans—caused a reluctant witness to remember the meeting and verify Dean's account. In short, Dean's testimony was being corroborated in every respect except one. There were no records or individuals except H. R. Haldeman and John D. Ehrlichman that could verify Dean's account of his meetings with President Richard M. Nixon.

We believed we had a brief reprieve when Dean's testimony was delayed at the request of the White House until after the San Clemente summit with Leonid Brezhnev. The delay provided yet another week to interview those close to Dean. Indeed, we got more corroboration, but not for Dean's meetings with the president. Dean testified for an entire week and was grilled closely by both sides. At the time, it was not clear to the majority staff how the minority members of the committee were quite as well prepared as they were. Certain details closely held by the majority until the last minute were appearing at the heart of well-thought-out (uncharacteristically so) questions by minority members Baker and Edward Gurney as well as by minority chief counsel Fred Thompson, not known for thinking on his feet.

Dean's story appeared to hold up, but it was rapidly becoming a case of his testimony against the president's publicly stated account to the contrary. During the following week, several witnesses, testifying in great detail about Dean's meetings with the president, suggested that Dean's account was largely correct except for his tendency to blame Nixon for the cover-up. That was Dean's idea, executed by Dean and kept from the president by Dean.

The temperature was in the nineties in Washington on Friday, July 13, 1973, as former attorney general John Mitchell testified publicly in the Senate Caucus Room in the Old Senate Office Building. As Dean's former boss, Mitchell was doing a splendid job of explaining away some of what Dean had said, admitting other parts, and flatly insisting he was lying about the rest. Downstairs and across the street in room G-334 of the new Senate office building (the Dirksen building), I was getting regular updates about the public hearings as I prepared to interview an obscure, retired air force colonel named Alexander Butterfield. Butterfield had worked closely with both Haldeman and Ehrlichman, the key witnesses who would be coming up two weeks later. Time was running out to find some corroboration for Dean's accounts of his meetings with the president. If anyone other than Haldeman and Ehrlichman knew the truth about those meetings, it was likely to be Butterfield.

Moreover, Butterfield might know about something else we had discovered just after Dean testified. Unknown to the majority staff, Fred Buzhardt, Nixon's special counsel to handle the hearings, had secretly dictated to Minority Chief Counsel Fred Thompson over the phone a listing of Nixon's meetings with Dean and a summary of Nixon's account of those meetings. Although plainly a summary, it contained extensive verbatim and near verbatim quotes. Although they were in most cases in agreement with Dean's testimony, they usually added a remark or two that suggested an interpretation more favorable to the president. The summary had been circulated only to key minority staff. But one of the minority staff had accidently left it out on a desk at night, where it was picked up by a majority staff clerk and provided to the majority staff, including myself, who were now trying to determine how best to use it strategically before the minority staff learned that we had it.

The fact that this summary had been prepared prior to Dean's public testimony suggested several interesting things. First, the passages chosen—almost exactly paralleling Dean's testimony—gave it a high likelihood that someone (I assumed Thompson and/or Baker) had leaked the summary of Dean's testimony about his meetings with the president back to the White House. Second, the president had personally corroborated most of what Dean had said or had evidence in the form of notes or dictated recollections that corroborated it, better evidence than the committee now had. Third, that evidence, if it vindicated the president in the same manner as the summary, would be a striking refutation of Dean if it could be authenticated as contemporaneous. And if it appeared to have been altered or to have been created after the fact, that could be a further step in the obstruction of the committee's inquiry and thus damning of the president.

Although he had recently left the White House staff to become the head of the Federal Aviation Administration (FAA), Butterfield, throughout the period about which Dean had been testifying, had been a deputy assistant to the president in charge of the paper work and records that moved into and out of the Oval Office. If anyone had seen notes of conversations or seen accounts of the conversations created later, it would probably have been Butterfield. It was my hunch that Butterfield could at the very least tell whether or not the Buzhardt account had been created from the president's recollection alone or whether there was evidence lying behind it. If there was evidence behind it, the committee would have a good claim to demand and perhaps even get the evidence before Haldeman and Ehrlichman testified. If it was from the president's own account, there were some important questions to be asked of Haldeman and Ehrlichman about how they refreshed their own recollections. In any case, the committee was building a case to request the president himself testify as a witness—a virtually unprecedented confrontation.

The room had only one small air-conditioning vent, and it was oppressively hot. The chairs and table were stained with grease from fast-food meals. Wastebaskets spilled over with cigarette butts and packages and sandwich wrappings. The carpet was filthy. (Janitors were barred from entering for fear that someone might plant an eavesdropping device.)

The session was to be conducted by myself, as lead majority committee investigator, and Donald Sanders, a former Federal Bureau of Investigation (FBI) agent who was the deputy counsel to the Republican minority and their lead investigator. Sanders was an example of the best the FBI can produce. A polished questioner, he was also an excellent listener. Whereas many investigators allowed their totally partisan views to enter their questions, Sanders was professional, playing it straight down the middle. He was also the only minority investigator willing to sit patiently through my long list of template questions. Other minority investigators, unable to stop such interviews, tried to obstruct them by leaving before I had completed the questions. That had hurt the minority several times when routine questions four hours into the interview hit pay dirt, which the minority did not learn about for days or weeks. (It was in this manner that the minority failed to learn for more than three months about the majority's discovery of the connection between the hundred thousand–dollar gift from Howard Hughes to Nixon's confidant Bebe Rebozo and the Watergate break-in and subsequent cover-up.) The interview recorder was Marianne Brazer, the most conscientious and competent of a highly talented stenographic pool. In addition, I was backed up by Gene Boyce, a majority counsel.

One of the few witnesses to appear without counsel, Butterfield impressed me with his military manner and his excellent memory. With his hands folded in front of him, he considered each question carefully. He looked directly at me; he spoke in calm and even tones. He had resigned his commission as an air force colonel to work for Haldeman in the White House. He described Haldeman and Haldeman's odd relationship with Nixon in candid, almost clinical terms. His respect for each had been deeply tempered by a contempt for their manner and style. We reviewed his daily routine. I asked Butterfield to describe every mechanism for documenting the president's day. He seemed to enjoy this rare opportunity to talk about the responsibilities with which he had been charged.

But his candor and memory were not much help in determining whether it was John Dean or Richard Nixon who was lying. Butterfield's job and his access to the president were matters of routine. "Did you see or hear anything which indicated to you that the president was involved in the alleged effort to keep the facts from the public?" I asked Butterfield. "No, but the way the White House operated it could have happened, certainly." Butterfield paused to reflect. "The series of meetings in questions [with Dean] didn't begin until February 1973. I was phasing out of my job and getting ready to leave for the FAA. I can't document anything or prove anything. I don't remember Watergate being anything," Butterfield said.

I was deeply disappointed that we were not going to get a more knowledgeable account of the Dean/Nixon relationship. I asked how good the president's memory was. Good, Butterfield replied, but he rarely had to rely on it. A talking points memo was always provided for the president, whether it was for a meeting of state, a telephone call, a postscript to a letter. Usually he was offered three alternatives — the middle one was always the one he was supposed to pick — but nothing was left to chance.

Butterfield told a joke about how rigid the system of preparing talking points memos for the president was. Butterfield recalled an instance in which the president and most of the senior staff were in Florida. Butterfield sent down a reminder that over the weekend Vice President Agnew would be celebrating his birthday. Butterfield suggested in a brief note to Haldeman that the president call Agnew and wish him a happy birthday. Back from Key Biscayne came the request from Haldeman for a talking points memo. Butterfield complied:

1. Happy Birthday to you.
2. Happy Birthday to you.
3. Happy Birthday Dear:
Alternative 1: Spiro   Agree _____ Disagree _____
Alternative 2: Ted   Agree _____ Disagree _____
Alternative 3: Mr. Vice President   Agree _____ Disagree _____
4. Happy Birthday to you.

Trying to make the most of the situation, I returned to Butterfield's expertise on the president's office routine and decided to spring the Buzhardt material. There were actually two documents: one memorandum listed the times, dates, locations, and participants for all the Dean-Nixon conversations; another described the substance of Dean's calls and meetings with the president. I started with the first. "We received a listing from the White House of the conversations between the president and Dean, which we understand are from the president's diaries," I began. Where could these materials come from?

"We have three types of back-up materials from which these listings could be constructed," Butterfield said. "The switchboard operators kept track of all phone calls to and from the president. Secret Service personnel, ushers, and secretaries record who comes and goes from the president's office. Staff members prepare memos for the president before each formal meeting with outsiders, outline the purpose and points to be covered, and then prepare another memo after each meeting, summarizing the tone of the meetings and any commitments made." All this was put together into a daily log for the president—where, when, and with whom he had met.

"Would there be a file on the substance of each meeting with staff members?" I asked, repeating the question he had previously answered. "If the staff member was in alone or only with other White House staff members, there would probably be no memo written. If there was a highly significant meeting, the president might say, 'Write this up.' " How did these results of meetings generally get recorded? Butterfield said if a guest, whether a head of state or an official from Capitol Hill, were visiting, the junior staff person attending the meeting would take notes and submit a memo for the record. Because most head of state meetings were not attended by any staff member besides Henry Kissinger, Nixon's national security adviser, Kissinger owed over three hundred such memos to the chron-file.

If there were no outside guests, the most junior staff person in the room would do a memo to the file, but only insofar as action was called for. Thus Haldeman would be the only source of notes in his meetings with the president. If Ehrlichman were there too, then he, not Haldeman, would decide what notes to keep and what to submit for the file. If Dean joined the three, then Dean would be the notetaker. Generally, each person meeting with the president kept the notes of his meetings in his own files.

I then turned to the second type of memo that Buzhardt had dictated to the Republican minority counsel—the president's version of his conversations with Dean. Pulling out a typed transcript of the summary, I asked Butterfield—without telling him where we had gotten it—where such an account might have originated. Could it have been from someone's notes of the meetings?

Butterfield glanced over the document. He paused several times to remark how detailed the account was. He lingered over it, picking it up off the table and setting it down neatly in front of him. Each time, he looked up at me and then Sanders, as if expecting us to say something more about the document. I thought Sanders seemed surprised that I had the Buzhardt summary, but he said nothing. It was not until that moment that it occurred to me that I did not know if Sanders himself had ever seen the document. It was possible the minority had not shared it with their own investigators.

"Somebody probably got the information from the chron-file and put it down," Butterfield said finally. As he continued to read, he was asked whether the summary described the kinds of meetings the president would ask someone to write up. No, he responded, again picking up the memo. I asked him if this type of information could come from any of the systems he had described to us before. In each case, he said no, it was too detailed.

Resuming his reading, Butterfield arrived at the account of the March 21, 1973, meeting and stopped. He noted aloud that the summary stated that Dean had told the president that E. Howard Hunt was trying to blackmail Ehrlichman. Butterfield was surprised. He pointed out to me that the next sentence included an actual quote: "The President said how could it possibly be paid, 'What makes you think he would be satisfied with that?' "

"Where did you get this?" Butterfield asked, glancing quickly back and forth between Sanders and me. "Mr. Buzhardt provided it to the committee. Could it have come from someone's notes of a meeting?" I asked. "No, it seems too detailed," Butterfield replied. "Was the president's recollection of meetings good?" "Yes, when I came I was impressed," Butterfield replied. "He is a great and fast learner. He does recall things very well. He tends to overexplain things."

"Was he as precise as the summary?" I asked. "Well, no, but he would sometimes dictate his thoughts after a meeting." Butterfield offered his earlier explanation. "How often did he do so?" I asked. "Very rarely," Butterfield said. "Were his memos this detailed?" I asked. "I don't think so," Butterfield said.

"Where else could this have come from?" I pressed. Butterfield stared down at the document. Slowly, he lifted it an inch off the table. "I don't know. Well, let me think about this awhile." He pushed the document toward the center of the green felt–covered table. He seemed troubled. I assumed he was reluctant to tell us about some file system that he had just remembered. I began drafting up sample subpoena language for these newly revealed systems. Gene Boyce asked a few follow-up questions.

Don Sanders began by turning the questioning into other areas. I was surprised he didn't follow up on possible ways to explain where the Buzhardt memo had come from.

"Did the president ever note an article in a news summary and write it in the margin?" asked Sanders. "Yes," Butterfield said. "Did he ever write 'Get this guy'?" "Yes. Not necessarily in those words. He is profane, but in a nice sort of way," Butterfield responded. "Do you recall when he said 'Get this guy'? Do you remember the phrase he used?" Sanders asked. "He said several times, 'I remember his — he's no good'— oftentimes referring to news people," Butterfield said. "Sometimes he'd write something like 'Ziegler should get wise to this guy.' "

Then Sanders began asking questions derived directly from Dean's testimony. I assumed that he was going to give his best shot at trying to document the president's innocence. I began to note the direction of Sanders's questions. He led to his question cautiously by recalling for Butterfield Dean's testimony. "Dean indicated that there might be some facility for taping," Sanders said. "He said that on April 15 in the president's EOB office he had the impression he was being taped, and that at the end of the meeting the president went to a corner of the room and lowered his voice as if he was trying to stay off the tape himself while he discussed his earlier conversation with Colson about executive clemency. Is it possible Dean knew what he was talking about?" Sanders asked.

I assumed Sanders was after additional examples that the Joint Chiefs of Staff were spying on the president, a fact that had been revealed earlier in our hearings, or trying to support Howard Baker's favorite thesis that the Central Intelligence Agency (CIA) arranged Watergate to entrap Nixon.

Butterfield thought for a moment, trying to frame a response to a complicated question. Then, glancing back and forth between Sanders and me, as if he were somehow trapped, he leaned over to the center of the table and picked up the Buzhardt account of the Dean-Nixon meetings.

"No, Dean didn't know about it," Butterfield said at last. Turning directly to me as if he were now answering the long-pending question, Butterfield continued. "But that is where this must have come from," Butterfield said, glancing frantically from one to another of us in the room to see if we had previously known what he was talking about. "There is a tape in each of the president's offices." Butterfield continued. "It is kept by the Secret Service, and only four other men know about it. Dean had no way of knowing about it. He was just guessing." "You do know about it, don't you; someone else must have told you about it?" Butterfield asked.

"Yes," I said, lying. "But we are not sure who knows what, so please tell us what you know and who else knows about it."

"Then, for forty-five minutes, Butterfield described the taping system in detail. Gradually he realized that he was not being trapped by us but that we had not heard about the system before. Butterfield became increasingly concerned that his trip the following week to the Soviet Union where he would sign the first civil air pact between the United States and the Soviet Union would be canceled. He did not want to be the one to publicly reveal the taping system. I assured him we would try to get someone else to testify to it. In the meantime, I asked him to say nothing to anyone until we called him. When the interview ended, I raced upstairs with Phil Hare to brief the Democratic majority's chief counsel, Sam Dash.

Dash was ready to leave for the evening; he was pulling his office door shut as we arrived. Followed by Gene Boyce, I pushed him back into his office over his objection. "I have to get home right away," Dash said. "Sarah [Sam's wife] insisted that tonight I must be home for dinner at a reasonable hour." I learned later that it was Sam and Sarah's anniversary.

"Sam," I blurted out, "Nixon taped all his conversations, apparently including those with Dean." Dash stood dumbfounded for a moment just as we had less than an hour before. "Let me call Sarah." Within a few minutes, I briefed Dash, and he called Senator Ervin to relay the news. Ervin asked Dash to brief his chief political aide, Rufus Edmisten.

Dash told us to move cautiously to verify the system's existence before the White House heard about Butterfield's revelation. I believed that the Watergate inquiry would be over one way or another in a matter of days or weeks.

Meanwhile, I had learned from a minority staffer that Sanders had located his boss, Fred Thompson, at a bar in the Carroll Arms Hotel, talking to two reporters. Later we learned that after Sanders relayed word of the discovery to Thompson, Thompson called and tipped off Buzhardt. Over the weekend Butterfield contacted Baker, who told him to contact the White House. Over the weekend, I briefed Terry Lenzner, Marc Lackritz, Jim Moore, and Lee Sheehy, key majority (Democratic) staff members, about the existence of the tape system. The five of us spent the weekend developing background information about the others who according to Butterfield, knew about the taping system.

A preliminary decision was made to attempt to verify what use had been made of the system and the status of the tapes since Butterfield had left the White House. We felt we needed to secure this information without tipping off the White House that the committee knew about the existence of the tapes and thus providing an opportunity for complete or partial destruction of this unique evidence. Our theory was that if we could document the existence of tapes of the crucial meetings with Dean and others, the president would be forced to choose, on one hand, between refusing to turn them over and immediately resigning or, on the other hand, turning them over to the committee and either being cleared or condemned in the committee's hearings. The key, we decided, was to get the Secret Service agent who had installed and maintained the system before the committee to testify in secret that the taping system existed, that the tapes were still in the custody of the Secret Service. If certain tapes had been checked out for use or were missing or were altered or destroyed, it was better to find out before the White House was aware of the significance of the inquiry. If others had heard the tapes, they could be questioned about their substance. If any of the tapes were altered or destroyed, the staff reasoned, the president would be accountable for tampering with evidence of constitutional magnitude.

Other staff were concerned that the Butterfield information had come too conveniently. Was it possible Sanders was orchestrating the discovery for Nixon's benefit? they wondered. I argued that the order and context of the interview led me to believe that Sanders had asked the question spontaneously and that Butterfield was truly caught unawares.

I called the head of the Secret Service unit that had installed the system, Al Wong. Wong agreed to appear for a secret staff interview on Monday. I called Haldeman's aide, Larry Higby, and asked him to come in on Monday afternoon. Steve Bull, Nixon's closest aide, was unavailable. After we had taken informal statements from each with a stenographer present, we would move quickly on Tuesday—before Butterfield was scheduled to leave for the Soviet Union—to get the best-informed and most authoritative witnesses to testify before an executive session of the committee. That way we would have the president boxed into a clear choice between denying or providing to the committee the best evidence available on his guilt or innocence.

The next Monday, Baker, without revealing his weekend role in urging Butterfield to tell the White House what had happened, urged the committee to call Butterfield as a witness immediately. With the exception of Dash and Edmisten, the other key majority staff were busy Monday morning tracking down other Secret Service agents, Higby, and Bull to testify. By the time they heard about Baker's proposal, it was too late to effectively oppose; I was instructed to call Butterfield to testify publicly that afternoon. I objected to Dash that by calling Butterfield publicly first we would lose our opportunity to find out from other witnesses what tapes did and did not exist and whether and by whom they had been used in preparing the president's defense, including the Buzhardt memo. I believed that if we did not get answers to these questions first, we would be bogged down in months of executive privilege claims. It was too late, Dash indicated. The committee had decided to proceed with the facade of bipartisan support.

Just before noon on Monday, I smuggled Butterfield into the small conference room in the basement of the Dirksen office building where we had interviewed him the previous Friday. He was still trying to talk us out of using him as the principal witness. Before he even completed his reasons, Senator Ervin and Sam Dash had arrived with Senator Baker and Fred Thompson. After recovering with Butterfield the basic elements of his testimony about the taping system, Ervin, Baker, and Thompson left. Dash took me aside and told me for the first time that Baker had claimed to Ervin that the Butterfield revelation had come spontaneously in answer to Sanders's question alone.

I repeated to Dash the context in which the interview had taken place. Butterfield had seemed to me to be a reluctant witness who had responded negatively to Sanders's question and positively to the pending question about the Buzhardt memo. While Butterfield was the best witness to the existence of the tapes, he was an even better witness on the subject of the Buzhardt memo and the attempt to use it secretly through the committee's minority. If Butterfield was to be called to testify, it should be in the context that he had revealed the tapes, i.e., that the tapes could be the only possible source of the detail contained in the Buzhardt memo. Butterfield should be questioned by Dash, the majority chief counsel, as a majority witness, I insisted. It was again too late, Dash explained. In the interests of comity, Butterfield would be treated as a minority witness.

I escorted Butterfield from room G-334. We had slipped unnoticed into the room, but a battery of television reporters greeted us as we emerged. I hurried Butterfield down the hall to the Senate Caucus Room. Leslie Stahl had the presence of mind to notice the name tag on his briefcase as we fled down the hallway. Why was the director of the FAA going to be testifying? she shouted after us.

I sat behind Ervin and Baker as Thompson questioned Butterfield, fuming that as a result of Baker's interference it would now take considerably longer to learn what was on the tapes. Butterfield concluded his televised testimony by noting, "This matter which we have discussed here today, I think, is precisely the substance on which the president plans to present his defense." Butterfield was, of course, right; that had been the plan all along. However, the president ended up spending more energy over the next thirteen months defending the tapes than using them in his defense.

Conversations between Alexander P. Butterfield and David Thelen about the Discovery of the Watergate Tapes

Introduction

The following document originated from a three-hour taped conversation between Alexander P. Butterfield and me at the O'Hare Hilton in Chicago, on June 22, 1988. After thinking over what he had said in Chicago, Butterfield called me on July 15 to elaborate his answer. We then taped a one-hour telephone call on August 8, during which he was at a motel in Cedar Rapids, Iowa, and I was at the *Journal* office in Bloomington. I then edited and spliced the two transcripts into a single document, which I forwarded to him for his comments and elaborations. On October 12 he returned a heavily edited revision. I then suggested revisions to his revision in which I left untouched most of his proposed changes but asked him to restore some of his omissions and inserted a few exchanges from our earlier conversations that I had not incorporated into the original transcript. Those changes he accepted with only minor alterations.

In my conversations with Butterfield I became acutely aware that what we were creating was not so much an accurate record of what Butterfield had said, done, and felt in 1973, but a collaboration based on our different needs in 1988. I wanted our product to illustrate for this special issue how he used his memory creatively, and he wanted to tell his story in his way. Over the course of the summer each of us came to understand and want to help the other meet his needs, but we were both conscious throughout of our different purposes.

The memories that informed our respective contributions to the collaboration were shaped by our different experiences and associations between 1973 and 1988. I had a vivid memory of the excitement I had felt as I had watched Butterfield testify on television that the White House had been taped. That revelation, not Butterfield as a person, was what I recalled. On the few occasions when I had thought back to the revelation—as when I read a published transcript to prepare a lecture or when I speculated about Nixon with friends (most of whom had not admired Nixon)—I had found only confirmation for my 1973 impression that Butterfield had only answered a question.

I would like to thank Matthew Derr for his assistance in the research and preparation for this project.

Butterfield's world, on the other hand, contained many Nixon supporters. He has had to formulate explanations to people who condemn him for contributing to Nixon's forced resignation, and, more importantly, to himself for the high personal and professional toll this revelation has taken. His memories in 1988 struck me as answers he has constructed over fifteen years to questions posed (and prices exacted) by those who think he never should have disclosed the tapes, not (as my memories have been) to the concerns of those who have cheered that revelation.

When I first approached Butterfield for what I expected would be a single interview, I expected that the transcript would be the triumphant, perhaps even inspiring, story of a truth teller. The story that is printed here certainly contains elements of that view, but it also is a rather sad story of a man whose life was badly, if temporarily, wounded by the events of 1973. The difference between my expectation and his story reflects the different ways the people we have associated with since 1973 have viewed his revelation. It also reveals how even now he tests, confirms, modifies, and reshapes his memory against new experiences, associations, and perceptions. He reported in 1988 that he would very much like to go on a camping trip with John Ehrlichman and John Dean in which they would test and compare memories of their White House years.

I got the clear impression that Butterfield has told, retold, and rehearsed many parts of this story many times since 1973. On several different occasions he used the same language to describe the same events. He has testified before millions of watchers and on the public record to some of these events. As he told his story in 1988, he seemed to be quoting some of these earlier accounts. Some of these rehearsed and public statements have not changed. There were a few times, however, when I asked things that led him to question his memory, to reflect in new ways about what he might have thought or felt. The best example is our lengthy exchange about whether he felt regret, as he expressed it in 1973, or relief, as he now thinks possible, at his revelation of the tapes. After we opened this question in our June meeting, he thought a great deal about it, calling me three weeks later to express his new recollection, and then drafting a statement that he read to me in August. By October he acknowledged that our particular collaboration had led him first to reconstruct things a bit differently and then to decide to make public his new conclusion.

The transcript itself was a collaboration. I spliced 130 double-spaced pages from two conversations into a single 20-page narrative in question-and-answer form. I had been particularly struck in our Chicago conversation by how much Butterfield's memories of that incident and of the White House generally seemed colored by the military culture from which he came. And I was struck by the prices he had paid for his revelation. Those impressions shaped the portrait that I edited from our conversations. He, in turn, was concerned that he not sound whiny or bitter (for many of his associates from that period had gone to prison) and that he sound responsive and articulate in his answers to my questions. Most of the changes he introduced were changes in style, not in substance or tone. They were so extensive, however, that fewer than half of his words in this printed transcript were the literal words he uttered during our conversations. He removed most of the references to the negative consequences of his revelation, but I persuaded him to reinsert them for the final draft. In each of our conversations about his 1973 Senate testimony about the taping system he brought up his 1974 testimony before the House impeachment hearing. I could not see the relevance, but when he prominently repeated the 1974 association in reacting to a transcript that omitted it, I decided that it was such a integral part of his memory of the Watergate revelation that our joint story should feature that particular recollection in his final summing-up of the points he wanted our story to tell.

In deciding to let the final product reflect an ongoing process of creation rather than a literal record of what we said on any particular occasion I have sided with those oral historians who emphasize the collaborative, cumulative, and creative aspects to the construction of memory. Even though I thought the record would be more revealing if it included a few of the things Butterfield said to me privately (and negotiated with him — sometimes successfully — to restore those points), I thought he deserved the right to put his story in the language in which he wanted it presented to *Journal* readers. At the same time I tried to illustrate the lines along which his memory evolved over time. I particularly wanted to report his conclusion that his recollections were vivid over the last fifteen years even as he interpreted his feelings in a new way.

Conversations

DAVID THELEN: What were some of your impressions of working in the White House in the years before Watergate?

ALEXANDER BUTTERFIELD: Well, I had worked even earlier in the Johnson White House, roughly twenty hours a week as a lieutenant colonel and military assistant for White House matters in the office of the secretary of defense. When the White House came to the Defense Department for anything at all — a press release, military airlift, a mercy mission, anything — the request would in all likelihood come to my desk; and I would attend to it, get it done. This was in the 1965–66 time frame. Then later, in January 1969, I became an appointee of President Nixon and served in a civilian capacity as Bob Haldeman's immediate deputy. Haldeman was what they call today the chief of staff or chief of the White House staff. But as a matter of interest, there was no such term then, and I'm surprised its use has become so common. To the best of my knowledge and recollection, the White House, by tradition, was not to have any military flavor. The point was always made not to publicize the fact that there were military people, apart from aides, working in the White House. Yet, it's true, there always are a good many military people assigned there sort of unbeknownst to the public. But to have come up with the title "chief of staff" for the president's principal or senior assistant was in my opinion highly inappropriate. It makes it sound as though you've got a Prussian army headquartered there, running America military style.

But back to my duties in the Nixon White House. In many ways I was a jack-of-all-trades, but responsible essentially for the smooth running of the president's official day, and for all White House administration. That, I think, pretty well sums up the essence of what I did on a day-to-day basis. Oh, I was also the secretary to the cabinet.

DT: Did anything strike you as noticeable about the atmosphere there as a place to work?

AB: As the son of a military officer and having been one myself for a full career, some twenty-one years in the air force, I was surprised by how many things were done for the president that had to do, not with the issues of the day, but with image, with manipulating the public's perception of the president. I was surprised by the emphasis placed on "image," and by the extent to which aides and image makers plotted and planned. For example, we had a number of people who did nothing but cut clippings from newspapers from cities and towns all over America just to get little human interest stories that they might inject the president into; human interest stories that would be sure to make big news in Dubuque, or Duluth, or Peoria. For instance, they'd have the president spend all one morning calling "little people" around the country who had made news in their own locales . . . like a call to a third grade school teacher in Nashville to tell her how wonderful he thought it was that she took her class to the museum or to the zoo, or whatever. And of course the fact that the president of the United States called a local (Peoria) schoolteacher

President Nixon watches while White House staff members
H. R. Haldeman and Alexander P. Butterfield are sworn in by
Chief Justice Earl Warren, January 21, 1969.

would play very big indeed in Peoria's newspapers and on Peoria's radio and TV sta-
tions. It was strictly an image-making activity to enhance the president's image, to
promote the president's humanism, to touch the people with his warmth and
thoughtfulness, and it worked. I remember on one occasion they planned a large
presidential rally. And someone, to give the president maximum visibility, said,
"Let's put him on top of a car." I was present at this session and I thought to myself,
"I can't believe these idiots." They're actually going to put the president on top of
a car, so the entire crowd can see him. And you probably know that the president
didn't stand very well on terra firma as it was. He was just not a graceful or athletic
man; and now, to want to put him up on a car roof and ask him to wave . . . well!
So in the pictures in the newspapers of this particular incident, there he is, doing
this strange balancing act on a Volkswagen roof and looking downright weird in the
process. He was sort of teetering backward and waving a funny wave. At any rate,

those kinds of things took up all kinds of time and were considered to be of great importance. And *that* I was not used to.

DT: Let's move on to the decision in 1971 to install a taping system.

AB: OK. There wasn't much to it. Bob Haldeman came into my office one day and said that the president wanted a taping system installed that would record everything that was said in the Oval Office, in the Cabinet Room, on the telephones he used most frequently (that would mean the telephones in the Oval Office, in the Lincoln Sitting Room, and [in] the president's office over in the EOB). And let me make a point here: He didn't have to tell me that it was for historical purposes. I just knew from working there and from being so close to the president that he was extremely conscious of history, of the historical aspect of things. As a matter of fact, we already had in place a system whereby a staff member, a particular staff member, would sit in on each meeting the president had, and then, immediately after the meeting ended, go back to his office and dictate a memo describing the meeting's substance and mood. That's how nuts, crazy, they were—or I should say, he was, the president—about history. These memos were called "memos for the President's file." So when I was asked to install a taping system, I said [to myself], "Ahh, another attempt to record history in the making. I wonder if the president realizes it'll duplicate the efforts ongoing to collect and maintain our memos for the president's file."

DT: You said they installed it for historical purposes.

AB: Yes. Without question.

DT: To keep a record?

AB: Yes, I was sure of that. The second thing Haldeman said to me, apart from giving me the basic assignment, was: "Be sure that WHCA doesn't do the work." WHCA was—and is—the White House Communications Agency, which was run then by a three-star army general named Starbird, General Starbird. But my point here is that Haldeman, who had this great and noticeable disdain for the military, who looked down on the military (as do a great many civilians in the higher echelons of the federal government), wanted to be sure that the military didn't install the taping system the president wanted. Many Kennedy holdovers on the Johnson staff just plain did not like the military. They thought that anyone in the military was an absolute dummkopf. Nixon was that way, too, incidentally. He felt uncomfortable around military people. He, too, felt deep down they were dumb bastards. Anyway, Haldeman said, "Have anyone but WHCA do the project." That meant that I was to call on the Technical Security Division of the Secret Service. The fellow who ran that division, Al Wong, said: "Well, Mr. Butterfield, we sure don't like to get into this, but of course we'll get it done right away." I said, "What do you mean when you say you don't like getting into this?" He then alluded to the fact that Johnson had had some kind of a taping system, and that other presidents had, too. He seemed only to intimate that over the years the experience was that such systems were more trouble than they were worth. He hinted, too, that technically it was wrong, maybe even a little illegal, to be taping officials of our government and other governments without their knowledge. I think that's a rather important point there. I don't think a lot of these young staff men who were asked to do things really sat down to think: Wait a minute. They're asking me to do thus and so. Now strictly speaking, in a legal sense, that's not cricket. But you don't think that. You think the man, the great man, wants me to do it. I can't do it fast enough. I should make it very clear here that Wong was not digging in his heels. He was only telling me what his views were—that these recording systems often became a pain in the neck, more of a waste of time than anything really useful.[1]

DT: Now here were these memos to the president's file, and here were these tapes. Did anyone ever listen to them or read them?

AB: No one ever listened to the tapes once the taping system was installed; that is, not while I was at the White House . . . up until March 15 of '73.

DT: They just accumulated in a pile? They were just not part of the working White House?

AB: No, that's right.

DT: I mean Nixon wouldn't say, Gee, I would like to go back and hear what the president of Mexico said or something like that?

AB: No, no, no.

DT: Did Nixon ever acknowledge to you your role with the tapes?

AB: No, but in fact it's funny because he is such a strange, strange fellow. I remember hearing Haldeman say in a 1975 interview that he thought Nixon was the strangest man he'd ever met. I was glad to hear Bob express himself that way. It helped me realize that I wasn't crazy, for I'd felt for some time, even then, that Nixon was the strangest man I'd ever met, too.

DT: What do you mean by that?

AB: Huh? What do I mean by that? I could give you a hundred examples, but we'd go too far from the subject if I started. Well, here's one example. You just asked me if Nixon ever mentioned the tapes once they were in. At the end of the day when the taping system installation was completed, Haldeman asked me to brief the presi-

---

[1] DT: In *Nightmare: The Underside of the Nixon Years*, J. Anthony Lukas writes that it was Higby who told you that the president wanted a tape recording system set up in the Oval Office and Cabinet Room and to make sure you don't go to the military and all that. Is that your recollection, too, that it was Higby who asked?

AB: Yes, it was Higby rather than Haldeman, personally. I may have said "Haldeman" a few times, but Higby, Haldeman's immediate or closest staff aide, was like Haldeman's spokesman. He issued instructions to most of the White House staffers almost daily, but you knew that if Higby asked something of you, it was being asked in the name of Haldeman.

DT: So when Higby talked you thought you were basically talking to Haldeman?

AB: Yes.

dent sometime before he left the Oval Office for the day. So I went in and said: "Mr. President, the taping system that Bob said you wanted is in place now, and I've thoroughly checked it out. It works fine, and I would like now to check you out, to at least brief you on the locations of the microphones, etc." He looked up, gave me a sort of blank stare, and said, "Oh, hmmm, ahh, hmmm, ahh, oh well, ahh." In other words, he didn't want to talk about it. That was the way he often communicated, and you had to know him awfully well to get his drift. Now in this case, his expressed disinterest wasn't because he viewed the taping system as a sinister thing. He just didn't want or need to get back into it. He had given the order. He was glad it was in, and that was that. But at the same time he knew he needed to know something about how it worked. It was the kind of petty little thing he didn't want to have to turn and talk to me about. So just to put the words in his mouth, so he wouldn't have to say the words himself or deliberate on this thing, I said: "We will do it about seven o'clock this evening, when you get ready to leave for the day." So, starting about 6:00 P.M., I kept an eye on him feeling pretty sure that he'd try to sneak away. When I thought he was ready to leave, I just barged in with the day's final batch of papers and walked him through it. And all the while, he never said a word. Now, is that strange?

DT: Well, there must have come a point—especially as John Dean started to appear—when you thought: I know a way that we can confirm or refute Dean's claims. The record is there on the tapes.

AB: Yes, yes, OK, yes. Several people who know this story and who look back on the events of July '73 have said, "Gee, didn't you think that?" I did, but only fleetingly. I don't recall ever pondering over the matter. Please keep in mind that everyone was working like a son of a bitch. People don't just sit around and discuss newspaper stories—not anyone I know. We all worked from early morning to 9:00 and 10:00 and 11:00 P.M. day in and day out. I was a loyal Nixon man and a strong supporter. That's another reason I wouldn't be inclined to doubt or wonder about the president's veracity. In March of '73 I became administrator of the Federal Aviation Administration and was especially busy getting settled in there when in June, I think, John Dean began his long testimony.

I'll tell you all I thought of as I listened to Dean. "Everything John is saying makes perfect sense. I know the 'White House System' as well as anyone, and everything he's saying fits." But again, strange as it may seem, I did not follow the thought any further. I didn't let myself take the time to look deeper into the matter. Subconsciously, I may have had some suspicions about Richard Nixon, even then, quite early on, but only subconsciously. Otherwise, I was totally loyal.

DT: Would there have come a time when you would have thought that these tapes—or maybe the memos for the president's file you were talking about earlier—would refute or confirm somebody's story?

AB: I knew about [Nixon's] suspicion of everyone. I had learned by working there in the inner sanctum for so long that this was part of Nixon—part of his strangeness.

He had deep resentments of people — resentments that seemed to have deepened over the years. If some senator or congressman weren't toeing the mark or were ultraliberal in his views or vocally anti-Nixon or had crossed Nixon in the past (he remembered those things like an elephant), he would say, "I don't want that son of a bitch to get any favors. Do you hear me? NOT a goddamned one."

I knew, for instance, that they felt Ted Kennedy might have a girl friend or two. The president wanted to, and did eventually, order the Secret Service to report on Teddy's activities. Naturally that's not the Secret Service's job; they (the agents) don't like to be put in those kinds of positions. But that's only an example of what went on — little sort of sneaky things like that were a far cry from my former "clean Gene" military world. But I must say, I took it in stride. I didn't, you know, think it was anything terribly shocking. I wasn't *that* naïve.

DT: But you knew one thing that very few people knew. You knew there was a tape being made of all these conversations to prove that either Nixon was right or Dean was right.

AB: Yes, and I thought about that. I thought that if those tapes were exposed — if that deep dark secret ever came to light — it would blow the whole issue, the whole national dilemma out of the water. When I was asked to come up to Capitol Hill [on Friday, July 13, 1973] and talk to some staff investigators of the Senate Watergate Committee, I knew very well that disclosure of the tapes information would be like a bombshell nationally and internationally. And because the taping system at the White House was known by only nine people, I made a conscious decision before going into that session not to reveal the taping system's existence unless, I want to repeat that, unless I were asked a very direct question pertaining to such a system. And of course I have to tell you I felt that that was highly unlikely. I never dreamed they would ask a question having anything to do with the subject of taping or recording conversations. But if I were asked a direct question about the taping system, I would, of course, answer appropriately. I knew in my mind that I would do that.

DT: Did you have any questions you thought they were much more likely to ask you about?

AB: No, I didn't prepare at all. I went up there on Friday afternoon directly from work. I didn't have to prepare. I knew what I knew, and I didn't know what I didn't know. They said they were going to ask me about how the White House works, how the staff functions. I guess I knew that about as well as anyone.

DT: Some people in that White House probably would have denied it or tried to evade it if asked. Why did you decide you would acknowledge it if you were asked?

AB: I never thought that I *couldn't* tell. You know what I mean? It seems so dumb now. People have pointed out to me that I could have taken the Fifth Amendment or something. I don't know about that kind of thing. I really don't. I mean I am not that kind of guy. This was a major investigation, and, if you want to get technical

Alexander P. Butterfield (far left) conducting daily staff meeting in the Adjunct Oval Office, 1971.

about it, Richard Nixon had said time and time again in public forums: "I want all of my people to come forward and be straightforward and open and honest. I want all the facts to come out." Well, I sort of knew that that was baloney, yet he was saying it, loudly and clearly.

The decision wasn't all that conscious. I simply knew I wouldn't lie. I would never lie. This may sound a little corny now, but this was an official investigation. I would never have *thought* of lying, whether under oath or not. But incidentally, I see now that I have been in the business world for a good many years that a hell of a lot of people do lie. Sometimes it seems that everyone lies, or would if money were involved. I didn't learn this until I was fifty-five years old. My whole upbringing was different. My father wouldn't have lied if his life had depended on it. I can't tell you how straight my parents were. In fact, I clearly recall my dad paying back the government a portion of his travel allowance when he spent less than was allotted, or authorized, for a particular trip. He was a career naval aviator, a Naval Academy graduate.

The Interview

[*This is the account Butterfield wrote six weeks after our interview in Chicago.*]

AB: The session with the investigators began around 2:00 P.M. on Friday, July 13, 1973. And almost immediately I was shown a paper which appeared to me to be a transcript from the tapes. Well, I couldn't have been more surprised, though I don't think I expressed or demonstrated my surprise to my principal interrogator [Scott Armstrong]. It was a typed, seemingly verbatim, conversation the president was having with someone (I don't recall the other initials; it seems to me it was John Dean now that I think about it) and the question put to me was, "Where would something like this have come from?" I suppose you could argue about how direct that was as a question, but no one had mentioned tapes, no one had mentioned recording devices, or even indicated that such was on his mind so I responded as though I too were puzzled. I allowed as how the president had quite a fantastic retentive ability, but that that particular paper I was holding in my hand seemed almost too detailed for one to have dictated its contents from memory. Then I mentioned that the president had kept a small mobile recording device in his desk drawer and occasionally dictated, on those small "tape belts," brief personal letters to friends, relatives, and others—letters which Rose Woods, his secretary, typed up for his signature. But I added that the transcript I was being shown was obviously not one of those "brief personal letters." So I sat there and scratched my head as though I were puzzled. And I was in a way. I couldn't believe that this was a transcript from the hidden recording system; yet what else could it be? Then, almost immediately, and to my great relief, the subject was dropped. It was as though the transcript had not been very important. The interview moved on to other matters, to things I knew very well. I am referring to the administration of the White House, how the office of the president and the president's staff really worked, what the president's relationship was to members of his staff, what the relationships were one staff member to another, that type of thing. Well, some four hours later, it had to be close to 6:00 P.M., Don Sanders, the staff member representing the minority counsel, spoke. He'd been relatively quiet up to that point. He said, "Mr. Butterfield, getting back to that paper you were shown at the outset of this session, you mentioned the fact that the president had a small mobile dictating machine in his desk drawer. Was there ever any other kind of voice recording system in the president's office?" Those are close to his exact words, and I think you'll have to admit, as I did at the time to myself, that that indeed constituted a direct question. And there was just no way that I could be evasive or give a vague answer. It was either yes or no. I recall precisely my response. I said, "I hoped you all wouldn't ask that question. Yes, there was another recording system in the Oval Office." "Where was it?" he said. "Well, it was a rather extensive system," I said. "In the Oval Office it was in two locations. There were microphones imbedded in the top of the president's desk and on fixtures over the mantel above the fireplace at the far end of the room, that is, at the opposite end of the room from the president's desk. There were also microphones in the Cabinet Room, and in the president's Executive Office Building (EOB) office, and on several of the president's most frequently used telephones."

Some people have asked since why I responded as I did, but that's an easy question for me to answer now. I thought it was easy to answer then, too. Because it was the truth; because he, Sanders, was a member of an official investigative body; because any other course of action would have been deceptive; because Richard Nixon (whether he meant it or not) had long since counseled his White House aides publicly to be cooperative and forthright with investigators; and, as if to emphasize his sincerity on that score, he had only some two months earlier released all of his aides from the executive privilege rule. Finally, I answered truthfully because I am a truthful person. I used to play that down to some considerable extent, but I see no reason to invent other reasons for having been open and honest and direct once the sixty-four-dollar question was put to me.

And the reason I prefaced my response to Don Sanders's question with the statement, "I hoped you wouldn't ask that question," was because of the adverse impact I knew the news would have around the world . . . within diplomatic and other circles. For instance, British prime minister Harold Wilson, Golda Meir, and a host of other world leaders would know that their conversations with our president, in his office, had been surreptitiously recorded. The nation would clearly suffer embarrassment, as would the president. That concerned me — the nation's image and the president's image. It concerned me greatly. But I didn't feel I had the luxury of choice in this matter.

DT: Did you feel relieved when they didn't get into the tapes after Armstrong finished? Or did you feel disappointed when they didn't get into the tapes?

AB: Now you've brought up an interesting question. You've touched on an issue I've never before mentioned. I was just thinking coming in here today that I would have to admit to some suspicion going back to my White House days. I didn't think a lot in mid-1973 about John Dean being right and the president being wrong; but I thought to myself—often, as a matter of fact—that the tapes ought to be brought to light so that we could clear up this long and debilitating national mess. I certainly didn't see it as a means to put the screws to a president I enjoyed serving and very much respected. I just kept thinking, "Why doesn't the president refer to the tapes? Why don't we get on with the simple process of clearing this matter up?"

So, as I say, you asked an interesting question there. I had already said to myself that I was going to answer the big question if it were put to me directly. And I had already diverted the one not-so-direct question, and now the same subject, the same question, was coming at me again. But this time, this fellow, Don Sanders, was asking about as directly as one could ask. Was there or was there not any kind of a taping system ever? Immediately after Sanders asked his question about a taping system, I said, "I am sorry you asked that question." Well, it's just possible that sub-consciously I wasn't sorry. It's just possible that my impatience for the facts of the matter to be known, and for the debating to end, had its influence. I don't know; it's a psychological thing. Perhaps deep down I was delighted he asked that question. But then the initiative was his, not mine. And I'm as sure as I know I'm sitting here that if he hadn't asked, I would never have volunteered.

AB: [*Butterfield elaborated on this answer six weeks later.*] I remember occasional, but only occasional, feelings of impatience at the time John Dean was testifying publicly in the summer of 1973. I found myself at times wanting something to happen, wanting the impasse, the debate, the stalemate, to end. What I'm saying, I think, is that I sense now in 1988 that I may have had a subconscious desire then, in 1973, to see an end to the debacle. There was a debilitating factor or aspect to the affair and knowing much or all of it could be brought to a close by the simple revelation of the hidden taping system, I was impatient. Do I think the subconscious impatience guided me? I'm not sure; I don't think so. I think I was guided by those things I mentioned early in our conversation. I was, however, strangely relieved. In speaking of this whole matter of impatience and the feeling of relief once the tapes information was out, I dare say that *most* people experienced a sense of relief. It was as though we had broken through a logjam and were now going to get on with it. I don't know if even the relief was a conscious thing in my case. It was just that I had this sense, subconsciously, that it sure would be great if everything would come out in the open. All one would have to do is expose the secret recording system. Then lo and behold, I'm in the docket and being asked the lead-in question. Does that mean that I somehow guided the event? I don't think so.

DT: After you revealed the tapes you must have thought something different than before Sanders asked the question. Did you think: Holy cow, the whole complexion of this issue is going to change, the Watergate Committee's actions are going to change, the press and so on, when it gets out?

AB: I knew very well that the complexion of the whole investigation was going to change, that the emphasis would shift immediately from who said what to whom to getting transcripts of the tapes, or the tapes themselves. I knew also how momentous the news would be. But perhaps naïvely, I thought the news, for a while at least, might be contained; and with that in mind, the first thing I did was gather Armstrong, Sanders, and the others right after the interview and express my hope that they would handle what they had heard from me wisely . . . because of the embarrassment such news would surely bring to the president and the country. I actually said to them (it really was naïve, wasn't it?) that it would never do for this to get out to world leaders and others. I recall feeling upset—maybe depressed is the word—that I had been forced by circumstances, to preempt the president. I didn't know what in the hell was going to happen. But then I felt that I needed to talk to someone on the committee so I went to see Howard Baker a day and a half later, on Sunday [July 15].

DT: Why did you choose Howard Baker?

AB: Because he was the Republican leader of the committee, and I felt I knew him sufficiently well to tell everything that was on my mind. Moreover, I wanted to go to someone senior on the Republican side.

DT: Did you assume that he would know right away what you had said and would be discussing it with the White House?

AB: I didn't know that. I was a little naïve about that, too. When I went to see him that Sunday afternoon, I told him the whole story as though he knew nothing. But of course he knew it all and had known it within hours of the event on the previous Friday.

DT: He acted like he hadn't heard it?

AB: Yes, and now that I think about it, had he let me know right away, he could have saved me a lot of time. After I went through the entire story, I said to Howard, "I wish this thing weren't out. It's so big. How are you committee members going to contain it?" "Well," he said, "it's going to have to come out eventually." Then I said, "I sure as hell don't want to testify before the [full Ervin] Committee [about the tapes]. Perhaps you could get Haldeman to do that. I'm so peripheral to this Watergate business. Haldeman knows about the system and he's already a central figure." "Oh," he said, "I don't think you'll have to testify before the committee."

DT: Baker said that?[2]

AB: Yes, he did. In fact, he said he'd lend a hand to quell the idea if it gained momentum. I felt pleased, as though I had a partner, someone in my corner. Then on Monday, July 16, I'm getting my hair cut prior to my scheduled departure for the Soviet Union the next day. I was at the barbershop at the Ritz-Carlton Hotel,

[2] Howard Baker argued before the committee that Butterfield should be called immediately as a witness, and he insisted—successfully—that Butterfield be a Republican witness because Donald Sanders, a Republican staffer, had elicited the crucial information. See Scott Armstrong, "Friday the Thirteenth," in this volume, pages 105–15.

watching the committee hearings on the barbershop TV. The phone rang, and it was for me. Committee staffer Jim Hamilton said: "Mr. Butterfield, we'd like you to come up to the committee. We are going to put you on this afternoon." Well, I was surprised to say the least. I'd felt comfortable after having talked to Howard Baker. Why hadn't I heard from Howard? What the hell was this all about? I felt myself getting angry. So, I said to Hamilton, "No way am I coming up there. I've talked to Howard Baker about this, and he said I probably would not have to testify publicly. So don't look for me. I won't be there. Besides you're interrupting my haircut." I then hung up. Then, within a half minute I saw this guy on the tube walk onto the dais where the committee members were sitting, walk back behind the row of senators, stop at Senator Ervin's chair, and lean over and whisper in Ervin's ear. I actually saw him whisper into the old man's ear, and Ervin—you know how he had those eyebrows?—I could see those eyebrows go whoop, whoop, whoop, up and down; and it was a strange feeling, for I knew precisely what he was hearing—this guy Butterfield said no way is he coming up here. Well, no doubt the senator wasn't used to having people talk to him like that, even indirectly, so sure enough, a minute or two later the barbershop phone rang again. It was Hamilton. He said very calmly, "Mr. Butterfield, I have talked to Senator Ervin about what you said." I said: "I know, I saw you on television." Hamilton replied, "Senator Ervin told me to tell you that if you aren't up here in his office by 12:30 today, he'll have federal marshals pick you up on the street." Well, having seen this fellow on TV was funny, and it made me lighten up a bit. I apologized for my tough talk earlier and told him I'd be there . . . which I was. We moved to a small room. There was Senator Ervin, Senator Baker, Sam Dash, and Mr. Thompson, plus, as I recall one or two of the underlings. Howard was sort of apologetic. I sat on the table and spoke first. I said, "I am a very peripheral person here, but this is so big. I meant it when I said I didn't want to testify publicly. I think that if the taping system has to be made public, one of you all should simply announce it; or you should ask someone like Haldeman, who is already one of your witnesses, to give you the details."

DT: Why were you worried about it coming from you rather than Haldeman?

AB: I don't know. I don't know. Maybe because in my view it would give the appearance of me sort of running in the back door. I just felt that it wasn't up to me. At any rate, they said no, we have talked it over and we understand your point, Mr. Butterfield, but no way is it going to be contained. It is going to come out, and the best way for it to come out is for you to reveal it just as you did last Friday. You are the one who told us; therefore you are the one who should tell the nation. So I said: OK, all right, let's go. I went in the washroom, washed my face, combed my hair, looked at myself in the mirror, and remember pausing for a second or two. Then I said to myself, son of a bitch, here goes. I didn't know precisely what I was going to say. But I knew I was going to answer questions, and I knew I wasn't going to have any trouble answering them. Yet I wanted to say more. I wanted to get a message to the president somehow. I wanted him—especially him—to know and appreciate how all of this had come about.

DT: How did this revelation, do you think now, in retrospect fifteen years later, change your life?

AB: It made it tough, I suppose, for a while. As it happened, I hadn't come to the White House to go on to a cushy job and make big money. That was not my motivation. Having come from a military family, and having been in the military, myself, for some twenty-one years, money was clearly not my orientation. It was hard for me to leave the military in a way because I had had my cap set to go to the top. And, admittedly, I had been on a fairly fast track. But, yes, I did think the White House experience would in some ways be an enhancement to my new civilian career. And, yes, as a result of Watergate, it was not. So, while I've had a few tough years, I can't complain too loudly. Just look at all the colleagues of mine who went to prison. They have to have had a hell of a lot tougher time than I did. My case, where Watergate was concerned, was so different. I was neither a good guy nor a bad guy. I was an enigma. Business executives didn't rush in to pick up those who were involved with Watergate and dust them off and give them nice cushy jobs out in the private sector. So, generally speaking, those first ten years for me were not happy. In fact, it was a fairly miserable period. I think the inner sanctum, the Nixon lovers, are down on me to this day, as I am sure he is, because I screwed things up. But I doubt they understand the context in which all of this occurred.

DT: Do you ever talk about these events with people from the Nixon White House?

AB: I see Ehrlichman every now and then. I have dinner with him occasionally in Santa Fe.

DT: Do you ever talk about this stuff with him?

AB: Yes, I have a little bit with him, and with John Dean, too.

DT: Well, what do you say as you think back?

AB: We haven't gotten into too much. But I'd like to. I'd like to get them both alone. I would love to go off on a camping trip with Ehrlichman and Dean and hash everything out, but of course those two wouldn't go on the same camping trip. My guess is that they dislike each other still.

DT: Thinking of your cold-shoulder treatment by the Nixon White House . . .

AB: And I'd have to tell you by the Ford White House as well.

DT: Do you think the reputation, this decision, affected your chances of getting jobs?

AB: Without question. As I said, CEOs of companies don't want anything to do with you if they think you may be the subject of new and surprising revelations. One has to recapture his self-esteem. I don't think I actually lost my self-esteem, but I had to keep thinking: I am a good guy, and I have had bosses in the past under different conditions who thought I did a superb job for them. But while thinking this and telling myself how great I was, I was noticing on the job market that CEOs I knew personally were shying away from me.

But I'm not going to sit here now in 1988 and be a bleeding heart. Things are just fine now. In fact, now I look back and feel very good indeed about the course of actions I chose—and about myself—and I rather enjoy looking the jerks, the people I know put selfish personal interests before probity, squarely in the eye. I feel that I have so much more than they do.

DT: Do you ever wonder why Nixon didn't burn the tapes after you revealed their existence?

AB: He didn't burn the tapes, when the chance was there, for one very simple reason. He didn't dream that he'd ever have to. He felt certain that there would be no need. He didn't know the snowball coming downhill was as big as it was, or that it was getting bigger by the day . . . nor did he know how fast it was moving. The president's perception of the mounting trouble was not accurate because the White House never listens. There's so much power there, at the White House; there really is. You can pick up the phone and call almost anywhere and people will get in line to talk to you. You can do so much. You can have such tremendous influence, and on such a scale. It's almost awesome. So I don't think Mr. Nixon ever dreamed that the Watergate issue would come unraveled or get to the point where it might be wise not to have tapes around.

Significance

AB: I guess I told you that in this Trivial Pursuit game I'm "the man who revealed the existence of the tapes." That will be with me always. And of course I don't like that description or identification because it connotes or implies a foreknowledge of wrongdoing. It leads people to believe that I may well have been out to dump the president, that I went to the investigators, not that they came to me. Well maybe in 1974, but definitely not in 1973. But getting back to the Trivial Pursuit game, to me it's a shame the identifying statement can't read, "He was one of the few people who answered questions honestly."

DT: Well, if you could write the Trivial Pursuit question for you, what would you say? "The man who just told the truth"?

AB: Yes, something like that. This is not worth belaboring, but suffice it to say that I'd like truth or honesty or integrity to be the emphasis. After all, that's the way it really was. Why should it now be twisted? I didn't go forward saying to myself, "Here's a chance to be famous because, like George Washington, I chopped down the cherry tree." It seems funny, strange actually, that what I did is exactly what all of us are supposed to do—what we teach our children to do—and yet that side of it, the simple motivation to be forthright, never came out. What came out was that things seem sinister, dirty, suspicious.

DT: Now, knowing all that happened, would you have tried to avoid the summons?

AB: No. I'm glad I didn't try to avoid the summons.

DT: You're glad?

AB: Yes. I felt good about it then because I knew in my heart it was right. It was perfectly OK to tell what I knew to be the case. And human nature being what it is, I'm not sorry that I might have some little place in history here, even though I realize that it's not the kind of place in history that might be admired by Nixon's progeny. It's not as though I went to my death for my country or burned at the stake like Joan of Arc or shot down thirty-nine enemy airplanes or something like that. My role was quite simple.

Butterfield added this comment when he returned the edited transcript in October 1988:

Let me summarize here the essence of the three principal points that I want to make:

1. In 1973 I did not go to the Watergate Committee; it came to me. I did not want to testify publicly and, in fact, refused until subpoenaed. I did not ask the questions; I only answered them.

2. While I do not feel that my memory of the events of 1973–74 has faded *or* that my perspectives have changed. I do realize *now* that during the fairly long period of John Dean's testimony before the Ervin Committee, I was, at times, impatient for the truth . . . which I knew the tapes would reveal. There was obviously a debate going on nationwide. Was the president involved, as Dean was telling us . . . or was the president free of complicity? I knew, of course, that the tapes would provide the answer, and in some strange, deep-down, almost subconscious way was relieved by having the direct question asked of me by Mr. Sanders . . . even though I heard myself say first in response, "I'm sorry you gentlemen asked that question." In fact, I was sorry—very sorry—for the several reasons I've already mentioned, yet simultaneously there was this sense of relief that at last the taping system would be known, and with it the honest answers to a myriad of questions concerning the commission of illegal acts.

3. While I was very much a Nixon man and fan and an ardent and loyal appointee up to and through my July 1973 testimony, I was quite less than that a year later when I went before Peter Rodino's House Judiciary Committee as its first of eight witnesses. I then had a purpose and a cause. I knew, or at least felt I knew, that if the committee voted one or more articles of impeachment, Richard Nixon, understanding that the House would follow, would be wise enough to close shop and step down. I was sure that what I had to say would greatly influence the committee membership and that no combination of wily tactics by Mr. St. Clair, the renowned Boston attorney representing the president, could throw me off course or render ineffective my factual contradictions of Nixon's oft-repeated lines about his negligence in monitoring and supervising his zealous aides, and about his preoccupations with the affairs of state.

The Timeless Past: Some Anglo-American Historical Preconceptions

David Lowenthal

The focus on memory in this issue of the *Journal of American History* reflects rising interest in a kind of past that historians seldom address explicitly, even though history is mainly grounded in memory. Scrutiny of the ways in which recollection and recall shape images of past and present could help historians to bring their own concerns more visibly in line with those of the public at large. The *Journal*'s editor suggests that since "the ways that individuals shape, omit, distort, recall, and reorganize their memories" closely resemble the ways that historians keep, interpret, and transmit social memories, "memory itself offers one possible way to link popular audiences and professional historians."

Individual and collective pasts have much in common, as attested by analogies frequently drawn between personal life histories and national chronicles. But the analogies should not lead us to overlook the profound differences. What we know of the past through memory is largely private and personal. What we know of the past through the study of history is mainly collective and capable of being tested against accessible sources. That is why likening these two routes to the past distresses those historians who "know history to be hard work while recollection seems passive, noninferential, and unverified."[1]

Other factors differentiate the professional study of history from that of memory. Psychologists, psychoanalysts, and other practitioners of memory focus on the processes of recollection and on the motives and biases that reshape memories. Historians and other practitioners of the collective past have traditionally inquired mainly into what may actually have happened, rather than reasons for imagining or pretending that things were otherwise.

The public at large, however, tends to view history through the same distorting lenses that filter their own memories. The collective past is apprehended as a per-

David Lowenthal was professor of geography at University College, London. Versions of this paper were presented at the seminar "Storia delle Idee" at the Lessico Intellettuale Europeo, Rome, October 1987; in the session "Imagined Pasts: History as Reconstructed," American Historical Association meeting, Washington, D.C., December 1987; and at a seminar on the Uses of the Past, University College, London, February 1988. The author is grateful for helpful suggestions from Michael Kammen and to his London seminar colleagues Robert Bud, Nicholas James, and Charles Saumarez Smith.

[1] Louis O. Mink, "Everyman His or Her Own Annalist," in *On Narrative*, ed. W. J. T. Mitchell (Chicago, 1981), 233–39, esp. 234; David Lowenthal, *The Past Is a Foreign Country* (Cambridge, Eng., 1985), 210–14.

sonal and deeply felt extension of the present, and the events and viewpoints of by-gone times are seen and judged in today's perspectives. Historical understanding among the general public, including most of the educated minority, embraces biases more closely akin to popular modes of memory than to procedures customary among historians.

My aim is to consider the perdurable perspectives on the historical past held by public figures, scholars in cognate disciplines, and the media generally in both America and Britain. It is not my intent to find fault with these patently anachronistic viewpoints, but rather to indicate their pervasiveness and their per-ceived utility. There is no true past out there waiting to be accurately reconstructed; as the editors say of memory, so is history "socially constructed, not an objective record to be retrieved." Everyone uses the past creatively, historians along with the rest. But Everyman does it differently, and if historians are to reach audiences be-yond the boundaries of their discipline, they need, as Michael Frisch so effectively shows elsewhere in this issue, to be cognizant of the screens through which historical information and ideas are commonly filtered.

Popular historical preconceptions embrace four often conjoined views. One is the notion of a timeless past until recently devoid of change, save for trivial or cyclic operations. Another is of a past that mirrors the present and that should be read back from it, reflecting eternal and universal causes, virtues, and vices. The third is of an unprogressive past to be disowned as a swamp of stagnant tradition or super-stitious error. The fourth comprises perspectives that sharply distinguish one's *own* national or cultural pasts from those of other societies, enabling one *either* to extol traditional stasis *or* to deplore primitives' lack of progress. These perspectives go be-yond the "Whig fallacy" immortalized by Herbert Butterfield, that is, history in which a triumphant elite legitimizes the present by using the past as origin, pre-cursor, and anticipation. All of these perspecirves are present-centered in a still broader sense; they misinterpret historical sources by viewing them through the cat-egories, even if not the values, of the present.[2]

Access to modern historical materials and insights has scarcely tempered earlier perspectives on the past and its bearing on the present; heightened interest in his-tory has, if anything, augmented these long-held preconceptions. Eschewing modern historical modes of explanation, professionals, policy experts, and public figures iterate ahistorical and unhistorical views. Thus Richard E. Neustadt and Er-nest R. May endorse Thucydides' dictum that "human nature remains constant [as do] dilemmas of human governance," and Britain's minister of the environment, time traveling in twentieth-century glasses, concludes that "a million years ago, this

---

[2] Present-centeredness or presentism goes beyond the present-mindedness implicit in any view we take of the past. See Herbert Butterfield, *The Whig Interpretation of History* (London, 1931); David L. Hall, "In Defense of Presentism," *History and Theory*, 18 (no. 1, 1979), 1–15; Adrian Wilson and T. G. Ashplant, "Whig History and Present-Centred History," *Historical Journal*, 31 (March 1988), 1–16; Adrian Wilson and T. G. Ashplant, "Present-Centred History and the Problem of Historical Knowledge," *ibid.* (June 1988), 253–74; and P. R. Coss, "De-bate: British History: Past, Present — and Future?" *Past and Present* (no. 119, 1988), 171–83.

country was not a place where you would have wanted to live."[3] The past is to be seen and understood, such statements imply, in the same terms as the present.

Custodians of public history, managers of heritage, teachers of schoolchildren, social scientists in general, even some professional historians articulate presentist, pre-historicist, whiggish, and other perspectives quite at odds with sophisticated historical understanding today. Such views are seldom consciously held or clearly articulated. And they often reflect mutually incompatible assumptions about the past, just as one 1950s history text showed the United States both as "perfect and yet making progress all the time."[4] Despite irreconcilable contradictions, these positions coalesce into conjoint tenets of faith.

Most of these perspectives were part and parcel of historians' own thinking a century ago, if not more recently. Dorothy Ross has shown how ranking nineteenth-century American historians grafted the Teutonic seed theory onto an older messianic exceptionalism. Revalidating Puritan millenarianism, they reanimated faith that "original sinlessness" secured Americans alone against time's corrosive influence. Since historians themselves continued well into the twentieth century to view American history as the unfolding of a divine and immutable mission, it is not surprising that many Americans still cleave to their redemptive escape from the toils of history.[5]

Indeed, popular politicians as well as the popular media assure us that American values and political institutions have remained constant since revolutionary days, if not before. It is Ronald Reagan's central credo that Americans are now, as always, God's chosen people, and George Bush has saddled the Founding Fathers with a Pledge of Allegiance that was in fact invented a century after their time. It is this supposed constancy that gives the American past its dynamic salience for the present.

Current debate over the meaning of the Constitution exemplifies this bent. Because it is less well known than the Revolution, the Constitution offers an even better template for remaking the past in the image of present ideals. By the late nineteenth-century, as Michael Kammen has shown, the Constitution had become a timeless credo, its framers shorn of their own historical context, much as former attorney general Edwin Meese III recently divested James Madison of eighteenth-century foibles. Finding in the Constitution the unaltered truths of American politics, believers in the doctrine of original intent attribute to it "timeless and universal meaning embodied in the philosophical aims of the Founders and discoverable through textual exegesis," much as Fundamentalist Protestants do with the Bible.

---

[3] Richard E. Neustadt and Ernest R. May, *Thinking in Time: The Uses of History for Decision-Makers* (New York, 1986), 265; Nicholas Ridley, "The Future of the Public Heritage," *Journal of the Royal Society of Arts*, 135 (1987), 675.

[4] Frances FitzGerald, *America Revised: History Schoolbooks in the Twentieth Century* (New York, 1980), 178.

[5] Dorothy Ross, "Historical Consciousness in Nineteenth-Century America," *American Historical Review*, 89 (Oct. 1984), 909–28; David Glassberg, "History and the Public: Legacies of the Progressive Era," *Journal of American History*, 73 (March 1987), 957–80. The term "original sinlessness" is from Garry Wills, *Reagan's America: Innocents at Home* (New York, 1987).

In their view, to treat ideas in the context of the times and places they occurred, as historians usually strive to do, is "obscurantist historicism" that precludes serious engagement with the ideas themselves. Lacking "any feel for history and what history does," such constitutional fundamentalists fail to recognize the differentness of the eighteenth century, the absence of deliberate consensus in the document that emerged, or the accretive processes that have subsequently transformed the meaning of the Constitution.[6]

But those who reprobate the original intent approach likewise read the present back into the past; their modes of historical explanation differ mainly in assigning credit and debit to different parties. To them the Framers are not saints but sinners, the Constitution itself almost as corrupt as William Lloyd Garrison's "covenant with Death and Agreement with Hell." Thurgood Marshall finds it disgraceful that the Framers proclaimed liberty in the name of a minority—excluding women and blacks. Another black judge assails the Constitution's "devastating ambiguity" and its drafters' "duplicity for high-sounding words about justice [while] maintaining a system of slavery." That Thomas Jefferson, George Washington, and Patrick Henry "could create a society where a slave would have her child snatched away from her" struck him as a "monstrous contradiction."[7]

Both sides seem unaware that the Founding Fathers did not create their society *de novo*, but were born into it, imbibed its values from childhood, and sought to codify most of them. They were folk of their time, no less than we of ours; for them to see slaves and women as inferior was not hypocritically discordant, but comfortably accordant, with their professions of liberty.

Similar anachronisms are legion. History is routinely modernized to render the past more accessible. The audiovisual show at Minute Man National Historical Park in Massachusetts presents the events of April 19, 1775, in the staccato style of modern newscasting. This achieves an intimacy that brings visitors into the act. But it fails to alert them to a crucial difference: news two centuries ago was spread at a different tempo and understood in ways quite unlike our own. Conned into thinking they are reliving the event exactly as it happened back then, modern audiences gain rapport with the revolutionary past at the cost of any awareness of temporal distance and hindsight.

Many outdoor history museums expressly liken past to present. The staff of the Stuhr Museum of the Prairie Pioneer in Grand Island, Nebraska, considers it "im-

[6] Michael Kammen, *A Machine That Would Go of Itself: The Constitution in American Culture* (New York, 1986); Gordon S. Wood, "The Fundamentalists and the Constitution," *New York Review of Books*, Feb. 18, 1988, pp. 33–40. Appropriated early on by the conservative establishment, the Constitution bicentennial engendered contempt—and boredom—among much of the intelligentsia, historians included. See Jamie Kitman and Ruth Yodaiken, "Celebrating (Yawn) the Constitution: Bicentennial Bust," *Nation*, July 2/9, 1988, pp. 1, 14–21; Warren Leon, "Some Thoughts on Museums and the Constitution," *Museum News*, 65 (Aug. 1987), 25–26; *New York Times*, Dec. 22, 1987, sec. B, p. 6.

[7] Kammen, *Machine That Would Go of Itself*, 98. For Thurgood Marshall's views, see *London Times*, May 22, 1987, p. 14. For Judge A. Leon Higginbotham's, see Jacqueline Tasch, "Black Americans and the Constitution: An Alternative Vision," *CAAS Newsletter*, 10 (Spring 1987), 1, 8–10. On the background to black views of the Constitution, see Leon Litwack, "Trouble in Mind: The Bicentennial and the Afro-American Experience," *Journal of American History*, 74 (Sept. 1987), 315–37.

portant that the visitors know that the problems of the people in 1880 are still very much the same problems of the people in 1980"—that is, farm prices and energy. The evident absurdity of that assertion highlights the reason for making it: erasing the time gap will put the visitor in the pioneers' frame of mind. A 1975 history text exhibits similar time warp empathy: "People in all our communities today have serious problems, just as slaves had problems before the Civil War." The past is made meaningful by being dragged out of context into the present.[8]

Equating history with fragments of popular culture familiar from memory and media replay likewise endears the American past. Famous film representations of historic features and events are more recognizable and convincing than the authentic, original lineaments. Many viewers seem less impressed by Charles Lindbergh's original *Spirit of St. Louis* in the Smithsonian Institution than by the plane Jimmy Stewart flew in the movie, for "this, after all, is the only one they *saw* crossing the ocean on film." The Alamo mural that until recently commemorated the battle there substituted Hollywood faces for those of the actual heroes, with John Wayne playing Davy Crockett. "Catch up on history!" urges a magazine from Connecticut, where "history comes alive in an unboring manner." Connecticut is "justifiably proud [of] the lollipop, the hamburger, the cotton gin, vulcanized rubber, and all-night 'I-love-Lucy' festivals"—all invented there; "the first American pizza was served in Connecticut."[9]

The pizza and the lollipop palliate the ponderous Constitution. The national chronicle is considered too large-scale, too abstract for most people to identify with; the public is led instead to focus on the private, domestic past. The first exhibit visitors see on entering Minute Man Park headquarters features a wooden darning egg, a needle holder, a detachable pocket, and an old comb, with the legend: "Life was a daily thing. Battles only temporary. But both went on while colonists waited out the war." This domesticates the Revolution. But it offers no historical events—only universal processes. At Valley Forge, history becomes timeless human nature. According to the display label, the soldiers encamped there over the winter of 1777–1778 "demonstrated the universal desire of the human spirit in its pursuit for freedom and self-determination." As Daniel Czitrom puts it for comparable Civil War displays, instead of social history we get "*Dynasty* set in the 1860s."[10]

Attributing present modes of thought and action to the past is not exclusive to judges and educators and park curators. Some archaeologists, presumably historically trained, interpret Narragansett Indian remains in a Rhode Island cemetery in much the same fashion. Continuities with earlier skeletal postures and grave goods

[8] Warren Rodgers, educational director, Stuhr Museum of the Prairie Pioneer, to David Lowenthal, Nov. 19, 1980 (in David Lowenthal's possession); FitzGerald, *America Revised*, 162n.

[9] Wills, *Reagan's America*, 375; Michael Wallace, "Ronald Reagan and the Politics of History," *Tikkun*, 2 (1987), 13–18, 127–31, esp. 128n; "Catch Up on Connecticut," *Connecticut*, 49 (June 1986), 100.

[10] Barbara Franco and Millie Rahn, "Who's Teaching History?" *History News*, 42 (Sept.–Oct. 1987), 7–11, esp. 11. On attitudes toward events and processes in history, see François Furet, "Beyond the *Annales*," *Journal of Modern History*, 55 (Sept. 1983), 389–410; Gertrude Himmelfarb, *The New History and the Old* (Cambridge, Mass., 1987), 16–18.

lead them to claim that seventeenth-century Narragansetts—remarkably like their descendants—maintained tribal identity and actively resisted white assimilation.

That interpretation suits present-day Narragansetts, for pride in identity and federal privileges reward modern continuity with like-minded ancestors. But how do the archaeologists achieve so neat a concurrence with current minority virtues? To legitimate the Narragansett as an autonomous group in the twentieth century and "reproduce social relations in the past as a mirror of social relations in the present," an archaeological critic charges, they "ignor[ed] certain dimensions of the ethnohistoric and archaeological database" and denied the known "history of interracial and intercultural synthesis." What moved them to posit "group solidarity and cohesiveness" against European pressures, he suggests, was not simply empathy with deprived native Americans; they needed to provide an explanation congenial to the Indians lest they subsequently be denied access to the site.[11]

Current minority virtues similarly explain past ethnography at the American Indian Archaeological Institute in Washington, Connecticut. Captions declare that "it is necessary to know that there never was oppression and colonization without native resistance"; the "it is necessary" alerts the visitor to the present-day import of the message. The "possible proof" is based on two presentist suppositions about the native American pottery figurines shown: that their "modest postures" reflect efforts to protect Indian culture and that the preponderance of women among them reflects tribal response to assimilation forced on the men (women "were so frequently symbolized in Shantok pottery" because they had become "leaders in a movement to reject the values, desires, and laws of the colonists").[12]

Thus archaeologists too remake the past in the mold they favor for the present. Today's Indianist and feminist values are ascribed to people of earlier times. The past is thereby rendered not only familiar and comprehensible but also accountable and controllable.

Many Americans thus conflate past with present only for particular cultures, notably their own. In this they echo Ross's nineteenth-century historians. The belief that Americans are uniquely exempt from temporal change and decay justifies ahistorical chauvinism of the Reagan variety noted above.

On the other hand, many vouchsafe historical progress to Americans and "advanced" Europeans alone, relegating "traditional," "primitive," and "backward" Orientals and Africans to eternal stagnation. In this exceptionalist vision, science

[11] Paul A. Robinson, Mark A. Kelley, and Patricia E. Rubertone, "Preliminary Biocultural Interpretations from a Seventeenth-Century Narragansett Indian Cemetery in Rhode Island," in *Cultures in Contact: The Impact of European Contacts on Native American Cultural Institutions, A.D. 1000–1800,* ed. William W. Fitzhugh (Washington, 1985), 107–30, esp. 109; Michael S. Nassaney, "An Epistemological Enquiry into Some Archaeological and Historical Interpretations of 17th Century Native American–European Relations," in *Archaeological Approaches to Cultural Identity,* ed. Stephen J. Shennan (London, 1989), 76–93, esp. 84–85.

[12] Exhibit captions, American Indian Archaeological Institute, Washington, Connecticut, July 1987; Russell G. Handsman, "Material Things and Social Relations: Toward an Archaeology of 'Anti-Structures,'" Conference on New England Archaeology *Newsletter* (Washington, Conn., 1987), 5. By contrast, the Euro-African decor of tobacco pipes from early colonial Virginia and Maryland, formerly thought to be Indian, is now held to "reflect close contact and cooperative craftsmanship between Africans and English on 17th-century plantations"; *International Herald Tribune,* July 14, 1988, p. 7.

and technology guide Americans toward material and moral perfection. Other peoples remain essentially unchanged over centuries, if not millennia. The distinction stems largely from WASPish racial ascription. American concepts of traditional backwardness have the same nineteenth-century roots as British relegation of native races to permanent, childlike dependency. Up to the fifteenth (1950) edition of his standard history of architecture, Sir Banister Fletcher dismissed non-Western buildings as unimportant, because "non-historical." Fletcher's views live on in the historian Hugh Trevor-Roper's imprimatur:

> Perhaps, in the future, there will be some African history to teach. But at present, there is none, or very little. . . . The history of the world, for the last five centuries, in so far as it has significance, has been European history.

In America, the technological advances of the twentieth century are held to "separat[e] modern man once and for all from his primitive ancestors"—and also from still-surviving primitive peoples.[13]

Archetypal images in the *National Geographic* magazine highlight the contrasting stereotypes of progress and stagnation. In images illustrating our own "evolutionary progress . . . by contrast with the evolutionary arrest of Others," American archaeologists are shown next to traditional peoples closely resembling their remote forebears who crafted the treasures (in National Geographese, all relics are treasures) that the archaeologists have recovered. The primitive lineal descendants appear unchanged or degenerated from the ancestral type: "Though kingdoms rise and fall, these Kurdish ferrymen carry on"; "Across the gulf of countless generations, the Minoan love of dance still finds expression in Crete." The emphasis is always on the changelessness of backward peoples. Joan Gero and Dolores Root note the reiterated equation "between what is unearthed and [contemporary] native material culture, between the indigenous technology and what was practised millennia before, between a modern physiognomy and physical characteristics depicted in antiquity." It is only *we* who continually evolve—an evolution that ironically enables *us* to unearth *their* past and reveal how timelessly unaltered is *their* present.[14]

Historical progress thus differentiates Americans, in their view, from traditional peoples. But not all Americans applaud such progress. Many consider it chimerical or destructive. Hankering after the preindustrial balance of peoples who supposedly aimed, not to conquer, but to live in harmony with nature, they regard historical change as an infection to be eliminated—once the life-enhancing past is restored. Resentment against, and rejection of, history as false progress is not solely American, of course, but it is most powerfully articulated in wilderness and environmental ethics movements in the United States.

---

[13] Bannister Fletcher, *A History of Architecture on the Comparative Method* (New York, 1950), 888; Hugh Trevor-Roper, *The Rise of Christian Europe* (London, 1965), 11; Arthur P. Molella, "The Museum That Never Was: Anticipations of the Smithsonian's Museum of History and Technology," paper delivered at the conference, "Collections and Culture: Museums and the Development of American Life," Woodrow Wilson Center, Smithsonian Institution, Washington, D.C., Oct. 1987, p. 15 (in Lowenthal's possession).

[14] Joan Gero and Dolores Root, "Public Presentations and Private Concerns: Archaeology in the Pages of *National Geographic*," in *The Politics of the Past*, ed. Peter Gathercole and David Lowenthal (London, in press).

Such proto-ecological perspectives echo an earlier faith in the ordered stability of nature and society, a pervasive dread of the contingent, the unpredictable, the uncontrollable—what Mircea Eliade termed the "terror of history." Historical change conjures up an unknown future from which many instinctively recoil.

Irreversible human damage to the biosphere—species extinction, the greenhouse effect, ozone depletion, nuclear radiation—now seem especially threatening. But environmental crusaders are not the only enemies of historical change. Following the nineteenth-century dictates of John Ruskin and William Morris, devotees of architectural and artifact preservation also enshrine a stable past never to be permanently altered. Restoration and renovation are allowed only insofar as things can be returned to their prior state; irreversibility is unforgivable.[15] Yet irreversibility is a constant and essential concomitant of life. We continually make decisions that preclude some prospects and foreclose others. History is by definition irrevocable.

Traditionalist nostalgia pervades social science too. Edwin L. Wade recounts how anthropologists in the 1920s and 1930s sought to erase the injuries of recent change from Hopi Indian folkways. To reverse history and promote the revival of purely traditional crafts, members of the staff at the Museum of Northern Arizona monitored goods at an annual arts and crafts fair to ensure their authenticity. Aniline dyes introduced by earlier traders were banned in favor of traditional vegetable dyes; basket shapes preferred by tourists were scrapped for old-time flat ware. When the reversions proved uneconomic and unenforceable, the museum introduced prehistoric Anasazi and Mimbres pottery motifs among Acoma potters; those thirteenth-century designs were touted as revivals of ancestral art, although the earlier and later cultures were demonstrably unconnected. Those efforts, revivalist and restorative, aimed to buttress tradition against modern change. Historical change in traditional cultures was considered a western taint—to be eradicated by westerners.[16]

When tradition is found, anthropologists are apt to exaggerate it. The old features, and hence the conservatism, of the "San Tomas" pueblo dwellers are emphasized by stressing their traditional hunting and gathering and agriculture, while avoiding any mention of the fact that most of them get their food by driving to Piggly Wiggly; traditional dance performances are closely monitored, but the same Indians' attendance at Anglo discos in Anglo clothes is ignored. The push for tradition came first and foremost from the whites. As an Indian informant put it:

---

[15] I discuss these views in David Lowenthal, "Awareness of Human Impacts: Changing Attitudes and Emphases," in *The Earth As Transformed by Human Action*, ed. B. L. Turner II et al. (New York, in press). See Mircea Eliade, *The Myth of the Eternal Return: Cosmos and History* (Princeton, 1954); Stephen Jay Gould, *Time's Arrow, Time's Cycle: Myth and Metaphor in the Discovery of Geological Time* (Cambridge, Mass., 1987), 12–13.

[16] Edwin L. Wade, "The Ethnic Art Market in the American Southwest, 1880–1980," in *Objects and Others: Essays on Museums and Material Culture*, ed. George W. Stocking, Jr. (Madison, 1985), 167–91. A recent effort to protect authentic Indian crafts against contamination by outside influences in what remains of Santa Fe's traditional market has come to similar grief. As in the 1930s, so in the 1980s, protection has resulted in restricting the scope and content of Indian crafts and freezing stylistic development. One potter complains she cannot now use a pottery wheel without being chastised as inauthentic. Deirdre Evans-Pritchard, "The Portal Case: Authenticity, Tourism, Traditions, and the Law," *Journal of American Folklore*, 100 (July–Sept. 1987), 287–92.

We have to learn how to be Indian again. First, the whites came and stripped us. Then, they come again and "find" us. Now, we are paid to behave the way we did when they tried to get rid of us.

But when tradition proves nonviable, old *National Geographic* stereotypes are trotted out in praise of American-style progress. "Maybe we made a mistake" in trying to maintain Indian cultures, Reagan confessed to Soviet students in 1988. "Maybe we should not have humored them in that, wanting to stay in that kind of primitive life-style." In Reagan's view, history is an Amtrak express that takes all passengers — but they must really want to travel.[17]

American exceptionalism is simply one variant of a widespread tendency to exempt one's own people (or other favored groups) from history's contingent processes. (It is apparently easier to recognize contingency — to see history as reflecting the play of chance, rather than proceeding from inexorable causes to predetermined ends — in the experience of people for whom one feels neither hatred nor love.) Disclaimers by British historians notwithstanding, the past as perceived and used in Britain exhibits biases and distortions as pronounced, as general as those among educated Americans.

Even British academics — some historians among them — remain attached to timeless or to presentist pasts. Consider the functionalist tradition until recently orthodox in British social anthropology. Following Bronislaw Malinowski, British anthropologists of the 1920s and 1930s studied tribal societies as closed and immutable systems, unchanged until European contact. Malinowski's heirs heeded his injunction to trace the regularities of all that was fixed and permanent in tribal life. Through native memories and mementoes they sought to reconstitute the precontact "ethnographic present" — the "authentic" tribal life held to have existed before European intrusion. In common with American salvage anthropologists, the British took on the duty of saving the relic folkways of holistic and timeless peoples uncontaminated by contact.[18]

Such societies *had* to be static because they operated as functional wholes: Émile Durkheim's concept of organic unity obliged functionalists to ignore historical change. And positing precolonial societies as stable over time enabled ethnographers to view *existing* primitives as survivals from earlier epochs, in line with the evolutionary uniformitarianism of E. B. Tylor. "While *we* had moved on to greater and greater technical, economic and political mastery over the environment," in Edmund Leach's words, "these 'other' people had somehow stood still." We recognize our primitive friends of the *National Geographic*.[19]

[17] M. Estellie Smith, "The Process of Sociocultural Continuity," *Current Anthropology*, 23 (April 1982), 127–35; *International Herald Tribune*, June 3, 1988, p. 3.

[18] Bernard S. Cohn, "Anthropology and History in the 1980s," *Journal of Interdisciplinary History*, 12 (Autumn 1981), 227–52, esp. 229–32; Robert Borofsky, *Making History: Pukapukan and Anthropological Constructions of Knowledge* (Cambridge, Eng., 1987), 45–46, 53; Marshal Sahlins, *Islands of History* (London, 1987), xviii; Jacob W. Gruber, "Ethnographic Salvage and the Shaping of Anthropology," *American Anthropologist*, 72 (Dec. 1970), 1289–99.

[19] Edmund Leach, "Tribal Ethnography: Past, Present, Future," *Association of Social Antropologists Monograph 27*, ed. Maryon Macdonald et al. (London, in press). (Note continues on following page.)

The ideal of a stable ethnographic present endured well into the 1970s. Even anthropologists who invoked history found it hard to shake off the image of unchanging native cultures; confining their histories mainly *within* tribes and archaic kingdoms, notes Bernard Cohn, "anthropologists still always end their narratives with the coming of the destructive Europeans."[20] And the persistence of the romantic illusion that an untouched primordial tribe might still survive somewhere accounts for the ease with which scholars were duped in 1971 by the "Stone Age" Tasaday of the Philippines.

Turning *National Geographic* perspectives on their head, British anthropologists (like their American counterparts) deplored European perversion of tribal folkways and sought to protect remaining "specimens of antique 'cultures.'" If it was too late to preserve the past, "you could write books about what you . . . imagined it had been like," and Leach adds that anthropologists wrote "as if they believed that the original pre-colonial tribal societies still existed inside a carapace of Western bureaucracy and technology. Chip the colonial shell away and you will get back to the traditional core."[21]

Indeed, many late nineteenth- and early twentieth-century administrators tried to do just that. Once the chaos of conquest was tidied away, British imperial officials in Asia and Africa undertook to reinstate previous tribal identities and revalidate age-old customs. Terence Ranger remarks that "what were called customary law, customary land-rights, customary political structures and so on were in fact all invented by colonial codification." Nonetheless, those inventions reflected British imperial faith that tradition was as immemorial among African tribesmen as in the hallowed precincts of English common law. From British officials, missionaries, and texts, for example, Fiji chiefs relearned their "true and ancestral traditions"—including the *Kaunitoni* migration myth tracing their Fijian origins by way of Tanganyika back to Thebes.[22]

It was to their own countrymen that British folklorists, following Tylor, attached the cachet of aboriginal survivals. In many English villages scholars found "ancient and unchanging links with a lost rural past when the folk in organic communities responded simply and directly to the rhythms of nature." Modern folklore observances unknowingly preserved fragments of primordial truths wrapped in later perversions; it was the folklorists' self-imposed duty to make the fragments whole and restore them to contemporary culture.[23]

See Margaret T. Hodgen, *The Doctrine of Survivals: A Chapter in the History of Scientific Method in the Study of Man* (London, 1936), 12–14, 38–53; Margaret T. Hodgen, *Anthropology, History, and Cultural Change* (Tucson, 1974), 21–24; Peter Munz, *Our Knowledge of the Growth of Knowledge: Popper or Wittgenstein?* (London, 1985), 45, 138–40.

[20] Cohn, "Anthropology and History in the 1980s," 252.

[21] Leach, "Tribal Ethnography." In a contrasting stereotype, prehistoric chiefs in Europe and the Aegean are now depicted as egocentric, pushy individualists stirring sluggish peasants toward civilization. See John L. Bintliff, "Structuralism and Myth in Minoan Studies," *Antiquity*, 58 (March 1984), 33–38.

[22] Terence Ranger, "The Invention of Tradition in Colonial Africa," in *The Invention of Tradition*, ed. Eric Hobsbawm and Terence Ranger (Cambridge, Eng., 1983), 211–62, esp. 247–51; Cohn, "Anthropology and History in the 1980s," 239–40.

[23] Georgina Boyes, "Cultural Survivals Theory and Traditional Customs: An Examination of the Effects of Privileging on the Form and Perception of Some English Calendar Customs," paper delivered at the symposium,

Since folk life was by definition static, the folk were ipso facto conservative and uncreative, "living depositories of ancient history." When folklorists realized that, contrary to this theory, folklore *had* changed and was changing still, they dismissed such alterations and accretions as degenerate. As late as 1968, leading folk song experts were asserting that "folk society and folk art do not accept, reflect, or value change."[24]

Since they considered only the most ancient elements authentic and valid, British folklorists exhorted villagers to strip off subsequent corruptions and replace them with original verities. And though few villagers had heard of the Celtic fertility rituals the professionals exalted, they often deferred to expert judgments and changed things accordingly. Thus the annual souling play at Antrobus adopted Arnold Boyd's theory that characters reincarnated the Halloween ghosts of their ancestors; Violet Alford revived (that is, inaugurated) the Marshfield Mummers' perambulation as an inviolate magic circle; and the current local belief that the Castleton Garland ceremony (which celebrates the restoration of Charles II) goes back to Celtic sacrificial rites stems only from the 1977 visit of a persuasive Celticist. Thus to understand present-day British folklore, one must retrace the recent peregrinations of the folklorists whose purifications these observances now embody. The 1938 president of the Folklore Society who reproached the leader of the Padstow Hobby Horse festival for "spoiling" what should have been an ancient and unchanging fertility ritual might have been mollified to hear a villager, half a century after her own minatory visit, affirm that "it still means the same to us as it did a thousand years ago."[25]

The fetish of folkloric purity is by no means unique to Britain. For example, to strengthen modern continuity with classical roots and to confute the taunt that Greeks are naught but Slavs, Greek nationalists have purged village tales of supposedly extraneous Turkish and Balkan elements; Hellenic folklore and other rural survivals are treasured as repositories of ancient Greek virtues. But the Greek crusade reflects the beleaguered identity of a new nation-state in thrall to nostalgic philhellenism; British folklore revision stemmed from no such immediate political needs. It merely reflected the deep-seated British preference for fixed tradition over the flux of history.[26]

In reanimating certain Cook Islands traditions, British anthropologists in the 1930s behaved much like British folklorists at home. While doing fieldwork on

"'Making Exhibitions of Ourselves': Limits of Objectivity in Representation of Other Cultures," British Museum, London, Feb. 1986 (in Georgina Boyes's possession). See Hodgen, *Doctrine of Survivals*, 52–53, 105, 141–50; Richard M. Dorson, *The British Folklorists: A History* (Chicago, 1968), 225, 441–42.

[24] Lawrence Gomme and [A. B.] Gomme, *British Folk-Lore, Folk-Songs, and Singing-Games* (London, [1916]), 10; Roger D. Abrahams and George Foss, *Anglo-American Folksong Style* (Englewood Cliffs, 1968), 11.

[25] Boyes, "Cultural Survivals Theory and Traditional Customs"; Georgina Smith [Boyes], "Winster Morris Dance: The Sources of an Oikotype," in *Traditional Dance I*, ed. T. Buckland (Crewe, Eng., 1982), 93–108; M. M. Banks, "The Padstow May Festival," *Folk-Lore*, 49 (Dec. 1938), 392–94; Channel 4 [U.K.], "The Future of the Past," television program, June 22, 1986. Ms. Boyes has kindly shown me a draft chapter, "The Folk and How They Were Constructed," of her forthcoming book on English folk song revival.

[26] Michael Herzfeld, *Ours Once More: Folklore, Ideology, and the Making of Modern Greece* (Austin, 1982); Michael Herzfeld, "'Law' and 'Custom': Ethnography in Greek National Identity," *Journal of Modern Greek Studies*, 3 (Oct. 1985), 167–85.

Pukapuka atoll, Ernest Beaglehole was disappointed to learn that the islanders were about to put on their annual biblical plays.

> I . . . visualized us sitting all day in the hot sun . . . and I felt that it needed something more than David and Goliath to keep interest alive. So I put it to Makirai: Why not play for a change old Pukapukan stories, the story of Malotini for example, or the eight men of Ngake, or the Slaughter of the Yayake people? . . . and besides, the acting of them would help us to remember them more vividly when we came to write them down.

So the village elders jettisoned biblical for Pukapukan legends, which are still being performed (now alongside biblical tales) a half century later.[27]

The British nurtured their own preindustrial past as an ideal type of heritage, with the crippling effects on innovation and competitiveness laid bare by Martin J. Wiener. And they continue to celebrate fossilized, antediluvian ways of life. Underlying the British embrace of the past is the assumption that change has been only superficial; the essentials remain untouched by time. Devotion to precedent is unabated. Eighty years after Francis M. Cornford's *Microcosmographia Academica*, all Britain still seems to share his view: "Every public action which is not customary, either is wrong, or if it is right, is a dangerous precedent. It follows that nothing should ever be done for the first time."[28]

A few years ago I wanted to look at the will of Sir Christopher Codrington, seventeenth-century governor of the Leeward Islands; the will is in the Codrington Library of All Souls College, Oxford, Codrington's major legatee. The librarian invited me there to see it. When I came we chatted; he brought papers to my antique table; half an hour later he came back, perturbed. "By the by," he asked, "you've used our library before, haven't you?" "No," I said, "I'm afraid I haven't." "Oh," he said, "then I'm afraid you can't use it now." (It was all right in the end; an All Souls Fellow was hauled away from his tea to identify me.)

Devotion to tradition overrides historical truth in public commemorations. Finding that Francis Drake was to be cut down to size in the 1988 Armada celebrations, city officials in Plymouth assailed the National Maritime Museum for its "prissy" insistence on scrupulous accuracy, a mantle of truth assumed so as not "to offend the Spanish now that they are in" the European Community. Plymouth was naturally outraged by the museum's determination to "dissolve old myths and prejudices," for "what Robin Hood is to Nottingham and Mickey Mouse to Disneyland, Francis Drake is to Plymouth."[29]

Devotion to precedent extends to the artifactual recovery of the past. Thus the raising of the Tudor flagship the *Mary Rose* resonated with traditions reinvoked for

[27] Ernest Beaglehole, *Islands of Danger* (Wellington, 1944), 174; Borofsky, *Making History*, 142–43.

[28] Martin J. Wiener, *English Culture and the Decline of the Industrial Spirit, 1850–1980* (Cambridge, Eng., 1983); Francis M. Cornford, *Microcosmographia Academica: Being a Guide for the Young Academic Politician* (1908; reprint, Cambridge, Eng., 1953), 15.

[29] *London Times*, Sept. 17, 1987, pp. 5, 11; *ibid.*, April 20, 1988; p. 22; *ibid.*, Jan. 30, 1988, p. 13; *London Sunday Times*, May 8, 1988, sec. G, p. 4.

the Falklands campaign. And traditionalism suffuses the heritage establishment, which portrays Britain as a nation with an already achieved historical identity that demands of the present only appropriate reverence and protection.[30]

The British working-class past is as timeless as the Tories'. When Labour leader Neil Kinnock excoriated the Conservative government's scheme for a poll tax as a reversion to the fourteenth century, he conjured up images of Wat Tyler and the Peasants' Revolt with which his party at once identified. Labourites too fancy themselves heirs to a timeless national tradition, a "continuity of struggles—by peasants, artisans, and workers for liberty, equality, and community," as one sympathizer put it. "The image of 'lost rights' which inspired popular movements from the fourteenth to the nineteenth century . . . may appear to be another Whig reading of the past," but at least "it is a Whig history from the bottom up." But Labourite traditionalism, conjuring up the vanished pre-Marxian solidarity of a proletariat spanning the centuries from Robin Hood through the striking Jarrow miners of 1928, has lost its appeal for many. Marxists, for example, now deplore the fact that "the Left remains profoundly wedded to the past."[31]

These examples reveal the chasm that separates "scientifically tested and literally accurate" academic history from the whiggish past deployed in British social science, politics, education, and heritage pursuits. The demise of the Whig interpretation of history is a widely accepted fact. But its arch-destroyer Butterfield himself later resurrected it during the dark days of World War II, for common law and the Whig interpretation "have worked together to tighten the bonds that hold the Englishman to his past—foster our love of precedent, our affection for tradition, our desire for gradualness in change." And David Cannadine finds present-mindedness in the 1980s as prevalent among Whig and Tory as among the earlier gentlemen-scholars "they so zealously disparage for precisely this error."[32]

These British perspectives on the past differ more in style than in substance from those in the United States, though whiggish chauvinism in the former and redemptive exceptionalism in the latter help to account for their distinctive national forms. The British take their heritage more for granted because it is largely indubitable, widely shared, and only slowly altered. Bygone feuds between Norman and Saxon, Celt and English, Protestant and Catholic scarcely disturb the general unanimity with which the past is apprehended, even from class to class. Given a consensuality

[30] Patrick Wright, *On Living in an Old Country: The National Past in Contemporary Britain* (London, 1985), 161–92; Patrick Wright, "Misguided Tours," *New Socialist* (no. 40, 1986), 32–34; Robert Hewison, *The Heritage Industry: Britain in a Climate of Decline* (London, 1987); Neal Ascherson, "Why 'Heritage' Is Right-Wing," *Observer*, Nov. 8, 1987, p. 13; Neal Ascherson, "'Heritage' as Vulgar English Nationalism," *Observer*, Nov. 29, 1987, p. 13.

[31] Harvey Kaye, "Our Island Story Retold," *London Guardian*, Aug. 3, 1987; Wright, *On Living in an Old Country*, 151–57; "New Times," *Marxism Today*, 32 (Oct. 1988), 3. The Left "past" referred to was that of 1945, the "backward, conservative . . . old social-democratic order."

[32] Herbert Butterfield, *The Englishman and His History* (Cambridge, Eng., 1944), 72, 4; David Cannadine, "Viewpoint—British History: Past, Present—and Future?" *Past and Present* (no. 116, 1987), 169–91, esp. 174–75, 190. See Wilson and Ashplant, "Whig History," 1–2. Many similar points about the history profession in America are made by Theodore S. Hamerow, *Reflections on History and Historians* (Madison, 1987).

so pervasive, it is no surprise that history in Britain engenders few heroes or villains and seldom requires professions of allegiance or gestures of dissociation.[33]

By contrast, American heritage seems a minefield of partisan emotions. Relative brevity, insistence on documentary credos, glaring and enduring disparities between the lot of native and colonist, black and white, WASP and ethnic, North and South leave less room for consensus, occasion more bitter disputes over historical rights and wrongs. Given such polarized views, it is no surprise that history in the United States throws up a profusion of exemplary figures and spurs anachronistic reiterations of long-gone issues.[34]

But those differences scarcely affect my central premise. Common modes of thought about the past on both sides of the Atlantic remain antipathetic to the perspectives of most professional historians. Few nonhistorians conceive history as contingent and unpredictable, or the past as a cluster of realms distinct from the present, each with its own mentalities and sociocultural determinants. Instead, the public tends to see the past — its own or others' or both — as undifferentiated and unchanging. Present-day aims and deeds are regularly imputed to folk of earlier times; history is either denied efficacy or held to be preordained. Progress either leaves us helpless agents of overwhelming historical forces or arms us with a fiercely righteous faith that history is on our side.[35]

For many Anglo-Americans the idea of history does not embody change but excludes it. The dismissive phrase "he's history" implies something over and done with. In praising the Tutankhamen treasures shown at the Metropolitan Museum of Art in New York as "so fresh they kind of wipe out time," Thomas Hoving, formerly the museum's director, celebrated the obliteration of time, not its passage. A writer in quest of the quintessential English village required of it "a sense of history — of time standing still."[36]

Ahistorical perspectives flourish among scholars as well as laymen. And archaeologists, anthropologists, folklorists, history museum curators, heritage site managers, even some historians shape the forms such perspectives take in wider public discourse. Adopting ethnologists' focus on "repeated and expected events," *Annales* historians among others have emphasized stability, structural regularity, the local, the common — the stuff of Claude Lévi-Strauss's "cold" societies. And in "hot" societies where change is rapid, cumulative, and transformative, scholars now often focus

[33] Those who contest British history seem to me to share, more than most Americans, a general understanding over what the contest is *about*. Wright, *On Living in an Old Country*, and Hewison, *Heritage Industry*, exemplify this consensus as much as they deplore it. For the view that British history is remote and unimpassioned, see Peter Laslett, "The Way We Think We Were," *Washington Post Book World*, March 30, 1986, pp. 5, 11.

[34] "The comparative lack of shared historical interest in the United States, or the weakness [of] *national* tradition — as opposed to particular ethnic, or religious, or regional traditions" is noted by Michael Kammen, *A Season of Youth: The American Revolution and the Historical Imagination* (New York, 1978), 3.

[35] Michael Wallace, "The Politics of Public History," in *Past Meets Present: Essays about Historic Interpretation and Public Audiences*, ed. Jo Blatti (Washington, 1987), 37–53, esp. 40; Glassberg, "History and the Public," 970.

[36] Wills, *Reagan's America*, 284. For Thomas Hoving's remark, see Peter Carroll, "It Seemed Like Nothing Happened," *Antioch Review*, 41 (Winter, 1983), 5–19, esp. 10. *London Sunday Times*, Nov. 15, 1987, p. 41.

on supposed remnants of the immobile past: engulfed and marginalized peasantries, women mired in domesticity, academics, artists, and bandits.[37]

Historical training and historiographical precepts leave embedded assumptions undisturbed even among those charged with applying and presenting history to the public. To employ the past as a stick with which to beat the present, or to deny it any efficacy whatever, or to exempt one's own past from processes at work in other cultures are entrenched and useful habits. They are unlikely to be displaced by sophisticated historians' perspectives that threaten to abandon claims to truth and relegate historical processes to limbos of uncertainty.[38]

It is no paradox that the growth of paraprofessional historical interests tends to foster, rather than to correct, such apprehensions of the nature of history. To justify and promote their own involvement with genealogy, antiquities, antiques, tourism, or the heritage of minorities and other special interest groups, many in the history business readily adopt unhistorical stances.

Meanwhile the technology and artistry of retrieving the past often fuel popular interest in bygone times to the detriment of historical understanding. And vivid experience gleaned through audiovisual displays, museum visits, heritage sightseeing, and reenactments has for many enhanced, if not replaced, bookish historical knowledge.

It is currently fashionable, especially within the discipline, to blame historians themselves for this trend. Professionalism, overspecialization, fragmentation, introversion, and the treatment of history as a science are held to have cost history much of its former audience: "more concerned with trivial truth than with fertile error, . . . academic historians [are] writing more and more academic history which fewer and fewer people are actually reading," is Cannadine's transatlantic judgment. "About any new history book . . . written by a professor," say two Harvard professors, "the presumption should be that its intended audience is other professors." As a consequence, Trevor-Roper's prediction that "the layman . . . will turn aside from us, and seek interest and enlightenment elsewhere" is held to have come true; the public has shifted "away from the scholarly and towards the recreational, with all the trivialization that that may imply."[39]

While "textbook authors seem forever doomed . . . to roll their hard little rock of historical dogma up and down the minds of bored students everywhere," Thomas Schlereth finds history museum curators increasingly imaginative and innovative.

[37] Jacques Le Goff, "The Historian and the Common Man," in *The Historian between the Ethnologist and the Futurologist*, ed. Jerôme Dumoulin and Dominique Moisi (Paris, 1973), 204–15; Cohn, "Anthropology and History in the 1980s," 252; Lawrence Stone, *The Past and the Present* (Boston, 1981), 91–96; Furet, "Beyond the *Annales*"; Smith, "Process of Sociocultural Continuity"; Marilyn Strathern, "Out of Context: The Persuasive Fictions of Anthropology," *Current Anthropology*, 28 (June 1987), 251–81, esp. 258; Sally Falk Moore, "Explaining the Present: Theoretical Dilemmas in Processual Ethnography," *American Ethnologist*, 14 (Nov. 1988), 727–36, esp. 728.

[38] Hans-Georg Gadamer, *Truth and Method*, trans. William Glen-Doepel (London, 1979), 258–74.

[39] Cannadine, "Viewpoint — British History," 176–79; Neustadt and May, *Thinking in Time*, 264; H. R. Trevor-Roper, *History, Professional and Lay* (Oxford, 1957), 26; Neal Evans, "Debate — British History: Past, Present — and Future?" *Past and Present* (no. 119, 1988), 194–203, esp. 202.

"Just as there are poor history books, there are poor living history museums, events, films, games," confesses a reenactment enthusiast, but at least "there are no *dull* historical simulations." Who would not exchange the ponderous tome for the walkie-talkie that lets you "really . . . imagine that you have been mysteriously transported back through the centuries [where] there's never a dull moment"—a veritable time machine that "will always give you the ringside seat . . . at the greatest events of history—as well as some of history's more intimate moments."[40]

That popular interest in the past has deposed written history seems to me at best a misguided exaggeration, however. Both the past's intimacies and its great events are conveyed to millions by professional historians, whose skillful re-creations are no less absorbing to modern readers than those of the Bancrofts and the Parkmans, the Michelets and the Macaulays were to previous generations. Many modern historians rival the media and the museums in bringing the past to life again; the worlds of *Montaillou* and *Martin Guerre* thrill modern audiences with romance lent added force by historical verisimilitude.

If historians still play a major role before the ringside seats of the past, they also share responsibility for the circus shenanigans. What readers and viewers gain from these exotic forays into remote lives, whether guided by historians or by historical showmen, is not historical actuality; it is voyeuristic empathy. The vivid intimacies promote historical sympathy but attenuate historical understanding, underscoring universal constants of human feeling while obscuring or ignoring the particular social and cultural trends that both link the past with, and differentiate it from, the present.[41]

Modern quasi familiarity with the past, or at least with its simulacra, commingles past with present in novel ways. In vicariously retrieving and reliving earlier modes of everyday life along with the past's momentous events, millions express a concern with historical authenticity, for example, that fundamentally alters how relic artifacts and works of art are perceived, valued, and used. For reenactors, authenticity is the cardinal goal; as the English Civil War Society says, "we hope to be able to justify *everything*." An American reenactment buff feels that "willfully ignoring authenticity is a crime." So much does the public insist on historical authenticity that heritage projects personnel at Oxford "spent weeks calling experts to find out if the figure of Edmund Halley . . . would have one eye closed when gazing through his telescope." To be sure, these scruples have more to do with material minutiae than with historical context.[42]

---

[40] Thomas Schlereth, "Afterword," *Museum News*, 62 (Feb. 1984), 65; Jay Anderson, *The Living History Sourcebook* (Nashville, 1985), 444–48; Christopher Matthew, "Walkie Talkies," *Punch*, April 2, 1986, p. 44; brochure for Time Machine Tours Ltd. cassettes, 1988.

[41] Natalie Zemon Davis felt she had to remake the film, *The Return of Martin Guerre*, into a book. "The film was departing from the historical record, and I found this troubling. . . . These changes may have helped to give the film the powerful simplicity that had allowed the Martin Guerre story to become a legend in the first place," but the film softened its contradictions and glossed over the sixteenth-century contexts. Natalie Zemon Davis, *The Return of Martin Guerre* (Harmondsworth, Eng., 1983), p. viii.

[42] English Civil War Society, leaflet at Kenilworth Castle garrisoning, Sept. 3, 1988 (in Lowenthal's possession); Jay Anderson, *Time Machines: The World of Living History* (Nashville, 1984), 192; *New York Times*, March 29,

Those unused to seeing historical processes as contingent and irreversible, yet also shaped by hindsight, can easily become obsessed with the notion that the past is timeless and pervasive, yet also personally accessible. The omnipresence of history in media and marketplace encourages the public to vacillate between nostalgic compulsion and self-protective amnesia.[43]

Nostalgia tempts people to see the past less as precedent than as alternative: not just what has happened but what could happen, an option still open. Characters in films like *Blazing Saddles* and *Blade Runner*, *Star Wars* and *Zelig* reenter the cinematic past as authentic natives; the popularity of *Back to the Future* reflects the prevailing penchant for reliving—and remaking—one's personal past. Until recently the believing time traveler—like Dorothy Eady (Om Seti), who "can't remember whether it's B.C. or A.D."—was a rare eccentric; today such people seem to swim in the mainstream. An otherwise serious California college student recently confided in her philosophy teacher, "You were once a Cheyenne warrior in a previous existence, and I nursed you back to health after you'd been wounded by an arrow through your heart" (all he could manage to respond was "thank you"). A "medieval kissogram" messenger hauled into court as a drunken rowdy refused to remove his costume on the ground that he was a medieval knight; the court usher had to explain, "This is not a medieval court."[44]

Seeming familiarity with even the least savory or commendable aspects of the past enhances its verisimilar appeal. Whatever the deficiencies of bygone times, they possess the supreme advantage of lacking the uncertainty of the present, because they are *over*. We can relive the past as a more satisfactory narrative because it is one that is completed. Because historians feel professionally compelled to give history a more rational shape than that of present crude experience, an ordered clarity contrasting with the chaos or imprecision of our own times, they themselves are partly responsible for confirming, if not generating, the illusion that the past has a pattern.[45]

The patterns we find in the past, whether historical or remembered, are patterns we ourselves fabricate on frameworks erected by intervening generations. But to suppose that something as precious as a received past is incapable of objective authenti-

1988, sec. B, pp. 1, 32. For other instances of authenticity, see Lowenthal, *The Past Is a Foreign Country*, 295–301. On the malign effects of the cult of authenticity among collectors, see Evan S. Connell, *The Connoisseur* (San Francisco, 1987).

   [43] The terror of a past that can thus invade the present is conveyed in a fictional interchange: "The past was somehow too much for me. It rose up and overwhelmed me." "The past would be too much for any of us, if it did not stay in its place." Ivy Compton-Burnett, *The Present and the Past* (London, 1972), 99.

   [44] Allison Graham, "History, Nostalgia, and the Criminality of Popular Culture," *Georgia Review*, 38 (Summer, 1984), 348–64; Lowenthal, *The Past Is a Foreign Country*, 18. On these themes, see David Lowenthal, "Nostalgia Tells It Like It Wasn't," in *The Imagined Past*, ed. Malcolm Chase and Chris Shaw (Manchester, 1989). On the Dorothy Eady story, see Jonathan Cott, *A Search for Omm Sety: A Story of Eternal Love* (New York, 1987); *International Herald Tribune*, Nov. 27, 1987, p. 5; *Harrow & Northwood Informer*, Feb. 19, 1988, p. 1.

   [45] Arthur Schlesinger, Jr., "The Historian as Participant," *Daedalus*, 100 (Spring 1971), 339–57, esp. 354; W. Walter Menninger, "Say, It Isn't So: When Wishful Thinking Obscures Historical Reality," *History News*, 40 (Dec. 1985), 10–13; Lowenthal, *The Past Is a Foreign Country*, 234–35.

cation goes against the grain. Hence we cling tenaciously to the past as a sanctuary for whatever versions of reality, particular or universal, progressive or unchanging, we seek to promote. And these old approaches seem validated not only by the *obiter dicta* of past historians but by uses of history common among today's social scientists, curators, and public historians. When the academic historian is unpersuasive, it is because the public finds his visions of the past not simply aloof, but deeply antithetical to traditional modes of utilizing the past — modes that confirm and celebrate the creatively supportive role of public memory.

INDEX